A CITY AT WAR

A CITY AT WAR

MILWAUKEE LABOR DURING WORLD WAR II

Richard L. Pifer

Wisconsin Historical Society Press
Madison, Wisconsin

Published by the
WISCONSIN HISTORICAL SOCIETY PRESS

Photographs identified with PH, WHi, or WHS are from the Society's collections; address inquires about such photos to the Visual Materials Archivist at the above address.

Publications of the Wisconsin Historical Society Press are available at quantity discounts for promotions, fund raising, and educational use. Write to the above address for more information.

Printed in the United States of America
Designed by Impressions Book and Journal Services, Inc.

07 06 05 04 03   5 4 3 2 1

Library of Congress Cataloging-in-Publication Data
    Pifer, Richard L., 1950–
        A city at war : Milwaukee labor during World War II / Richard L. Pifer.
        p. cm.
    Includes bibliographic references and index.
    ISBN 0-87020-338-X
1. Industrial relations—Wisconsin—Milwaukee. 2. Immigrants—Wisconsin—Milwaukee. 3. Milwaukee (Wis.)—Economic conditions. I. Title.
HD8085.M53 P54 2002
331'.09775'9509044—dc21
                                                    2002070693

To

Marge, Rebecca, and Christopher

and to

Herbert and Margaret

you sustain me

CONTENTS

ACKNOWLEDGMENTS

I owe a debt of gratitude to the many individuals who played contributing roles in this project. As teacher and mentor, John Milton Cooper at the University of Wisconsin–Madison taught me to think critically about history and helped guide the first drafts of this book. Robert Asher, University of Connecticut–Storrs, urged me to publish my manuscript and contributed early editorial guidance. Paul Hass and Kent Calder, editors at the Wisconsin Historical Society, shared their deep experience and helped shape a more interesting and readable narrative.

Without the devoted assistance of archivists and librarians at the Wisconsin Historical Society, Milwaukee Public Library, Milwaukee County Historical Society, and National Archives, this history could not have been written. As historians we often mistakenly believe that we control the past, when in fact we create history by writing about the past. The true shepherds of the past are the archivists who preserve the records necessary to write history and the librarians who organize existing knowledge into usable systems.

For their help in gathering the images in this book, I thank Bob Blessington, Wisconsin AFL-CIO; and Devan Gracyalny, West Allis Historical Society.

In ways too numerous to count my family has contributed to completion of this project. Writing a book requires emotional sustenance. To my wife,

Marge Hannon Pifer, who never flinched at the long hours devoted to research and writing, and to my children, who were young when I began, I owe a debt too great for words.

As with all such endeavors, the words, interpretations, and errors are mine alone.

Richard L. Pifer
Madison, Wisconsin

On December 7, 1941, an aroused America went to war. An evil force was loose in the world, and the time had come for the United States to marshal its industrial might, enter the fray, and crush the Axis. Americans won the war on the battlefront, in the factory, on the ration committee, and in the kitchen. America's workers willingly shouldered their tools in the name of the war effort. They and their unions made daily sacrifices on behalf of the war and sought victory like everyone else on the home front. They bought bonds, donated scrap, and participated on numerous boards and committees. Their patriotic response to the world crisis fueled the production miracle that won the war.

Nonetheless, the nation did not rush to victory with single-minded devotion. The story is more complex. American society certainly was united in its effort to defeat Germany, Japan, and Italy; but that great common goal did not end industrial conflict any more than it eliminated social unrest or racism. Heroic posters promoting production symbolized labor's and the nation's support for the war, but these posters did not reflect the stresses of war, the industrial conflict that emanated from a lack of common interest between labor and management, or the concern workers felt about their future in the postwar world.

This book is about two responses to war. The attack on Pearl Harbor ended any illusions Americans may have had about the war in Asia and Europe. Americans greeted the onset of war with the resolve to see the conflict prosecuted to victory. On the home front they displayed this commitment through a myriad of daily actions ranging from participation in civil defense, to cooperating with rationing, to bond purchases, to working harder and longer hours. Women cared for their families and went to war in America's factories. Patriotism was displayed in a willingness to forgo accustomed activities and commodities, as well as luxuries, until the future. Oddly, this same orientation to the future also produced a counterpoint to the national unity of wartime society. Americans look to the future. As powerful as wartime unity may have been, as dire as early losses on the battlefield were, Americans never really doubted that victory would be won and that they would get on with life. Americans sacrificed to win the war, but they never lost sight of the fact that the war would end and peace would return. As a consequence, actions during the war were shaped not only by patriotism and a commitment to the war effort, but also by a commitment to the future and a society returned to normal.

Industrial conflict, almost inexplicable to many observers at the time, stemmed from the fact that neither management nor labor was willing to sacrifice future economic security in the name of the war effort. They never lost sight of the fact that when the war ended companies would still be striving to produce good products at the lowest cost, and workers and their unions would be struggling with management to protect basic rights and economic security.

Strikes and less visible forms of industrial conflict continued throughout the war. Workers and unions, managers and companies protected their interests for the postwar future. As wartime wages fell behind inflation, workers and unions worried about jobs and earning power in a postwar world. In turn, as managers and companies profited from the war, they worried about low cost production and postwar competitors. Ultimately, wartime industrial conflict emanated from the fact that the postwar goals, interests, and concerns of workers and unions on the one hand and managers and companies on the other were incompatible. Workers looked to the future and sought to protect earning power while managers sought to maintain a competitive edge.

Because wars tend to unite people in a common cause, studying the home front during such conflicts offers an opportunity to understand not only what unites a population, but also what is perceived as important by groups within society. When a society is in crisis, conflict between groups within that society focuses on basic differences between those groups. World War II provides an ideal setting for understanding the nature of labor-management conflict and the issues that were most important to American workers and their unions. Several issues transcended the war itself and can be defined as basic to labor, because those issues marked the point beyond which workers would not compromise simply in the name of the war effort. Industrial workers reached such a point when they perceived that their future economic security was at stake. Similarly, unions refused to compromise their future power and existence on the altar of the war. Nor was labor unique in this regard. Management also balked at measures that limited traditional managerial prerogatives, and industrial leaders continually focused attention on their profit margins. Industrial conflict occurred because the basic interests of workers and unions never fully coincided with the basic interests of managers and companies.

During the war workers took concerted action to protect their interests, even when such action temporarily impeded the war effort. There were some sacrifices that many workers (and their unions) would not willingly make. They would not commit organizational suicide in the face of challenges from employers or rival unions. They would not sit idle while employers did as they pleased on the shop floor and undermined the union's standing with its members. Even when their average weekly earnings skyrocketed, workers refused to mortgage their future by placidly watching the cost of living outstrip hourly wage rates. Male workers—who represented the overwhelming majority of workers—sought to protect their job and wage security as women filled jobs once considered the private domains of men. Men who labored in war industries accepted women into their ranks, but they also resisted management's efforts to use the presence of women to cut pay rates.

When workers, male or female, reached the outer limits of sacrifice, they took actions designed to protect their interests. These actions ranged from personal confrontations on the shop floor to formal meetings across the conference table; from nondisruptive arguments over pay and working conditions to outright strikes that stopped production until the dispute was resolved. The press routinely, almost reflexively, harped on labor's strike record, but the number of disputes settled quietly through negotiation greatly outnumbered the disputes that resulted in work stoppages. The absence of a strike, however, did not mean the absence of conflict. Despite the war, workers and unions still fought to protect wage rates, job security, and contract rights. Likewise, employers still sought the most profitable way to manufacture their products and were unwilling to compromise managerial prerogatives or jeopardize their peacetime competitive edge merely to achieve industrial peace.

The lack of consensus on economic issues was compounded as workers sought greater control over their own workplaces and participation in the establishment of work rules, grievance procedures, seniority systems, and apprenticeship programs. Greater worker involvement in production decision-making inherently threatened traditional management prerogatives to control the workforce and threatened the social structure of the factory. During the first years of the war, management found itself trapped between the need for increased production and the manpower shortage caused by the imperatives of the selective service system. Managers watched as their control over the shop floor—and over production itself—was eroded by official and unofficial arrangements made to preserve labor peace and keep the production system flowing. The industrial hierarchy seemed to be changing as workers and their unions gained greater control than ever before over their work environments. Whether it was through the implementation of labor-management committees, the development of more frequent consultation with union officials, or the unofficial controls imposed on production by workers, managers often saw their prerogatives threatened and their old freedom of action curtailed.

Even more troubling to industrial managers than the unofficial controls placed upon them by the exigencies of the war effort was their perception that organized labor had undertaken an attack on their right and ability to manage. Union attempts to guarantee fair treatment of workers and to protect them from arbitrary dismissal looked like the beginning of a battle to control management's right to hire, discipline, and fire workers. By the time military production was declining late in 1944, many business leaders were prepared to counterattack and regain the initiative from their union opponents. Indeed, the rising number of strikes as the war drew to a close was in part an outgrowth of management's desire to protect its authority from further union encroachments.

Patriotism and appeals for national unity might have held conflict at bay if the workers involved were only concerned about the present; but workers and union leaders looked to the future and saw the threat of a declining standard of living because wartime wage rates had failed to keep pace with inflation. The key to understanding industrial conflict during World War II lies in perceiving that the basic relationships between worker, union, and company remained unchanged by the war. Likewise, the driving forces behind conflict remained unchanged. Patriotism and wartime unity acted to limit industrial conflict, but those factors were seldom strong enough to outweigh workers' concerns for their future economic well-being. Conflict might have been eliminated if workers, unions, and employers reached complete consensus on the goals they wished to achieve. Wartime unity and appeals to patriotism did not create such a consensus.

By World War II labor organizations increasingly operated within a quasi-judicial system to resolve conflict, a system that included contracts and negotiations, grievance procedures, arbitration and mediation panels, and government boards. The war itself hastened the formalization of such mechanisms for channeling conflict into this judicial system and away from overt expressions of aggression. Some unions, especially in the construction trades and well-established AFL (American Federation of Labor) unions such as the Operating Engineers and the Pulp and Sulphite Workers, were well along this road before the war arrived. For many of the large, militant CIO (Congress of Industrial Organizations) unions that had existed for only a few years, the war hastened the acceptance of formal channels for the expression of conflict and the bureaucratization of union controls over workers who chose to express their concerns through spontaneous slowdowns and "wildcat" (unauthorized by the parent union) strikes.

On the national level unions tended to become more bureaucratic during the war. At the local level as well, the wartime emergency increasingly forced unions to rely on formal government channels such as the War Labor Board or the National Labor Relations Board for assistance in resolving disagreements with management. Nonetheless, workers had it within their power to take independent action when it appeared that the formal systems for resolving disputes were not working, or when management or their own unions were not sufficiently responsive to their demands. When workers in a factory or a department were ready to take action, but their union was unready, unwilling, or unable to act, workers might strike or take less visible measures to protect themselves.

Union leaders reacted to local events based, in part, on a set of institutional imperatives that at times differed from what the workers themselves perceived as their own interests. The two labor federations adopted policies against strikes shortly after Pearl Harbor. The AFL, the CIO, and the international unions that comprised those federations generally believed it necessary to adhere to the "no-strike pledge" out of patriotism and a sense of self-preservation. Neither federation officially sanctioned any strike during the war, and union leaders often worked diligently to resolve labor conflicts peacefully. Nonetheless, as pay rates lagged behind inflation and as government boards slowly resolved conflicts, workers themselves increasingly concluded that it was in their best interest to ignore the pledge.

Wartime industrial conflict fed on perceptions of both present and future, perceptions that were reinforced by the tensions that pervaded life on the home front. To be sure, the unity people remember was real, and Americans responded by sacrificing their lives, time, and money. Although war workers, whether men or women, reaped the financial benefits of factory overtime, they found that their extra take-home pay bought little in the way of a more nutritious diet, better housing, higher standard of living, or future economic security. The sacrifices resulting from rationing, housing shortages, and transportation problems forced many to give up what they believed were necessities. Pundits wrote of juvenile delinquency, neglected children, and the apparent disintegration of family and community structure. Doomsayers wondered whether working mothers might reject their children and their family duties and refuse to return to their kitchens after the war.

The fear that women might eschew traditional roles was groundless but highlighted the ambivalence with which many Americans viewed the massive influx of women into war jobs. Young women, unmarried women, and women supporting families had always been a part of the industrial workforce, but the war brought these workers into many new jobs not previously held by women and brought large numbers of married women and women with small children into the workforce as well. The wartime economy required their participation as more and more men joined the armed forces. Union leaders responded to these changes by seeking to protect male union members, the recognized breadwinners. Unions approached the issues of equal pay and seniority within the context of protecting male workers, not only for the present but for the postwar era as well. Many women accepted the limits these attitudes implied. They understood that their war jobs would likely last only for the duration and would be terminated by either changes in production or the return of soldiers to their old jobs when the war ended. As the fear of a generation of motherless children suggested, the social changes implied by large numbers of married women and mothers in the workforce raised numerous questions about the care and nurturing of children and the management of families. As a group women never rejected their nurturing roles, but they faced the daily reality of juggling household duties, child care, and work.

Many such issues that emerged during the war could neither be addressed nor solved until peace dawned. The war turned pressing social problems into secondary issues to be solved at some future date. These unresolved problems produced tensions that went hand in hand with the overall unity of the war years, and they gave the home front a more varied complexion than many people remember.

This tension was particularly poignant for factory workers. Like most citizens they made sacrifices, but all too often their reward was not praise but condemnation. Day after day war production workers read in the press a litany of the problems they were causing for the home front and for military production. When paychecks grew fat from working extra hours, workers were blamed for fueling inflation. When they gave up holiday and Sunday double-time pay some pundits criticized them for hindering production by refusing to give up overtime pay as well! Industrial workers, most of whom abided by the no-strike pledge, often read editorials in their daily newspapers attacking their unions and fellow workers for hindering the war effort in much-publicized work stoppages. Despite the fact that wartime strikes consumed less than one-tenth of 1 percent of available work time devoted to American industrial production during 1942, 1943, and 1944, strikes regularly made headlines and were criticized by politicians and editorialists as incompatible with the war effort. In short, a workforce that had endured a decade of hard times during the Great Depression was routinely pilloried for seeking compensation for its wartime efforts—and for looking ahead to preserving its wartime gains in an uncertain postwar world.

This study focuses on the home front, organized industrial workers, unions, and labor unrest in one of America's great industrial cities: Milwaukee, Wisconsin. It deals with both major labor federations, with skilled and unskilled workers, with men and women in industrial factories, and with conditions on the shop floor and on the home front generally. Although this study reflects the many ways Americans supported the war effort, the nature of national unity and the history of the home front during World War II cannot be wholly understood by seeking only the evidences of selfless patriotism. One must also uncover the sources of tension and conflict and pursue the relationships between home front life and industrial disputes.

The Milwaukee community, with its skilled workforce and stable business environment, offers an ideal setting in which to study wartime society, the concerns of industrial workers, and the nature of industrial conflict. Although popularly known as the nation's beer capital, its economy was built on heavy industry and a workforce of German and Polish heritage. The men and women who worked in Milwaukee's factories not only made the products that built city fortunes; they also made strong unions. Most studies of wartime labor have focused on communities or industries dominated by the youthful and energetic CIO. By contrast, Milwaukee's industries were organized by strong AFL unions as well as by CIO unions. For example, Allis-Chalmers, Milwaukee's largest manufacturer, was organized by Local 248 of the United Auto Workers (CIO). Workers at A. O. Smith, the city's second largest manufacturer, belonged to Federal Labor Union 19806, affiliated directly with the AFL. Both labor federations were strong, healthy, and vigorous defenders of their members' interests. Milwaukee thus provides a setting within which to study not only the relations between labor and management but also to compare the activities of unions affiliated with the CIO and the AFL.

This study places labor's experience in the context of the home front by focusing on a community that was not a wartime boom town; by studying the CIO *and* the AFL; by analyzing women's experiences in unionized factories in relation to the perceptions and goals of male workers, union leaders, and society itself; and by combining a social history of wartime Milwaukee with a history of its workers. It seeks to understand the nature of industrial conflict and the issues most basic to workers by studying them through the lens of a society at war.

Milwaukeeans greeted the advent of war with the same determination as other Americans. They did not want to be at war, but once the conflict was forced upon them, they acted with patriotic fervor to win it as speedily as possible. For those on the home front, participation in the war effort took many different avenues. Everyone felt the effect of the war, whether through concern for loved ones in danger, longer work hours, consumer shortages, or participation in war service organizations. Everyone hoped for the day when the Axis would be defeated, the killing would end, and society would return to "normal."

Throughout the war, Americans made rational decisions regarding the best way to support the war effort. Whether they served on Office of Price Administration ration boards, Red Cross relief committees, civil defense groups, factory fire brigades, or scrap and bond drives, people chose their war work very carefully. They avoided projects that held little relevance for their daily lives and supported projects that touched them directly or promised to yield tangible benefits for the war effort.

Milwaukee's workers were like everyone else in their hopes and desires. In more than ample measure, they filled the vital role of producing the goods necessary for victory—the vehicles, weapons, munitions, and components for all the machinery of war. Like housewives and accountants and schoolteachers, they took part in those home front activities that seemed most likely to protect their homes and families or hasten the end of the war. Like many others, Milwaukee's workers looked toward the postwar future.

This future orientation provides one of the best explanations for the existence of industrial conflict during the war. Businessmen sought to protect their investments and secure new markets for the postwar era. Workers looked to the postwar era and the protection of their living standards. Unions sought to preserve their hard-won gains. When the employer's future goals and the worker's goals were incompatible, conflict almost inevitably ensued. By and large, both workers and employers sought private, rather than public, ways to solve problems and protect war production from disruption. When workers in Milwaukee went on strike, they struck as a weapon of last resort to preserve economic security or to protect their unions. Like their employers, the workers viewed the war as a transitory condition. In their own ways, both labor and management sought to ensure that prosperity, not depression, would follow the end of the war.

In Milwaukee, as elsewhere, industrial conflict received harsh criticism at the time. Wartime strife between labor and management was incomprehensible to many observers, but Milwaukee's industrial employers and their workers understood it at the time. To them, industrial conflict was not unpatriotic any more than it was unhealthy or immoral. Conflict existed before the war and would continue afterward; it was simply a condition of daily life, like the noise, heat, and controlled chaos of a mill or foundry. It signified the acquisitiveness and prudence of businessmen with their eyes on future production and profits, just as it signified the vitality and farsightedness of workers with their vision of future security and prosperity.

CHAPTER ONE

INDUSTRIAL GIANT—READY FOR WAR

In 1830 Milwaukee was little more than Solomon Juneau's trading post at the mouth of the Menomonee River. Within the brief span of a hundred years, the village became a city, passing through an era in which German culture dominated the social scene and commerce in wheat dominated the local economy to become a major industrial center with strong ties to national and overseas markets. By December 1941 Milwaukee industries largely had recovered from the Depression and were producing turbines, cranes, construction equipment, motorcycles, small engines, electrical controls, machine tools, hosiery, and leather. As war clouds darkened the horizon after Germany invaded Poland, local companies began converting production to meet the growing defense needs of the federal government. With a highly skilled workforce and a reputation as the "Machine Shop of the World," Milwaukee was ready to go to war.[1]

During its first thirty years, Milwaukee's economy focused on the trading of agricultural commodities rather than manufacturing. The growth of Wisconsin's hinterland, the completion of railroads from Milwaukee to the Mississippi River, and the improvement of harbor facilities made the city a center for the milling and transshipment of wheat and flour. In 1846 two years before statehood, Milwaukee exported 213,448 bushels of wheat and 15,756 barrels of flour—significant amounts to be sure. In 1857 the Milwaukee & Mississippi

Railroad alone delivered 1,678,000 bushels of wheat to the city. Grain elevators and flour mills dotted the city's landscape. During the Civil War Milwaukee surpassed Chicago as the world's greatest shipper of wheat, and the *Milwaukee Sentinel* told its readers: "The business of a large share of our citizens has been to dispose of the manufactures of other people, and to traffic in the rich products of our own broad, fertile prairies." In 1869 the city's merchants shipped over 16 million bushels of wheat and a million barrels of flour.[2]

The Civil War decade also marked the emergence of Milwaukee as a manufacturing center. From wheat came flour; from iron ore came steel; from livestock, meat and leather; from wood, farm implements and vehicles; from barley and hops, beer. The availability of raw materials, the existence of markets, the influx of workers, and the construction of transportation systems coincided in the 1860s to transform Milwaukee from a center of agricultural commerce to a fledgling industrial giant. The eastern United States and Europe provided markets for wheat, flour, and leather. Westerners needed wagons and farm equipment; millers needed grinding mills. Lumbermen needed saws and steam engines; the railroads, endless miles of track. European immigrants, many of them skilled in metalworking and toolmaking, provided the labor force to run factories and foundries; the development of railroads gave industrialists the incentive, and the wherewithal, to bring raw materials to Milwaukee and to ship finished goods to markets both east and west. Metal-based manufacturing slowly grew in importance as Milwaukee became an industrial center. Fifteen years after the Civil War, Milwaukee had the nation's sixth highest concentration of industrial workers, 45 percent of the workforce. By 1910 the products of Milwaukee's iron and steel mills, foundries and machine shops, and tool-and-die establishments constituted the city's broad, rock-solid industrial base.[3]

By the time of World War II, few, if any, of the city's major companies could trace their origins as far back as Milwaukee's most popular manufacturers, the brewers. The brewing industry originated in the 1840s—a time when German immigrants were settling in Milwaukee, when Wisconsin was forming its state government, and when the grains and hops necessary for the brewer's art were supplied by farms in Wisconsin.

During Milwaukee's first half-century, Germans such as Jacob Best, Joseph Schlitz, Valentin Blatz, and Frederick Miller made Milwaukee beer world-famous and created an image of the city that, in conjunction with its German heritage, entered the popular consciousness. To serve an ever-growing national market, Milwaukee's brewers steadily expanded production from 58,666 barrels in 1865 to 3,724,937 barrels in 1910. Drawing as it did upon immigrant expertise and agricultural products from Wisconsin's hinterland, growth of the brewing industry was no accident—and neither was the linking of Milwaukee with its most famous product. Frederick Pabst's slogan, "Milwaukee beer is famous—Pabst has made it so," appeared on walls, wagons, and streetcars in New York. By 1898 Schlitz advertising used the slogan, "The beer that made Milwaukee famous." Beer had become associated with the city.[4]

Brewing grew out of the link between immigrants and local raw materials. Other early industries likewise originated from the convergence of new settlers and local supplies. By the end of the nineteenth century, Milwaukee was one of the nation's major producers of packed meats and of leather. Not only were raw materials easily accessible, but the national rail system also carried Milwaukee products to eastern markets.[5]

Milwaukee's iron and foundry industry best illustrated the important relationship between access to raw materials and to markets. Milwaukee, like other industrial cities of the Great Lakes, was an ideal place for the marriage of iron ore from Michigan and Minnesota and coal and coke from Pennsylvania. In 1880 Milwaukee ranked sixth in the nation with annual iron and steel production valued at nearly $5 million. Although meat packing ranked as Milwaukee's single most important industry that year, iron, steel, foundry, and machine-shop production combined equaled $7.2 million annually, outstripping the packing industry by over $1 million.[6]

The Allis-Chalmers Manufacturing Company represented one of Milwaukee's most important firms engaged in heavy industry. The company began in 1847 as the Reliance Works, founded by Charles Decker and James Seville as a manufacturer of cast-iron products and flour-milling and sawmill equipment. The company prospered for a decade but fell on hard times during the depression of 1857. When the firm was sold at a sheriff's auction in 1861, Edward P. Allis took possession. Between 1861 and his death in 1889, Allis built the business from production valued at $31,000 to production of over $3 million. He expanded operations by taking risks to enter local markets and by innovating to meet the needs of national markets as well. When Milwaukee built a water system in the 1870s, Edward P. Allis supplied most of the pipe, pumps, and engines. He surprised and excited city observers when he bid on the pipe contract, for at the time he made the bid, the Reliance Works had no foundry in which to make the pipe. As he rushed to build the foundry and meet the contract schedule, Allis hit upon a business formula that served him well: hire the best men available and provide them with the tools they needed to create new products. Among the first of many experts he hired were John Pennycook, a Chicago pipe expert, and William Wall, a skilled foundryman. In addition to the pipe contract, Allis soon specialized in sawmill equipment for northern Wisconsin and millstones for local gristmills. In 1873 he hired George Madison Hinkley, a millwright with extensive experience in the Michigan lumber industry, to revitalize his sawmill department. Successful innovations in the use of band saws and electric motors soon made the company a major manufacturer of sawmill equipment.

Four years later Allis hired William Dixon Gray, an expert in flour milling with whose help he introduced the roller system of grinding flour to America. In 1878 Allis supplied Cadwallader C. Washburn, a former governor of Wisconsin, with an all-roller flour mill for his operations in Minneapolis—what eventually became General Mills. Publicity generated by this event brought new orders and made the Reliance Works a major builder of flour-milling equipment. In 1877 Allis hired engineer Edwin Reynolds from the Corliss Steam Engine Company of Providence, Rhode Island. Reynolds was capable of designing the new engines and power plants necessary for mines, lumber mills, and public works that were becoming a staple of the company's national business by the turn of the century. By the time of Allis's death in 1889, the Reliance Works employed 1,500 men.

To improve its ability to serve national and world markets, the Edward P. Allis Company,[7] then the largest manufacturer of steam engines in the United States, merged with two Chicago companies and a Pennsylvania firm, all manufacturers of engines and heavy machinery, to form the Allis-Chalmers Company in 1901. At that time the new company's annual business exceeded $10 million and employed a total of five thousand workers at five plants.

Unfortunately, a decade of mismanagement resulted in receivership by 1912. Reorganization in 1913 elevated Otto H. Falk to the presidency of the Allis-Chalmers Manufacturing Company. Falk, a retired brigadier general in the Wisconsin National Guard and vice-president of the Falk Company, a Milwaukee foundry, brought to the company his considerable managerial skills and a strong interest in agricultural machinery. Expansion of the company's tractor production reflected Falk's belief in mechanization, his anticipation of changes in many aspects of American life, and his desire to diversify the company's product line.[8]

Unlike Allis-Chalmers, Milwaukee's second-largest manufacturer began as a producer of consumer goods rather than of heavy industrial machinery. In 1874 when C. J. Smith, founder of A. O. Smith Corporation, established a machine shop in Milwaukee, he specialized in making bicycle frames and parts for baby carriages. By the 1890s the company was the nation's largest producer of bicycle frames. Innovation brought the company success. While other producers relied on solid iron bars for bicycle manufacturing, Smith developed a technique for making frames using tubular steel. By 1910 the company had adapted its work with bicycle frames to become the nation's largest producer of automobile frames.

During World War I the A. O. Smith Corporation turned its attention to making welded bomb casings. In the postwar era the company combined its experience with bicycle frames, pressed-steel automobile frames, and welding to become one of the leading suppliers of large-diameter oil and gas pipes. The company also produced vessels made of numerous layers of welded tubular steel capable of containing materials under high pressure. In seeking a way to contain the corrosive compounds often stored or manufactured in these pressure vessels, the company began lining its casings with a variety of alloys and with glass. By 1940 company engineers were deep in the development of a new use for their process: the glass-lined hot water heater. Whether the product was steam engines and tractors at Allis-Chalmers or bicycle frames and large-diameter pipe at A. O. Smith, Milwaukee's two largest manufacturers built their success and reputations on new products and processes that became essential to twentieth-century industry.[9]

The manufacturers for whom Milwaukeeans worked in 1940 made beer, leather, clothing, steel, automotive products, tractors, electrical relays, generators, water heaters, batteries, kitchen utensils, and industrial cranes. As with Allis-Chalmers and A. O. Smith, many of these companies dated back to the nineteenth century. Filer and Stowell evolved from a machine shop established in the late 1850s to serve the sawmill industry. Geuder and Paeschke Manufacturing Company was founded in 1880; by 1940 it was making kitchen utensils, milk cans, and steel shipping packages. Alonzo Pawling and Henry Harnischfeger founded their machine and pattern shop in the early 1880s; it evolved into the Harnischfeger Corporation, specializing in heavy industrial cranes.[10]

All of these companies contributed to Milwaukee's growing industrial importance. By the end of the first decade of the twentieth century, the city was more committed to industrial production than were many other cities of the same size. With a population of 373,857 Milwaukee ranked twelfth in the United States, but the city's manufactured products were valued at over $208 million, placing it tenth in the nation. Approximately 15.9 percent of the city's population were industrial wage earners. Of the other top ten cities, only Detroit and Philadelphia had a greater concentration of their populations involved in manufacturing.[11] More than 50 percent of Milwaukee's labor force worked at industrial jobs in 1910 and 1920. In 1940 even after the dislocation and retrenchment caused by the Great Depression, almost 40 percent of the labor force worked in factories.[12]

Milwaukee's high concentration of industrial workers, as well as its significant German population,[13] shaped city politics in ways conducive to the development of a strong, vibrant labor movement. In the early twentieth century an alliance of workers, Germans, and socialists (with much overlapping) created a reform movement that shaped Milwaukee politics for forty years. In 1910 after years of agitation and campaigning, a coalition of socialists and organized labor defeated David G. Rose, the corrupt mayor and Democratic political boss, and replaced him with Emil Seidel, a Social Democrat.[14]

Although he was a socialist, Emil Seidel was elected because of the reputation of socialists in Milwaukee for reform rather than revolution. The foundation was laid during the 1880s by the careful work of Victor Berger (1860–1929). An Austro-Hungarian by birth, Victor Berger resigned his teaching job in 1892 to devote his attention to socialist organizing and newspaper editing. He took over the *Arbeiter-Zeitung* in 1893, renamed it the *Wisconsin Vorwarts,* and soon made it the official voice of the Milwaukee Federated Trades Council (founded in 1887) and the Wisconsin State Federation of Labor (founded in 1893).

Berger preached a moderate, evolutionary socialism. He organized an informal group known as the *Sozial-Democratischer Verein* at about the same time he took over the *Arbeiter-Zeitung.* This small group attracted German-speaking socialists, many of whom were leaders of Milwaukee's fledgling trade unions.

The link between socialism and the trade unions was perfectly clear when Berger formed the Social Democratic party in 1897. Almost immediately, the Federated Trades Council endorsed the new organization. After an internal struggle between the socialists and the non-socialists, the Federated Trades Council ended the century by electing an executive committee made up solely of socialists, among them Victor Berger. Although unions offered opportunities for socialist organizing, he admonished his colleagues that the labor movement must include "Democrats, Republicans, Populists and Prohibitionists" as well as socialists or risk failing in its mission to represent the interests of workers.[15]

Thus was forged an alliance between organized labor and the Milwaukee socialists that lasted well into the twentieth century. The years before World War I marked the alliance's heyday—a time when major figures in the Milwaukee Federated Trades Council such as Frank Weber and John J. Handley also played prominent roles in the Socialist party.

When Emil Seidel won the mayor's seat in 1910 and another Social Democrat, Daniel Hoan, won it in 1916, the victories represented the strength of the socialist-labor alliance, the importance of the German vote, and the power of reform politics in the Progressive era. When voters in Milwaukee supported socialists, they were voting not so much for ideology as for honest government over corrupt machine politics.

Daniel Hoan won the mayor's office in 1916 with the strong support of organized labor. Seidel's socialist administration had demonstrated the value of having an ally in the mayor's chair. The administration had insisted on the use of union labor for city printing jobs, enforced the city's factory safety and sanitation ordinances, raised the wages for common laborers working for the city, and kept the city's anti-union police chief under control in 1911 when the Garment Workers Union went on strike.

Hoan himself came to office with impressive credentials. During the garment workers' strike he refused to prosecute a picketer who called a strikebreaker a "scab." As city attorney, he had vigorously enforced ordinances designed to force utilities to bear their fair share of the municipal tax burden. Besides his role as a member of the Seidel administration, he had been the attorney for the Wisconsin Federation of Labor and had helped draft a proposal from which the state legislature created the nation's first workmen's compensation law.[16]

Remarkably, Hoan served uninterrupted from 1916 to 1940. His record amply justified labor's support. He seldom had a socialist majority on the city council, but he shaped an administration renowned for its fairness, humanity, efficiency, and honesty. Unions and workers alike became accustomed to an administration that was concerned about the welfare of working-class people and that assiduously worked to resolve labor-management troubles amicably.

Dan Hoan believed that industrial violence occurred either when the civil authorities were demonstrably anti-labor or when the employer refused to bargain in good faith with the workers. During his tenure the Milwaukee police remained a neutral force prepared to protect the rights of picketers and employers alike. He assumed that workers were basically rational, law-abiding citizens who were not seeking special privileges but rather were seeking to exercise legitimate rights. When the mayor talked about reforming the police department during his administration, he emphasized the importance of using the police fairly in labor disputes. He argued that Milwaukee's modern record of nonviolent strikes[17] was due to the fact that workers knew their rights would be protected and employers knew that the mayor would countenance no abrogation of those rights.[18]

A similar commonsense approach marked the Hoan administration's attempts to mitigate the worst effects of the Great Depression. The First World War had fostered rapid expansion of Milwaukee industry. Between 1910 and 1915 the value of manufactured products in Milwaukee increased by 7.5 percent. By contrast, manufacturing increased by 158 percent between 1915 and 1920. Wartime orders created tremendous demands for iron, steel, heavy machinery, motor vehicles, packed meats, and leather—all Milwaukee specialties. The early postwar prosperity and economic growth were hurt by an agricultural depression that began in 1920 and ended with the crash of the stock market on Thursday, October 24, 1929.[19]

Milwaukee's economy was partially insulated at the onset of the Great Depression by the fact that orders for heavy machinery did not decline as rapidly as did consumer orders, and the fiscally conservative municipal government closed 1931 with a $4 million surplus. Nonetheless, by 1933 Milwaukee felt the full impact of the Depression. Employment dropped to only 66,010 wage earners—a decline of 44 percent since the crash in 1929. Manufacturers of iron, steel, and heavy machinery in particular had borne the brunt of declining orders placed by railroads, farmers, and the general public. Building construction had plunged to only 12.5 percent of the average annual expenditures during the previous twenty years. Once hard times came to Milwaukee, the city's experience mirrored that of the nation. The economy improved somewhat in 1935 and 1936, then worsened during the recession that began in August 1937 and ran to September 1938. It was not until 1939—as global tensions mounted—that the economy finally rebounded.

In the early years of the Depression, Milwaukee met relief needs by converting an old armory into a kitchen and dining facility and by transferring available city funds to departments prepared to provide work for the unemployed. During 1931 more than 12,000 men worked at least one ten-day shift improving the city's parks and playgrounds. During 1933 the burden of meeting growing relief needs shifted from the locality to the federal government and Franklin Roosevelt's New Deal programs. With federal money, bureaucrats, planners, and legions of workers created the middle-income Parklawn and Greendale housing projects, constructed school buildings, paved city streets, laid new sewer lines, and renovated city buildings.[20]

As city, state, and federal governments sought solutions to the Depression and attempted to ameliorate the suffering, Milwaukee's trade unions stirred, sought their own solutions, and came to life with new organizing campaigns. Beginning with a union-mounted drive to organize common laborers in August 1933, labor-management friction increased and began to place stress on Daniel Hoan's approach to industrial relations. In 1933 there were only six strikes involving a total of 482 workers in Milwaukee. The following year there were forty-two strikes involving almost 14,000 workers.

The bitterest of those strikes resulted in the unionization of the Milwaukee Electric Railway and Light Company, operator of the city's transit system. The strike began when the company refused to abide by a National Labor Relations Board order to reinstate thirteen employees who had been fired for their union activity. Soon it paralyzed the city's electric trolley transportation system. Large crowds of Milwaukeeans supportive of the strike gathered at the car barns, riots broke out, and Mayor Hoan made plain his support of the workers. To protect company property, the railway company electrified its grounds with live wires. On the evening of June 29, 1934, a demonstrator entered the grounds and an employee turned a fire hose in his direction. There was a flash of light, and the young man was electrocuted. The crowd that had gathered at the car barns quietly disbanded in stunned disbelief.

This grisly incident rapidly solidified public hostility toward the company, and railway officials soon met with union leaders for the first time. The negotiations resulted in recognition for the union and the rehiring of both the strikers and the workers who had originally been discharged unfairly. The city government and the people of Milwaukee played an important role in supporting unionization of the Milwaukee Electric Railway and Light Company.[21]

Similar support was provided in 1935, when workers began a seventeen-month-long strike at the Lindemann-Hoverson stove works. The company refused to meet with representatives of the workers or with federal conciliation officials and insisted on keeping the plant running. The police found it impossible to control the large crowds that gathered at the factory. As conditions worsened, Mayor Hoan said that he feared a "breakdown of local authority and . . . the intervention of the state militia and the declaration of martial law."[22] To bring conditions under control, the common council adopted an ordinance empowering the mayor or the chief of police to close a plant if an employer refused to bargain with his or her employees and if large crowds gathered at the plant on two successive days. Although the Boncel Ordinance—so called for its author, alderman Frank Boncel—was never used and was repealed by the council after the socialists received a stinging defeat in the elections of 1936, it caused Lindemann-Hoverson to close its factory voluntarily. Thereafter the level of hostility subsided.[23]

As the Depression decade wore on, the Federated Trades Council (FTC) and the American Federation of Labor (AFL) achieved notable success not only in organizing trade unions but also in organizing industrial unions. Socialists in Wisconsin's labor movement advocated organizing the workers of a factory into a single union, regardless of specific worker duties or skills, when that factory or industry relied largely on assembly line production or on workers who completed only a small portion of an assembly job. With its focus on building unions based upon an industry rather than on the craft of an individual worker, this position was a departure from the way unions had been organized during the nineteenth and early twentieth centuries. The Milwaukee Federated Trades Council had been quite sympathetic to the concept of industrial organizing. Similarly, the Wisconsin State Federation of Labor had been in the forefront of those advocating a compromise between the old AFL craft unions and the rapidly growing industrial unions of the Committee for Industrial Organization (CIO), which had been so successful elsewhere in the automobile, steel, and rubber industries.

The most important Milwaukee organizing drives resulted in the formation of Federal Labor Unions (FLU, meaning industrial unions directly affiliated with the AFL and not with a craft union) at Milwaukee's largest manufacturers, A. O. Smith and Allis-Chalmers. Success at these companies symbolized the contrasting results of industrial organizing. At A. O. Smith, Milwaukee's second-largest employer, management readily accepted craft unions. When the AFL organized a Federal Labor Union in the 1930s, the company quickly accepted it as the bargaining agent for workers not already represented by craft unions. Throughout World War II AFL Federal Labor Union 19806 (also known as the Smith Steel Workers Union) coexisted with nearly a dozen older craft unions at A. O. Smith.

By contrast, Federal Labor Union 20136 (later to become United Auto Workers [UAW] Local 248) at Allis-Chalmers, led by members of the electricians' union, began absorbing craft workers, much to the displeasure of several of Milwaukee's most powerful craft unions. Those AFL unions had experienced little success in organizing Allis-Chalmers's workers, who often resented the entrance requirements, elitism, and high dues of the craft unions. When Allis-Chalmers workers greeted FLU 20136 enthusiastically, it put the union on a collision course with the FTC.

Unfortunately, the leaders of established craft unions such as the carpenters, electricians, and teamsters in Wisconsin and nationally feared that unions organized by industry or factory would harm their craft-based organizations. After the 1935 AFL annual meeting refused to sanction industrial organizing, John L. Lewis of the United Mine Workers and leaders from the garment and textile unions formed the Committee for Industrial Organization to pursue this new approach. Technically a committee within the AFL, the group was the embryo of a new national labor federation headed for a confrontation with the dominant craft unions of its parent organization. At the AFL annual meeting in 1936, delegates voted to suspend the rebellious unions. Two years later, in recognition of its standing as a new national force in the labor movement, the Committee for Industrial Organization changed its name to the Congress of Industrial Organizations and was known thereafter as the CIO.

The same rivalry between craft and industrial unions resulted in an irreparable rift in the Milwaukee Federated Trades Council. Shortly after the AFL expelled the CIO unions, the FTC expelled the union at Allis-Chalmers, the largest local in Wisconsin. The split developed when Molders Local 125 and Electrical Workers Local 494 complained that Trades Council representatives from the Federal Union at Allis-Chalmers were former members of the Molders' and Electrical Workers' locals. In the weeks that followed, the Trades Council debated the issue, the Allis-Chalmers Federal Union joined the UAW as Local 248, and the FTC expelled the local from its ranks. The gigantic Allis-Chalmers union threatened the established craft unions and the balance of power in the Federated Trades Council. Eventually sixty-two locals withdrew from the FTC and formed the Milwaukee Industrial Union Council (IUC) under the leadership of Harold Christoffel, president of Local 248. The stage was set for an intense struggle as the FTC and the IUC competed for workers' loyalties in a new wave of organizing activity.[24]

Thus, as war broke out in Europe in September 1939, the Milwaukee labor movement was at war with itself. The rivalry between the two labor federations fostered organizing as never before. The movement signed up thousands of workers who were unorganized prior to 1932. That year Milwaukee's unions had 20,000 members. Four years later, they had 60,000. Following the split between the AFL and the CIO in 1936, the pace of organizing accelerated nationwide, and Wisconsin became one of the most significant battlegrounds. The Wisconsin Labor Relations Board concluded that renewed organizing drives had doubled AFL membership in Wisconsin during the year between the 1936 and 1937 AFL conventions. At the same time, the CIO officially came into existence and brought thousands of members into the fold of organized labor. In a thinly veiled attack on AFL critics, the Wisconsin edition of the *CIO News* made this very point in 1938:

> Take a look at Wisconsin. If we had not had this "tragic split" at least 125,000 men and women enrolled in CIO or AFL unions would still be unorganized. The 8,000 Allis-Chalmers workers would still be at the mercy of wrangling craft union leaders. Harley-Davidson, Fairbanks-Morse, Evinrude Motors, Milprint, Louis-Allis, Gisholt, Highway Trailer, Marathon Electric and more than 100 other industrial plants would today be open shop . . . strongholds, instead of organized in powerful, industrial unions.[25]

The AFL and the CIO enrolled thousands of new members as the Great Depression drew to a close and industry and manufacturing revived. In many instances labor's greatest victories occurred when organizers, both of the AFL and of the CIO, emphasized the industrial union rather than the craft union approach. The CIO auto, steel, and electrical workers' unions were particularly successful in Milwaukee. Federal labor unions and the AFL auto workers, both of which sought to organize unskilled production employees, were equally successful at A. O. Smith, Briggs and Stratton Corporation (small gasoline engines), and the Harley-Davidson Motor Company (motorcycles). These were not truly "industrial-style" unions, because the AFL craft unions bargained for their own narrow memberships; but it was the unskilled workers who dominated labor-management relations at Milwaukee's biggest factories, whether organized by the CIO or the AFL. Craft unions representing the machinists, electrical workers, carpenters, and operating engineers remained powerful forces in Milwaukee; but the vitality of the labor movement resided in those who were organizing workers who normally fell outside the old craft-union structure.

By 1940 Milwaukee was a thriving city of 587,472 residents, with an adjacent county population of approximately 766,885. Nearly 40 percent of the city's labor force was employed in manufacturing, making Milwaukee one of the most heavily industrialized cities in the nation. Manufacturers of iron, steel, and heavy machinery continued to dominate. Packed meats, leather products, textiles, chemicals, and beer trailed far behind heavy industry.[26]

As Britain and Russia teetered on the brink of disaster in Europe, and the United States edged toward war, industries in Milwaukee and other Wisconsin cities rapidly converted to war production. During 1941 the state garnered $450 million in orders for military goods. At first, industry responded slowly to these orders as it converted civilian production facilities to meet military needs. By December 1941 however, war conversion and production were moving at a rapid pace, and Wisconsin manufacturers had delivered finished products to the federal government valued at over $225 million.[27]

Well before the Japanese attack on Pearl Harbor, Milwaukee's industries were committed to military production. Milwaukee factories received more than $175 million in arms contracts by November 1941. Total industrial production in Milwaukee reached $940 million in 1941, topping the previous high from 1929 by $28 million. The total number of workers employed in Milwaukee factories rose from an average of 86,400 in 1940 to 108,180 in 1941.[28]

As the economy converted to war production, Milwaukee's industrial corporations expanded their operations, depleting local labor supplies and drawing thousands of workers to the city in search of war jobs. Allis-Chalmers with 11,610 employees and A. O. Smith with 6,499 dominated the industrial scene in July 1941. A year later Allis-Chalmers employed 20,632 workers and A. O. Smith employed 8,594. In response to the demands of the war economy, each company eventually reached peak employment in 1944, with over 25,000 and 15,000 employees, respectively.

In July 1941, on the eve of war, the United States Employment Service (USES) surveyed more than two hundred Milwaukee-area companies, including most if not all of Milwaukee's major manufacturers. Of the 98,854 people employed by these companies, 53,416 (54 percent) already worked in plants producing ordnance or small-arms ammunition.[29] In fact the USES probably underestimated the number of workers already engaged in war production because it listed companies such as Allis-Chalmers as making non-war machinery. The Allis-Chalmers turbine department produced equipment valued at more than $1.6 million in 1939. By 1941 the same Milwaukee plant was heavily committed to manufacturing steam turbines for navy warships. Thanks in large part to government contracts, the value of production in this department increased

165 percent during 1940 (to $4.2 million) and another 72 percent in 1941 (to almost $7.4 million).[30]

News from other companies reinforced perceptions of a vibrant defense production economy in Milwaukee. A. O. Smith showed third-quarter earnings of $1,382,688 in 1941—some 356 percent higher than for the same quarter in 1940. Even before the attack on Pearl Harbor, Allis-Chalmers, Nordberg Company, Cutler-Hammer, Inc., and the Harnischfeger Corporation already operated their plants twenty-four hours a day, six days a week, turning out machine tools, propelling equipment for ships, torpedo tubes, electrical controls, and industrial cranes. Chain Belt Company, A. O. Smith, and Square D Company, makers of artillery, aerial bombs, and electrical controls, operated on a similar basis in some departments. The Falk Corporation was on a seven-day, round-the-clock schedule working on naval contracts, as was the Kearney and Trecker Corporation, which reported being "swamped" with orders for milling machines essential for industrial conversion to war production. In an attempt to extend defense production to small contractors, the Heil Company subcontracted over $175,000 in orders for repair tools to service Pratt and Whitney aircraft engines to ninety-four companies employing between three and eighty workers throughout Milwaukee. Heil itself had received a $25,000 order for airplane service trucks. Four days before the United States entered the war, the Heil company received a $10 million order for aircraft gasoline and oil tanks. The company already devoted 90 percent of its output to defense production and estimated that the new order would keep its 2,400 employees busy around the clock throughout 1942.[31]

When war came, the United States stood poised to become what would be known as "the arsenal of democracy"—in fact, the biggest arsenal on earth. For the next seven months Milwaukeeans were treated to a spectacle that implied, by its very nature, that America would win the production battle. Through its news columns and monthly "General Business Pulse," an index of local economic conditions, the *Milwaukee Journal* carried the message of rising industrial production to its readers. The nation rushed to meet its war needs, and millions of dollars in new contracts poured into Wisconsin. The Milwaukee shoe industry took its first government contracts; the Massey-Harris Company purchased a major plant in Racine to begin tank construction; Allis-Chalmers began work on two new factories. The latter company hoped to have a $9 million plant ready to produce turbo-superchargers for high-altitude bombers before June and had laid plans for a $2.25 million steam-turbine plant as well. In March, Captain Frederick Hansen, director of the Milwaukee suboffice of the Chicago ordnance district, reported that Wisconsin military production had improved markedly—by 400 percent in some cases—since December.[32]

Small companies as well as large ones benefited from the war-induced prosperity. One small firm, the Taylor Manufacturing Company—makers of drill presses, production drills, and hydraulic dynamometers for measuring the power developed by engines—stood on the verge of bankruptcy in September

1939. By May 1942 the company had expanded to a new factory, employed over fifty workers, and was thriving.[33]

Stories about production bottlenecks, corporate inefficiency, and broken production schedules provided a sobering counterpoint during the days after Pearl Harbor, but such stories paled next to those of successful production. Entire industries retooled in record time and began to produce critical war supplies ahead of schedule. The automobile industry provided the best single example of America's awesome productive power. Through careful planning, the major automobile manufacturers prepared for converting their plants to military uses even as civilian vehicles continued to roll off their lines at full speed. By March, for example, General Motors's Buick plant was turning out bomber engines at the rate originally scheduled for December of 1942. At a Fisher Body plant in Detroit, gleaming new auto bodies—the last of their kind for "the duration"—were still on the assembly line as workers began converting the factory to tank production. Forty-seven days later the first of many thousands of all-welded M-4 Sherman tanks rolled off the line under its own power. To achieve this miraculous transformation, company engineers and workers designed and built many of their own tools, drew their own blueprints, and adapted their old knowledge to new purposes. Likewise, by the end of May, Henry Ford's new bomber plant at Willow Run completed its first B-24, the first aircraft to be built solely by an auto company. Ford's huge four-engined bomber symbolized what Americans and Europeans had been waiting for: mass production of war matériel by the world's greatest industrial power.[34]

The initial phase of war production demonstrated unmistakably that the Depression was over. Unemployment rose briefly during the conversion period, but more than three-quarters of those who were laid off immediately found other jobs. Curtailment of automobile production hit Milwaukee factories harder than any other single development during the conversion period. Major Milwaukee companies such as A. O. Smith, Briggs and Stratton, and Seaman Body (Nash-Kelvinator) were closely tied to the production of cars and trucks. The first two firms, however, had already secured major defense contracts, lessening the need for layoffs. In addition, in 1941 A. O. Smith established a retraining program that allowed many workers who would otherwise have been laid off to prepare for new jobs in the plant.[35]

Seaman Body workers were not so lucky. In January 1942 the company laid off approximately 3,000 workers as it retooled to accommodate aircraft orders. Nash-Kelvinator, the parent company, expected employment at Seaman Body to return to 3,200 by fall; but conversion problems, poor planning, and contract cancellations delayed full production at the plant until the fall of 1943. In the interim, workers and union officials alike complained of the mismanagement that was preventing their reemployment. When Seaman Body called its workers back, they returned with memories of the hardship and discontent bred by eighteen months of unemployment. Many companies had been reluctant to hire laid-off workers who might soon be recalled to work by their original employers.[36]

Happily for most workers, the dislocation at Seaman Body was the exception, not the rule. Most factory workers displaced during the conversion period soon found new jobs in similar plants or were recalled by their original employers. In May, for example, Allis-Chalmers advertised for workers to fill jobs opened as men went into the armed forces or took jobs created at the company's new supercharger plant. The response reflected the basic health of the local economy: only five hundred workers applied for some six thousand jobs! Presaging future developments, J. I. Onarheim, Allis-Chalmers's employment supervisor, anticipated that the necessary workers would come from those employed in nondefense work and from women not employed at the time. Onarheim told a *Milwaukee Journal* reporter, "We are running out of people with even a minimum of training . . . and fellows like [Donald] Pulley will have to be trained to supply the necessary force."

The Donald Pulley named by Onarheim had grown up on a farm near Highland, Wisconsin. In August 1941 he moved his wife and two children to Milwaukee in hopes of finding a defense job. With no prior factory experience, Allis-Chalmers rejected his first application for work. Instead, he found work in a Milwaukee restaurant. Nine months later Pulley applied again for one of the jobs being advertised by the company. This time, as Onarheim told the *Journal* reporter, Pulley probably would get a job despite his lack of experience.[37]

When Donald Nelson, head of the national War Production Board, proclaimed an end to the conversion period in July 1942, most Milwaukee workers engaged in vital war work could look forward to several years of uninterrupted employment in factories committed to turning out military supplies. During the first year of the war, Milwaukee industry increased the value of its output by 27.5 percent and set a production record for the city. One year later, local industry topped the record by another 21 percent and produced almost $1.5 billion worth of products.[38] As the war economy hit its stride, Milwaukee factories were producing seagoing tugs, electrical controls, plane refueling units, leather goods, giant diesel engines, torpedo tubes, aircraft and tank parts, artillery pieces, and all manner of ammunition.[39]

For many companies, wartime production meant unprecedented expansion. Allis-Chalmers was not alone in opening a new plant in Milwaukee. Ben Froemming, a Milwaukee building contractor, began producing 1,000-ton seagoing tugs at a shipyard on the Kinnickinnic River. On the site of the old Eline Candy Company on the Port Washington Road, the federal government built a huge ordnance plant to be operated by the U.S. Rubber Company. A. O. Smith built a new facility to manufacture airplane propellers, and the Harnischfeger Corporation, maker of industrial cranes, tripled its production without even building new facilities. With the aid of the Smaller War Plants Corporation, a federal agency created to help manufacturers with fewer than 500 employees to secure war contracts, a wide variety of small machine shops and businesses carried out subcontracting work for major war factories. Likewise, several hundred basement mechanics and small shop owners formed A-M, Incorporated (Ability and Machines), in order to take advantage of subcontracting assignments. The war economy presented numerous opportunities for the small, highly skilled manufacturing enterprises that abounded in and around Milwaukee.[40]

For the first time in more than a decade, Americans did not have to worry about layoffs or plant closings. Factory work was easy to find, and it paid well. During the first year of the war, the "General Business Pulse" index maintained by the *Milwaukee Journal* rose 22 percent. Employment was up by 21 percent from 113,800 in December 1941 to 137,700 a year later; payrolls rose 54 percent during the same period. Between December 1941 and December 1942, average weekly earnings in Milwaukee rose by 20 percent—from $36.10 to $45.20. As the war began, manufacturing employees were working an average of 43.3 hours a week and earning an average of 83.6 cents an hour. A year later they were working 47.4 hours a week and earning an average of 95.8 cents an hour. The rise in average hourly pay reflected both an increase in hourly pay of approximately 12 cents and the overtime pay received for the extra four hours a week being worked.[41]

Prosperity and wartime social tensions, high profits and high wages, energetic and growing unions, confident and thriving businesses; all of these factors comprised the fabric of life on the home front during World War II. Milwaukee companies and their workers helped make possible the production miracle of the early 1940s; but the record of those years reflects a history more complex than simple devotion to national duty and the war effort.

In Milwaukee labor relations were influenced by the fact that, although the city prospered during the war, it was not a boom town. Unlike Willow Run, Michigan, which sprang up in an empty field, or cities such as Seattle and Birmingham, which underwent sudden, dramatic changes with the rapid growth of the aircraft and steel industries, Milwaukee's wartime expansion did not entail extreme, overnight social dislocation. Approximately 70 percent of the city's industries continued to produce their standard products during the war, but instead of serving the private marketplace, they served the war effort.[42] Milwaukee's war plants tended to draw upon local sources for industrial workers: women, employees in nonessential jobs, retired workers, young people, and racial minorities, mostly black. As a consequence, the social structure of neighborhoods, kinship, and friendship remained largely intact—a resource to be drawn upon as Milwaukeeans dealt with wartime demands that placed pressures on home and family.

Labor relations also were shaped by Milwaukee's long heritage of skilled craftsmanship and craft unionism and by the recruitment of assembly-line workers by vibrant new industrial unions. Workers unaccustomed to dealing with employers from a position of strength found themselves negotiating with managers equally unaccustomed to negotiating *anything* about how to run their companies. Friction inevitably occurred as labor and management worked out the details of this new relationship. The results of this process ranged from the relatively cooperative relationship between the union and management at A. O. Smith to the highly combative relationship between UAW Local 248 and the management of Allis-Chalmers.

By the time the United States went to war, these relationships had solidified in Milwaukee. Much of labor relations during the war—the rhetoric and the politics of boardroooom and shop floor, the compromises and the obduracy, the continual jockeying for advantage and the sometimes bitter wrangling—can be understood only by examining those relations in context and in detail. No matter how patriotic and self-sacrificing both parties were, nor how great were their achievements, labor and management possessed fundamentally different visions of the best way to guarantee themselves a bright future in the postwar world. In Milwaukee, as elsewhere, the resolution of those differences proved to be a complex and frequently misunderstood chapter of wartime history.

CHAPTER TWO

UNITY AND TENSION
ON THE HOME FRONT

"**T**hey went out for a holiday and found war."¹ Sunday, December 7, 1941, was "children's afternoon" on Wisconsin Avenue. The day was sunny. After church thousands of Milwaukee families strolled the avenue, admiring Christmas displays in shop windows, listening to Christmas chimes over the loudspeakers, laughing with Santa Claus. There were only fourteen shopping days before Christmas. "Sergeant York" was drawing crowds to the movie theater. Radios carried music, football, learned discussion, and the first news of war into homes and automobiles. As news of the Japanese attack on Pearl Harbor slowly spread, people reacted with shock and surprise. By late afternoon, newsboys heralded war.

Small groups discussed the news in taverns and hotels. Although many people found the reports hard to believe, they viewed the outcome as certain. Edwin Hellmich, a local cab driver, typified the prevailing mood when he told a *Milwaukee Journal* reporter, "There's no question but that the United States, with unlimited resources, will win." Margaret Felch, who told a reporter that she worked as a "demonstrator," commented, "The war is a shame and it's too bad, but how beautiful we're going to beat those Japanese. We'll wipe them out. I stayed up until 1:45 A.M. listening to the radio. I have a son and three sons-in-law who will be ready to go if they're needed."

The same certitude was expressed in Milwaukee's small Chinese community. With American involvement in the war, the cause of supporting their former homeland against an invader merged with the interests of their new home. When news of the attack on Pearl Harbor arrived, a meeting to discuss aid to the poor in China and the purchase of United States defense bonds was already in progress at Jack King Wong's importing house. The group immediately turned to the radio for news. "We decided to offer ourselves to the United States," Jack Wong announced to a reporter. "All of us promise to do everything we can, financially and physically, to help. We want Uncle Sam to take any of our boys who can serve in the army and navy. The rest of us will work hard at home."

The Japanese attack even brought old enemies together. Lansing Hoyt, leader of the Wisconsin chapter of the America First Committee, responded by announcing that Japanese cities should be bombed "to the ground. . . . We have been for defense all along. . . . Now we are for offense. It looks like war against the Axis." Edmund Shea, president of the Wisconsin Committee to Defend America and a staunch opponent of the isolationist position of America First, urged all Americans to support the defense of the nation.[2]

For Dorothy Tuchman the evening of December 7 was supposed to be a joyous time. A party was planned as a send-off for a good friend who had been drafted and was leaving for military service. As she recalled, "the whole tenor of the evening changed because all of a sudden we were in the war and it was an entirely different feeling about his leaving. There was much more stress and much more worry. He was the first one that was actually going into the service. So it was a traumatic day."[3]

As people began to adapt their lives to the war, city and company officials posted armed guards to protect industries, utilities, and railroad facilities from sabotage. Eager young recruits swamped recruiting offices—the first of many thousands of young men and women who would heed the nation's call to arms. In all, some 330,000 Wisconsinites would serve in the various branches of the military.[4]

All over the city on December 8, Milwaukeeans listened to the broadcast of President Roosevelt's address to the joint session of Congress requesting a declaration of war. Pedestrians paused as loudspeakers on Wisconsin Avenue broadcast the President's words. The day before, these same speakers had played Christmas carols. Elsewhere traffic halted so pedestrians could catch the news broadcast from car radios. Public library patrons lingered in front of a replica of the Declaration of Independence to listen to the radio, as did the customers of Frank Geier's tavern and Jacob Stockinger in his butcher shop. The district court suspended proceedings so judges, attorneys, court workers, policemen, and prisoners could hear the Presidential address.[5]

In a way few people expected, the attack on Pearl Harbor answered the question of whether America could avoid involvement in another European war. Ironically, conflict in Asia brought the United States into the Second World War. Since 1932 episodes such as the Japanese slaughter of civilians in

Shanghai had appalled Americans but did not divert their attention from economic problems at home. When Japan's aggressive behavior erupted into war in China in 1937, Americans strongly supported the Chinese but still did not favor active involvement. Soon thereafter, events in Europe overshadowed Japanese conquests in Asia.

Since September 1939 American attention had focused with growing apprehension on Germany's rapid conquest of Europe. When Germany invaded Poland, Americans did not want to enter the war, but they had no sympathy for Germany. Scandinavia, the Low Countries, and mighty France were the next to fall, leaving Great Britain alone in the fight. Although organizations such as America First vocally opposed entry into the war on the side of the British Empire, most Americans favored an Allied victory. Unlike World War I, there was never any meaningful support for the German cause among the American population. By late 1941, with Hitler's armies at the gates of Moscow and victorious in North Africa, Americans had concluded that war was preferable to German victory.

While Hitler's forces advanced across Europe, the Japanese army established a strong presence in French Indo-China. By the summer of 1941 they threatened the Dutch East Indies with its rich oil fields, a resource the Emperor's armed forces needed badly if they were to pursue their war. President Franklin Roosevelt took an increasingly hard line on Japanese aggression and had embargoed oil and scrap metal. In July the United States, Great Britain, and the Netherlands completed the economic isolation of Japan by freezing that nation's assets—a virtual act of war. Diplomatic negotiations during the summer and fall failed to resolve the differences between the United States and Japan.

By late November a slight majority of Americans believed the United States would soon be at war with Japan. On the very morning of the day war broke out, the newspapers in Milwaukee reported that 125,000 Japanese troops were massed in Indo-China and a major Japanese fleet was headed toward the Gulf of Siam. President Roosevelt had sent a message directly to Emperor Hirohito, protesting the troop concentrations. The *Milwaukee Journal* quoted Lieutenant General Teiichi Suzuki, president of the cabinet planning board, as saying: "We Japanese are tensely watching to see whether President Roosevelt and Prime Minister Churchill will commit the epoch making crime of further extending the world upheaval." Karl H. Von Wiegand, chief foreign correspondent for the Hearst Newspapers, reported: "Completely shut off by America and Britain from the Dutch East Indies, Japan today was grimly confronted by the more immediate question of whether to shed national blood for oil. . . ." The *Milwaukee Sentinel* titled the article "Von Wiegand Says: Japs Face Choice of 'Blood for Oil.' "[6]

The fact that the United States was finally at war was not what surprised Americans; rather, it was the manner of our entry into the war. Overnight, the devastation in Hawaii made the entire nation seem vulnerable. Suddenly American attention focused on the common purpose of defeating the Axis.

Anxiety and outrage over the "day of infamy" were quickly replaced by a national sense of purpose, of participation in a heroic crusade against a common enemy. The sense of purpose engendered by the phrase "national unity" meant that Americans shared a determination to destroy an evil force in the world. Although "national unity" meant many different things to those who stayed on the home front, no other single phrase better described the national mood.

Milwaukeeans greeted the advent of war with the same determination as other Americans. They did not want to be at war, but once the conflict was forced upon them, they acted with patriotic fervor to win it as speedily as possible. Everyone felt the effect of the war, whether through concern for loved ones in danger, longer work hours, consumer shortages, or participation in war service organizations. Everyone worked toward the day when the Axis would be defeated, the killing would end, and society would return to "normal."

Work, volunteer activities, and financial contributions to wartime agencies provided the basic mechanisms through which most people on the home front participated in the war effort. Popular images of Americans united in an effort to defeat the Axis often include men and women in overalls at factory benches, campaigns for war relief or war bonds, air-raid wardens in steel helmets patrolling darkened streets, and children collecting scrap metal. These activities represented the most obvious and symbolic ways in which civilians supported the war.

Nonetheless, Americans did not share a universal view of the best means by which people on the home front could serve the cause; nor did they possess a common vision of the world of the future and the best way of achieving it. They interpreted the demands of the nation in light of what they perceived as important. Throughout the war people made rational decisions regarding the best way to support the war effort. Whether they served on Office of Price Administration (OPA) ration boards, Red Cross relief committees, civil defense groups, factory fire brigades, or scrap and bond drives, people chose their war work carefully. They avoided projects that held little relevance for their daily lives and supported projects that touched them directly or promised to yield tangible benefits for the war effort. For example, attempts to devise a civil defense system in Milwaukee demonstrated that residents did not blindly respond to the rhetoric of community leaders concerned about the lack of defense preparations. The majority of Milwaukeeans viewed the threat of enemy air attacks as unlikely, and instead they assisted activities such as blood drives and conservation campaigns which had a clear purpose and an immediate impact on their daily lives.

"National unity" masked diverse and sometimes contradictory individual reactions to the war. Americans willingly supported the war effort, but their sense of unity and devotion to that effort could not produce consensus where none existed. At times the sense of national purpose could bring about compromises that helped the war effort, but it could not heal the wounds of prewar industrial conflict, nor could it solve serious social problems that plagued the nation.

For organized labor, the war presented significant opportunities for cooperation with management, but also new venues within which to fight old battles. The success of blood drives and bond drives in Milwaukee clearly illustrated the power of cooperation between labor and business interests in achieving common wartime goals. In contrast, years of conflict between the Milwaukee Industrial Union Council (CIO) and local business leaders lay behind a protracted struggle over CIO participation in local Community-War Chest campaigns. In a corollary to wartime disputes on the factory shop floor, CIO leadership maintained its support for the War Chest and at the same time fought for participation and recognition in the Chest campaigns against business leaders intent on limiting labor influence.

Industrial conflict during the war also must be viewed in the context of the social tensions inherent in wartime life. Americans contributed to winning the war in subtle ways through the sacrifices they made. Rationing, housing shortages, and transportation problems disrupted established patterns of daily living. Rationing made it difficult to buy meat and butter in the quantities many people believed necessary for good health. It sidetracked the American love affair with automobiles and forced workers in cities such as Milwaukee to find alternative means of getting to work. Likewise, the housing shortage, which had developed during the Depression, reached crisis proportions as workers flocked to Milwaukee's war plants. Although they were often taken for granted and borne with a certain grace and humor, these changes in everyday life added to the inherent tension of wartime society.

The attack on Pearl Harbor and the rapid Japanese advances in the Pacific riveted attention on domestic security as well as the war overseas. Within forty-eight hours of America's entry into the war, federal, state, and local officials detained forty-nine Germans and one Italian in Wisconsin as enemy aliens. Guards were placed on Milwaukee's filtration plant and pumping stations. Defense factories began requiring identification badges and were placed under twenty-four-hour guard.[7] Likewise, the embryonic civil defense network began preparing for air raids. The call went out for thousands of volunteers to act as spotters, wardens, and air patrol pilots. Preliminary plans had already been laid for evacuating parts of the city, caring for the population, establishing a radio communication system, and providing an emergency water supply.[8]

Despite the initial appearance of efficiency, Milwaukee's civil defense system was seldom able to recruit enough people to fill its needs because relatively few demonstrated sustained interest in this effort. Attempts to mobilize local residents for defense activities largely went unheeded. The county's defense requirements called for approximately 49,000 auxiliary police, auxiliary firefighters, air-raid wardens, aircraft spotters, rescue personnel, and medical aides; only 7,082 volunteered. (By contrast, 16,266 people enrolled in the salvage and the morale-building committees and in other branches of the welfare services.)[9]

Two and a half months after the war started, Milwaukee had not established an air-raid signal, indeed did not even have a siren system over which to broadcast such a signal. There were only a handful of air-raid wardens and no rescue, bomb, or decontamination squads. Preparations to handle medical problems resulting from an air raid had advanced only a little beyond normal conditions. The police department was training an auxiliary force of 2,100 men, but this was less than half its goal. The fire department made even less progress toward meeting its goal of 2,000 auxiliary firefighters. Not only had few people volunteered, but the department was ill-equipped to teach large numbers of people to fight fires. Their most successful program involved training factory workers, who returned to local companies and created fire brigades. Milwaukee was simply unprepared to deal with an air attack—and seemed not to care.[10]

This problem was never completely resolved. The last of four wartime blackouts, on May 27, 1943, demonstrated that the defense council and the public had finally learned how to darken the city; but that was the only major achievement of the protective services. The defense council enrolled a credible force of air-raid wardens and auxiliary police who faithfully enforced blackouts, but the council never brought the city's inadequate warning system up to code.

The areas in which the civil defense system functioned best were those in which it had always been strong: auxiliary police, medical personnel, and services and supplies. All three of these areas drew their strength from existing organizations. In the first days of the war, the council of defense channeled large numbers of volunteers to the police department, which was prepared to train and utilize them quickly. The strength of the emergency medical service was founded on the organizational work of the county medical society. The supply branch drew its manpower and equipment from the Transport Company, the Yellow Cab Company, the trucking lines, and the public utilities.[11]

Of the protective services, only the air-raid wardens grew to any appreciable strength without the assistance of some well-organized patron group. Most other civil defense services struggled to secure volunteers. This was not for lack of publicity. Repeatedly officials warned of Milwaukee's vulnerability to air attack and called for more volunteers.[12] By 1943, as the Allied counteroffensives rolled back the enemy tide worldwide, warnings about Nazi warplanes over Milwaukee took on a decided aura of unreality. They seemed designed to keep American spirits committed to civil defense as the real need for such measures declined. When a German broadcast stated that Washington, Boston, and New York were not safe from attack, James Landis, national director of civilian defense, warned, "The enemy wants pictures of burning American cities to show his people. The enemy will strike wherever the element of surprise is in his favor. WE MUST NOT ASSUME THAT THE THREE CITIES MENTIONED ARE THE ONLY ONES IN DANGER."

The *Civilian Defense News,* official bulletin of the Milwaukee County Council of Defense, used Landis's remarks to demonstrate that Milwaukee was open to attack. Indeed, the defense publication argued, Milwaukee was closer to Norway than was New York, and even more vulnerable to Japanese planes based on Kiska in the Aleutian Islands![13]

Leon Gurda, Milwaukee's building inspector and chairman of the civilian defense committee on air-raid shelters and demolition, also pointed to the city's vulnerability when chastising the citizenry for its failure to take civilian defense seriously. According to Gurda, people seemed to think that air-raid preparations were a joke. He had been informed by military officials that Milwaukee, Chicago, and Detroit might be bombed during the summer. Gurda intended to act upon the advice and warned, "To do anything else is not common sense. Nor is it logical for civilians who know military strategy to be so cock-sure that 'it can't happen here.' "[14]

As with business and professional organizations, labor unions participated in the protective services in a variety of ways. Labor officials were appointed to state and local defense councils and participated on many of the committees that assisted these organizations.[15] Unions also attempted to mobilize their members to support the protective services. Early in 1942 the women's auxiliary of UAW-CIO Local 248 at Allis-Chalmers launched a campaign to enlist women in the civil defense effort. In the case of Flat Janitors' Local 150-B, the entire local joined either the air-raid wardens or the fire wardens, while members of Local 494 of the Electrical Workers' Union offered their assistance for clearing high voltage wires that might be downed by an air attack. In addition, the International Ladies Garment Workers Union provided first aid instruction for its members, a basic requirement for anyone wishing to serve in the protective services.[16]

As widespread as such activity may have been, it had little impact on preparedness. The demolition squads provided a poignant example of the problems faced by the protective services, even when they benefited from strong organizational support. In November 1942 Laborers' Local 113, Teamsters Local 200, Operating Engineers Local 139, and Iron Workers Local 8 formed a squad of 300 construction experts to deal with air-raid destruction, shore up buildings, clear debris, and help defense work run smoothly. The *Labor Press* article announcing formation of this group also contained an appeal by Leon Gurda for enrollment of enough construction workers to bring the demolition squadron up to its full strength of 3,000. Four months later Gurda could count only 181 volunteers on the combined rolls of the demolition, rescue, and air-raid shelter crews.[17]

Americans were not apathetic, as some bureaucrats charged at the time. Virtually everyone, children as well as adults, was engaged actively in some aspect of the war effort; but most tended to choose activities that directly touched their lives. Thus, a woman might join the workforce to help her brother or husband in the armed forces or to make ends meet, and a storekeeper might subscribe to an extra bond because the neighbor's son was a prisoner of war. The air-raid warden program successfully recruited volunteers without relying on any preexisting institutional support because it operated at a level with which everyone could identify: the neighborhood.

Similarly, measures to protect factory facilities had a particular impact on the daily lives of most factory workers and met with more success than the defense council's protective services. The contrasting record of the auxiliary firemen and the factory fire brigades provide the best example of this phenomenon. About a month after Pearl Harbor, 235 employees of Kearney and Trecker began a fire-fighting course offered by the West Allis fire department. The program was purportedly the first such effort in the nation, and 100 workers from other West Allis plants immediately asked to participate. On February 2, 1942, the Milwaukee fire department opened a "fire college" to train auxiliary firemen and factory fire brigade members. By June it had trained 475 industrial workers, 880 auxiliary firemen, and 2,168 employees of the Transport Company, operator of Milwaukee's bus system.

Although the number of industrial firefighters met with general approval, city fire officials remained concerned over the low auxiliary enrollment. The 880 who had been trained constituted less than one-third of the civil defense requirement, and defense officials were troubled by the high turnover rate among auxiliary firemen. By contrast, many of the industrial trainees were fire brigade leaders who returned to their plants to train fellow workers. By the end of 1942 the number of industrial firemen trained by this program had increased almost fivefold and involved workers from over 130 Milwaukee plants. The seventy-seven auxiliary firemen who graduated from the school in December swelled the county's auxiliary fire-fighting force to only 450 men. In other words, while participation in the industrial program soared, participation in the auxiliary program fell by nearly 50 percent.[18]

The reasons for this dichotomy lay in the fact that factory fire-protection units often garnered the support of unions and management alike. In many cases, companies paid workers a small stipend while they attended training meetings on their own time. More importantly, the threat of a factory fire was well within the realm of possibility, while few Milwaukeeans took the threat of an air raid seriously. Factory workers could identify with a fire-protection squad much more readily than they could with a civil defense demolition squad. A factory fire caused by a stray spark or a careless action could kill fellow workers and cripple a factory's ability to produce war supplies.

Although the level of industrial preparation for an air raid never satisfied defense officials,[19] the growth of factory protection programs compared favorably with the stagnant civil defense system. This contrast highlighted the problems inherent in trying to form volunteer organizations for which many people saw little need. People participated in the wartime welfare services—blood donation, salvage drives, bond sales, and relief activities—because these activities clearly relieved suffering, saved lives, and furthered the war effort. While defense officials bemoaned the public's apathy, the citizens of Milwaukee demonstrated their commitment to the war effort through participation in war bond purchases and the community chest campaigns.

Unlike during the First World War, when bond sales were limited to special drives, the publicity to buy bonds during the Second World War was continuous. The federal government advocated the purchase of bonds as a mechanism to reduce the inflationary pressure of consumer spending by encouraging saving. Store window displays, radio programs, and newspaper advertisements constantly urged people to devote a greater portion of their financial resources to the war effort by buying bonds through participation in payroll savings plans or by purchasing them independently.

Virtually everyone on Milwaukee's home front felt the pressure to buy bonds. Bond drives and payroll savings plans provided a means by which the average person could participate directly and clearly in the war effort. They provided a tangible means of expressing support for friends and relatives on the battle front. Purchasing a bond served as a statement of national unity.[20]

The success of appeals for war bond purchases or charitable contributions in general depended heavily on the cooperation of companies and unions in Milwaukee. When both the company and the union, two agencies that touched workers' lives almost every day, issued a cooperative appeal to employees, the results could be astounding. When one factory labor-management committee, established under the auspices of the War Production Board, became concerned over the rate at which workers were curbing their purchases of war bonds through the company payroll savings plan, a joint effort involving the company and the union successfully tackled the problem. The committee interviewed every worker who wanted to cut his or her bond purchases, and attempted to find other ways to meet the employees' financial difficulties. As a consequence, only 25 percent of the reductions in the payroll savings plan requested by workers in this plant were actually carried out.

Labor-management cooperation could be equally successful when it came to selling bonds. Local 47 of the Fur and Leather Workers teamed with the management of Albert Trostel and Sons to set the pace for the last bond drive of the war. The labor-management committee offered the workers a full-course dinner at noon on Wednesday, March 21, 1945, to kick off the campaign. The drive actually started on March 20, and by the time of the dinner, the workers had already subscribed to the company's goal of $44,000. Trostel was the first company in Milwaukee to meet its goal for the 7th War Bond Drive. Cooperation in the building trades produced similar results during the seventh war loan drive. With a quota of $1 million, the Joint Committee of the Building Construction Industry in Milwaukee sold nearly three times that amount.[21]

An Office of War Information report issued in the summer of 1943 underscored the significance of labor's role in the promotion of bond sales. Half of the 27 million workers enrolled in the payroll savings plan, it claimed, came from the ranks of organized labor. For all practical purposes, this meant that virtually every union member in the nation participated in some way in the payroll program. In addition, 70 percent of the $425 million in bonds purchased each month through the payroll savings plan came from the pay envelopes of union members. Although bond purchases never reached the level desired by the government as a curb on inflationary spending, these purchases provided a partial curb on buying power. In 1944, for example, the participation of millions of Americans in the payroll plan siphoned 7.1 percent of the national income after taxes out of purchasing power and into series E bonds.[22]

Many other appeals besides the bond drives also bombarded Americans. Appeals went forth for the community chest, the Red Cross fund, and foreign

relief. In all of these campaigns the workplace, the company, and the union became focal points for soliciting contributions. In Milwaukee the Federated
Trades Council and Industrial Union Council successfully sought support for a
wide variety of humanitarian programs, but the cooperation of union locals
was equally important. The parent organizations could promote and advertise,
but they could achieve little without the active cooperation of local unions. As
with the selling of bonds, many of the best examples of organized blood donations came from those factories in which the union and management had a
sound working relationship. Thus, at A. O. Smith the company provided
workers with transportation to the blood center and assisted in circulating
donor cards through the plant. At International Harvester the company and
the union were honored with certificates commending their cooperation with
the Red Cross. To promote blood donations, United Electrical Workers' Local
1131 and the Louis Allis Company organized "Louis Allis Buddies Week," the
immediate goal of which was to secure a pint of blood for every employee in
the armed forces. Before the drive posters went up throughout the plant and
letters went out to all employees. The company provided numbered buttons
indicating how many times an employee had donated and attached donor
reservation cards to each time card so that workers could indicate the best time
to donate. Nearly five hundred workers responded to this cooperative call, and
donors were listed on an honor roll that was distributed to company employees in the armed services.[23]

Just as in the case of bond drives and blood campaigns, contributions to
the Community-War Chest of Milwaukee County illustrated the willingness of
Americans to contribute more than their labor to the war effort, and it provided graphic examples of how effectively unions could mobilize their members. In 1942, for example, labor was expected to contribute $850,000 during
the War Chest campaign, approximately one-third of the goal of $2.4 million.
When the contributions were tallied, 550 AFL locals in Milwaukee County had
given $358,728, nearly triple their pledges of the previous year. Employees of
approximately ninety factories organized by the CIO contributed $320,092,
topped their quota, and quadrupled the previous year's donation. In other
words, workers at factories in Milwaukee County organized by the major labor
federations contributed almost 80 percent of labor's quota for the drive.[24]

The success of the 1942 Community-War Chest campaign reflected not
only the value of labor-management cooperation, but also the power of
wartime unity to bring labor and management together despite their conflicts.
Relations between the Federated Trades Council and the Community-War
Chest were cordial throughout the war. On the surface, the county Industrial
Union Council was also on good terms with the charity organization. Beneath
the surface, cooperation was threatened by a disagreement between the Milwaukee CIO and major industrial supporters of the Community-War Chest
over the role the CIO would play in the 1942 campaign. Nonetheless, no one
wanted the conflict to become public, because a public airing of the problem
would not have been in the interest of the fund drive or the war effort.

The 1942 problem began when the CIO and the AFL negotiated an agreement with the Community Chests and Councils, Inc. sanctioning a cooperative solicitation program for 1942 and encouraging local groups to reach agreements under which such solicitations could operate. These local agreements were to give organized labor due credit for funds raised. The Milwaukee AFL quickly reached such an understanding based on the standard of soliciting 10 percent of one week's pay (equivalent to four to five hours annually depending on overtime) as a Community-War Chest pledge. Reaching an agreement on local CIO participation was more difficult, despite the fact that the national CIO was proposing standard pledges of one hour's pay per month (twelve hours annually). The local CIO insisted that 40 percent of the money raised (four hours) be distributed to the American Red Cross and to international relief agencies, such as Russian War Relief, in which the CIO had an interest. This formula left eight hours' pay for the local Community-War Chest, almost double the amount per contributor planned by the AFL in Milwaukee.[25]

The local agreement almost floundered because it recognized CIO interests and clearly identified the CIO as a participant in the solicitation campaign. The day after Milwaukee Community-War Chest officials reached an agreement with local CIO leaders, Edmund Fitzgerald, vice president of the Northwestern Mutual Life Insurance Company, told Fred Goldstone, "I think we have reason to feel better about the C.I.O. matter but I still have very husky reservations about the reception we will get from employers." He believed the CIO representatives were too optimistic and that "we may find a number of spots where there will be a definite objection to too much cooperation with them." He recommended that Goldstone meet with plant captains at Allis-Chalmers, Harnischfeger, Nordberg, Heil Company, Chain Belt, and Phoenix Hosiery as soon as possible to explain the situation and resolve any misunderstandings.[26]

Fitzgerald's concerns were well founded. Upon learning of the special arrangement with the CIO, Walter Harnischfeger informed Fred Goldstone that the Harnischfeger Company would not contribute to the Chest that year. Goldstone sympathized with the irate industrialist's view and acknowledged that several businessmen on the executive committee of the Chest felt the same way. Nonetheless, these other businessmen had accepted the plan "in the interest of the community and the War Chest." Harnischfeger agreed to think it over for a few days before making any recommendation to his executive committee. Later, Mr. Moorbeck of Nordberg Manufacturing Company called Goldstone about the same issue. After the joint solicitation program was explained, Moorbeck indicated that he thought it would work well. Shortly thereafter, "Buck" Story, vice president of Allis-Chalmers, also called. Although he did not like the situation, Story agreed that the Chest had little choice but to cooperate with the CIO. After these encounters and the lengthy explanations they required, Goldstone told William Coleman of the Bucyrus-Erie Company that "There are 79 CIO plants in Milwaukee and I think probably I should install a public addressograph system in order to reach all of them at once."[27]

A second major dispute arose over who should represent the CIO on the Community-War Chest Board of Directors. The Chest required that participating organizations submit at least three nominees for each position on the board of directors, from which the Chest would pick one. The Federated Trades Council followed this requirement,[28] but the Industrial Union Council insisted on appointing its own representatives to such organizations. When the matter was discussed in July 1943, CIO leaders emphasized that their nominees were in the best position to carry the campaign back to the members of the CIO in Milwaukee. Nonetheless, Harold Christoffel, president of the Milwaukee Industrial Union Council, suggested a possible compromise. If the Chest would nominate members of the public, trying to achieve a representative cross-section of the city's population, Christoffel suggested that the Chest might nominate CIO members, and the Industrial Union Council might accept these nominees.

Edmund Fitzgerald recommended privately that the Community Chest accept part of Christoffel's offer as a solution to the representation problem. Instead of nominating members of the board of directors from a cross-section of the public, Fitzgerald proposed an alternative slate of CIO representatives consisting of Alex Scrobell (Vice President of the Milwaukee County Industrial Union Council), Walter Burke (Secretary-Treasurer of the State CIO), Anthony Carpenter (regional director of the CIO Committee for American and Allied War Relief), and Mel Heinritz (Legislative Representative of the State CIO). "In this way," Fitzgerald noted, "we avoid any of their nominations, we get men who have had experience in our organization, and we have the Vice President of the Industrial Union Council as a Director." Apparently nothing ever came of Fitzgerald's suggestion, for the County Industrial Union Council again proposed its original slate of nominees in December 1943.[29]

While the CIO maintained its policy of selecting its own representatives, officials of the War Fund believed that they were under legal and ethical obligations as a public agency and as a corporation to maintain ultimate control over the selection of individuals to serve on the board of directors. All other organizations had complied with this policy, and the Chest insisted that the CIO do the same.[30]

The debate was complicated by the Industrial Union Council's insistence on Harold Christoffel as its representative. Christoffel was an intelligent, militant unionist who was disliked by much of Milwaukee's business community. At the same time, he was the logical CIO representative. Christoffel was instrumental in creating the Milwaukee Industrial Union Council, and he had succeeded in building a strong UAW local at Allis-Chalmers despite continuous opposition from the company.

Throughout the dispute, the Industrial Union Council never wavered in its support for the Community-War Chest; but CIO leaders would not relinquish what they perceived to be labor's prerogatives, nor would businessmen forget old hostilities. Milwaukee's labor leaders sought community recognition for themselves, their unions, and the workers they represented. When such recognition seemed to strengthen the union movement, as in the case of the CIO and the Community Chest, businessmen resisted this encroachment on what they perceived to be their prerogatives as entrepreneurs and as community leaders. Wartime "unity" had its limits. The dispute between the CIO and the Community-War Chest was a fight among leaders defending their perceived rights and prerogatives. It demonstrated that national unity seldom meant an absence of conflict.

Campaigns for charity asked people for their money; blood drives literally asked for a part of their bodies; welfare services asked for their time. These were public sacrifices, made in the name of the war effort. The war also imposed significant but subtle social costs on Americans. Workers found their freedom to change jobs sharply curtailed by manpower controls, and they underwent the stress and fatigue imposed by expanded working hours. Despite their ability to buy or rent good lodgings, many workers suffered from poor housing conditions for which no remedy existed as long as the war continued. Likewise, they rode transportation systems overburdened by people who, because of wartime shortages and patriotism, no longer used their cars. They endured rationing programs that curtailed the ability to gratify needs and desires deferred because of the Depression and prevented the purchase of meat, sugar, and butter in quantities that many Americans deemed essential. The United States was not ravaged by the war, but its citizens nevertheless made sacrifices for the national cause. These sacrifices helped create a common bond among Americans who were working for victory.

Americans daily made sacrifices to meet demands of the war, but the prosperity of the wartime years and the fact that Americans never suffered from direct attacks at home tend to mask these sacrifices. Compared with the London blitz, the brutality of German occupation, the Holocaust, or the hardships of military life, conditions in the United States were rosy. Nonetheless, such comparisons tend to devalue the role American civilians played in the war effort and to obscure the realities of life on the home front. The war wrought changes—often for the worse—in living conditions and placed stress on the industrial workers who made the "arsenal of democracy" a force for victory.

Few Milwaukeeans suffered for want of food or shelter, but the war forced many people to sacrifice. Rationing facilitated the equitable distribution of most consumer goods, but it also postponed the immediate gratification of many consumer desires. Likewise, use of the family automobile became a luxury, and getting to work could become a challenge, especially for those who did not live close to their place of employment. Despite newfound economic well-being, the housing shortage made it difficult for recently arrived war workers to find a place to live, and it prevented many of those in substandard housing from moving to more adequate quarters.

Wartime population pressures stretched Milwaukee's housing capability almost to the breaking point. During the Great Depression construction of dwelling units averaged only 722 per year—well behind the average of 2,550 units necessary to keep pace with marriages and population growth. A housing survey conducted in 1935 found a vacancy rate of only 2.5 percent compared with the 4.6 percent rate that city and real estate officials considered necessary for a healthy real estate market. Approximately 4 percent of all city dwelling units contained families who were doubling up because they could not afford adequate single-family accommodations.[31]

Another study four years later concluded that 29 percent of the city's dwellings were substandard. Of these 48,479 substandard units, almost half lacked permanent heating equipment. In thousands of other cases, families shared toilet facilities or lived in dwellings that lacked flush toilets, running water, or electric lighting. Poverty was the dominant factor preventing most occupants of poor housing from moving to better conditions. The median annual income of families living in substandard housing was between $600 and $799.[32]

The war brought little relief. The influx of workers and the rise in personal income created "a tremendous demand for additional dwelling units and . . . relegated many of the families of low income to the least desirable of the many substandard dwellings in the county."[33] Indeed, by February 1942, only 0.7 percent of the dwelling units in the Milwaukee metropolitan area were "for rent, habitable and with standard facilities." More than 6,000 rooms were available for rent in already occupied dwellings, but they were of use mainly to single men and women. Milwaukee was suffering from a severe housing shortage—a condition it shared with almost half the major defense areas in the United States, but which provided little comfort for a family trying to find decent shelter.[34]

A housing committee appointed by Mayor John Bohn presented a bleak picture in May 1942. Since the summer of 1940 Milwaukee industry had received war contracts exceeding $1 billion, and the industrial workforce had grown by 40,000 employees. Employment had increased by 13 percent since early 1941; paychecks had risen 35 percent over the same period. The figures illustrated Milwaukee's ascent out of the Depression. Approximately one-quarter of this increased workforce was comprised of in-migrants, many of whom were single men; but now employers were hiring increasing numbers of skilled, middle-aged men, many of them with families. The city needed 5,000 units immediately and would need to accommodate 12,000 more workers within the next year. Although the congestion could be relieved by encouraging workers to use mass transit instead of moving nearer their jobs, by inducing residents to rent extra space to war workers, by converting Civilian Conservation Corps and National Youth Administration barracks to worker dormitories, and by acquiring an increased construction allocation, the committee concluded that it would be impossible to solve the housing shortage without damaging war production. Milwaukee would have to live with crowded conditions.[35]

The city's rooming houses and light housekeeping units were almost filled to capacity, and industrialists reported a continuing need for in-migrants. When the housing council of the Milwaukee Real Estate Board began registering housing units for rent, it recorded only six apartments, twenty houses, and 150 rooms. Callers who wished to rent property as soon as it was registered hampered the council's work. The housing register was not meant for individual public referral. Instead, the Real Estate Board intended to provide mimeographed lists to factory personnel officers so that war workers would have the first chance of rental. John Roache, secretary of the Milwaukee Real Estate Board, concluded that the registry program failed because virtually all available housing was already in use.[36]

Construction of new houses and apartments, and the conversion of existing facilities to use as apartments or duplexes, eased the housing shortage somewhat, but these measures never met the need created when thousands of workers migrated to Milwaukee in search of war jobs. For the war worker seeking a place to live, the housing shortage meant long hours of searching. If the worker was single, a room could be rented without much difficulty. For a married couple the search might take longer, but for a family with children the situation was almost hopeless. Letters pleading for assistance poured into the mayor's office and into the *Milwaukee Journal*'s "From the People" column. The writers consistently complained of landlords who would not rent to families with children, of apartments priced out of reach, and of the lack of housing in "decent" neighborhoods.[37]

A *Journal* reporter posing as a working man of moderate income with four children discovered that it was indeed almost impossible to find housing. Numerous upstairs apartments existed within the right price range, but landlords were afraid that the children's noise would disturb the downstairs residents. The duplexes he investigated tended to be in high-rent districts. He found some affordable apartments in other areas of town but they were in such deplorable condition that no one would want to rent them.[38]

Carl Mucklinsky and his family encountered the same problem after he got a defense job in Milwaukee. In frustration his wife wrote the mayor,

> Maybe people like us are supposed to live in one of the 'hell holes' of which I hear Milwaukee has quite a few. . . . Can't apartment house owners be made to understand that just because one has a job in a defense plant, he isn't making a fortune, that *children must live somewhere,* and that besides paying rent, we must eat, clothe ourselves, and gain a few permanent possessions such as furniture?[39]

Families who failed to find adequate shelter faced serious repercussions. In the worst cases, the housing shortage forced parents to break up their family unit. One worker sent his wife and children home to Detroit; other parents distributed children among friends and relatives in Milwaukee. In one week during June 1942 thirty-eight adolescents entered the county home for dependent children because their parents could not find them shelter. Although this was a particularly serious week, the phenomenon was not considered unusual.[40]

An untold number of Milwaukeeans found solutions that provided less than ideal shelter but at least kept their families together. In some cases they moved in with friends or relatives who had a little extra space. In addition, over 1,500 residents of Milwaukee County made their homes in trailer camps. The majority of trailer inhabitants accepted the change in lifestyle as a necessary sacrifice for the duration. Although many of these camps maintained sanitary conditions, the Milwaukee County Health Department fought a running battle to preserve decent living conditions. None of the county camps provided trailer hook-ups to running water. Showers, toilets, and washing machines were located in central service houses, which in some cases were in good condition and in other cases were quite unsanitary. With trailer lots of 1,000 square feet, play space also was limited, and no camp provided community houses, recreation rooms, or playgrounds. Despite the stigma attached to trailer life, the demand for housing kept these facilities full. Building inspectors found it particularly difficult to enforce regulations or to close camps, because their residents had nowhere else to go. Only local regulations and an inadequate supply of trailers limited camp expansion.[41]

Most residents of Milwaukee, of course, were not migrants looking for work. Nonetheless, wartime housing conditions had a direct impact on their lives. The mayor received numerous complaints about unreasonable rent increases during the months immediately following the attack on Pearl Harbor. Likewise, the regional OPA received daily complaints of rent increases and evictions.[42] To help solve the problem, the OPA froze rents in Milwaukee. As of August 1, 1942, the government required landlords to register their property with the OPA and to limit rent to the level charged on March 1, 1942. The OPA would approve rent adjustments if the owner made extensive improvements to the property or if fixed costs such as taxes and utilities rose substantially.[43]

Rent control succeeded admirably, though never perfectly, in Milwaukee. After nearly two years, rents in the city stood at about the same level as in March 1942. Rent control officials attributed the success to the stiff penalties levied on violators. Tenants could sue for three times the amount of the overcharge or $50, whichever was greater. Two or three damage suits charging rent violations were filed each week in civil court, and conferences with rent officials secured over a thousand voluntary rebates by landlords. Nonetheless, one small survey easily demonstrated the difficulty of enforcing rent regulations. In March 1945 the unions at A. O. Smith and Seaman Body surveyed their members and discovered that approximately 4 percent of the renters were being overcharged, and approximately 9 percent of the landlords had failed to register their rental units with the OPA rent office.[44]

Evictions presented an even more troubling problem, for which no adequate solution was ever found. Although OPA regulations made it difficult to remove a tenant except for nonpayment of rent, creating a nuisance, or to allow owner occupancy, the housing shortage complicated the situation. Workers with surplus income created a house-buying boom as they sought a secure place to live. In many cases they purchased houses that had been rental units, and the evicted tenants faced the problem of finding a new place to live. This problem became particularly acute in the summer of 1944. The number of eviction cases peaked in April, when 486 new owners petitioned the civil court for eviction writs so they could occupy their properties. In June new owners filed 466 petitions, more than double the number submitted during the same month of 1943. On one day, the court heard fifteen eviction cases. Nine of these cases involved owners seeking to occupy their own property. OPA rules required new owners to wait three months while their tenants looked for new quarters. Of the nine families being evicted, only one had found a place to live during the three-month waiting period. That family had purchased a home and was waiting for the tenant to leave. The Milwaukee housing shortage had thus created a vicious circle. People seeking security bought houses, which put other people out on the street. In turn, some of the evicted families decided to buy their own homes, which created a new wave of evictions.[45]

Not only was housing in short supply, but many workers could not afford the housing that was available. Based on requests handled by the Milwaukee housing center, 82 percent of the families seeking housing had children. On average, they were willing to offer $35 a month for a five- or six-room apartment. According to Frank Kirkpatrick, the center's director, it was "almost impossible to find decent housing in Milwaukee for $35 a month."[46]

In recognition of the city's serious housing problem and bowing to political pressure, the Common Council established a housing authority on January 24, 1944. This action sparked a heated debate over the powers to be exercised by the authority and the role of private enterprise in renovating the blighted areas of Milwaukee and providing housing for low-income families. The debate focused on the Sixth Ward (bounded by the Milwaukee River on the east, West State Street on the south, Twelfth Street on the west, and North Avenue on the north), home to almost 83 percent of the city's African American population and site of some of the oldest housing stock in Milwaukee, where the wartime housing shortage had made a bad situation worse. Although there were other congested areas in the city, the Sixth Ward was one of the most dilapidated. Almost half of its residents were African American, and the number grew by two thousand between April and October 1942. With little chance to live elsewhere and with white residents in surrounding neighborhoods openly hostile to any expansion of minority housing, black workers migrating to Milwaukee for war jobs found themselves limited to living in slums.[47]

Representatives of the Milwaukee Real Estate Board attributed slum conditions to the slovenly habits of the tenants themselves and argued that private enterprise could supply housing as cheaply as the government. Public housing advocates, especially leaders of the CIO and the AFL, responded with indignation to the first charge and incredulity to the second. After almost thirty years, private developers had accomplished little in the Sixth Ward, where housing remained essentially as it was in 1916, when Milwaukee's health commissioner had warned of slum conditions among the neighborhood's eastern European population.[48]

When discussing the plight of the Sixth Ward, William Kelley, president of the Milwaukee Urban League, told a *Milwaukee Journal* reporter that "The average age of the homes occupied by our people is 65 years. In 101 units surveyed recently, 79 were without hot water, 45 without baths of any kind, and many without sufficient sanitary facilities." Even though prosperity meant that many African American families could afford to pay more for housing, they found it difficult to rent or buy homes in other areas of the city. Thus they were confined to the worst housing district in Milwaukee. At the same time, Kelley suggested that landlords often refused to upgrade their properties because rent ceilings prevented their charging higher rent.[49]

Dr. E. R. Krumbiegel, the city's health commissioner during World War II, surveyed the Sixth Ward during the fall of 1944 and classified housing in that neighborhood as 45 percent "good," 25 percent "fair," 17 percent "poor," and 13 percent "dilapidated." When opponents of public housing used these statistics to support their claim that drastic renovation was unnecessary, the *Milwaukee Journal* immediately pointed out that Krumbiegel's report offered no such hope. Conditions were much worse than a superficial reading of the commissioner's report indicated, the *Journal* argued, because of Krumbiegel's conservative subjective rating system. The doctor clearly defined "good" as pertaining to structures that were painted and repaired as needed. Everything rated less than "good" had to be considered substandard housing, according to Krumbiegel. Thus, based on a survey the *Journal* considered too generous, 65 percent of the housing in the Sixth Ward was substandard by December 1944.[50] Milwaukee made little progress toward solving the housing problem during the war. Even in the Sixth Ward, with all the publicity generated by the debate over urban blight, little was accomplished.[51]

The movement of suburban families back into the central city in response to gasoline rationing and overtaxed transportation facilities made the housing problem even worse. During the 1920s American society wedded itself to the automobile. Within two months of the attack on Pearl Harbor, the federal government froze new car sales and imposed tire quotas. Cars, tires, and gasoline were not essential in a city like Milwaukee, but being deprived of their use placed an additional strain on wartime life. Problems arose not because a luxury had been curtailed, but because the city's transit system was never designed to handle a population without automobiles.[52]

The war overwhelmed a transit system designed for peacetime operation. The problems of overcrowding, slow service, and inadequate equipment could not be solved while the nation was at war. New, essential services could be implemented only after long delays. Faced with tire and gasoline rationing, workers turned to a mass transit system that was designed primarily to bring people to the center of the city and was built on the assumption that many people would travel by automobile. They began using a transit system that was never designed to carry them from neighborhoods on one side of town to factories on the other side, and they were angered when the system broke down under the weight of their travel.

Spurred by tire rationing and poor weather, the daily passenger load on Milwaukee's buses and streetcars increased by more than 20,000 riders (8.8 percent) between December 14, 1941, and January 11, 1942.[53] The growth in ridership signaled the first phase of a long struggle to maintain an adequate transportation system for the city. The Transport Company, operator of the bus and trolley system, moved from crisis to crisis as the passenger load increased without adequate supplies of equipment to meet the demand, the government rationed gasoline, and labor leaders and local government officials pressured the company to provide service to new factories outside its normal service area.

During January 1942 the mass transit system in Milwaukee carried over 3.9 million passengers a week. To handle the new load, the Transport Company operated virtually all available equipment during rush hour and added new trolleys and buses daily as the equipment arrived. During peak travel periods 60 percent of the buses had at least half their standing room taken. This passenger load left pitifully little room for future expansion.[54]

Summer brought a brief reprieve for the overtaxed system. More people walked to work, the city implemented a staggered work hours program, and drivers began sharing rides. Although carpooling, or "share-the-ride" as it was called during the war, had mixed success,[55] it was the implementation of staggered hours for government offices, stores, schools, and businesses that provided substantial relief to Milwaukee's mass transit system. Beginning in July 1942, employees of the city government and of the public utilities came to work at 8:30 A.M. and left at 5:30 P.M., a half-hour later than usual. Most retail stores shifted their hours by a half-hour as well, opening at 10:00 A.M. and closing at 6:00 P.M. Employees of the Northwestern Mutual Life Insurance Company and students in the city's business colleges and parochial schools made comparable changes. In addition to affecting approximately 12,000 employees and students, the plan placed shoppers on a delayed schedule and alleviated the burden they placed on the transit system. For the first time in months, rush-hour passengers found empty seats when they boarded the city's buses, trolleys, and streetcars.[56]

Under normal conditions, the staggered hours program might have sufficed to meet the growing demand for mass transit. By late November the Transport Company carried 25 percent more passengers than at the same time in 1941, but its fleet of trolleys, streetcars, and gasoline buses had grown by only 9 percent. Only through efficiency measures had the transit system been able to keep pace with demand.[57]

The first day of December 1942 brought gas rationing and a winter storm. The passenger load seemed comparable to any other storm day. Over 100,000 new passengers pushed the transit system to its limit, but relatively few serious problems resulted. December 2, the second day of gas rationing, coincided with a cold snap. Swamped with much larger crowds than normal, the transit system bogged down, thirty-five minutes behind schedule on many lines. Snow interfered with electrical equipment, a trolley line broke at West Fond du Lac Avenue and North 32nd Street, and traffic became snarled on the Lisbon-Wisconsin line when a streetcar door froze open, preventing the car from moving. George Kuemmerlein Jr., superintendent of transportation for the city, reported that "The situation was far worse than on Tuesday. . . . There were far fewer automobiles on the streets Wednesday and their owners poured in on us, expecting us to carry them with ease. But it wasn't that easy." Boarding buses jammed to capacity became a matter of "survival of the fittest."

An improvement in weather conditions eased some of the strain on transit facilities, but there was little relief from long waits at bus stops and from standing-room-only on the buses themselves. Record cold and severe storms in January of 1943 caused even more transit delays and underscored the seriousness of the problem.[58]

The problems encountered during the winter of 1942–1943 were replayed in the succeeding winters of 1943–1944 and 1944–1945. The passenger load grew from 28,749,014 in October 1942 to 35,351,927 in October 1943 to 36,124,193 in October 1944. Although the Transport Company faced shortages of equipment, tires, and trained operators, they were able to meet the growing demand through more efficient use of their equipment. Nonetheless, only the end of the war could solve the long-term problems faced by the Milwaukee transit system.[59]

For many workers, reliance on the transit system represented a material alteration in their way of life. Not only were they less mobile, but bus riding often meant hours of waiting, long rides, and crowded conditions. Workers who once drove quickly to their jobs found that use of mass transit required long walks because the existing system failed to meet the needs of wartime society in Milwaukee. The problem was particularly acute for workers at new factories on the city's outskirts and for West Allis workers who lived in Wauwatosa and the far northwest part of Milwaukee. For all practical purposes, buses remained on their peacetime routes well into 1943. These routes provided excellent service to shoppers headed downtown but poor service to employees at outlying factories. Thousands of workers at the Allis-Chalmers Supercharger plant and at the Pressed Steel Tank Company, for example, relied on their own devices as they traveled to work. Unable to use their cars, employees of West Allis plants had no alternative but to ride downtown, transfer, and ride out to the satellite community. Workers on the night shift or on odd schedules often had long waits to catch a bus home.[60]

The problems that plagued implementation of a new crosstown transit line illustrated the difficulty of improving any form of transportation service during the war. The new transit line required ten new buses and approval from the Office of Defense Transportation (ODT). Neither the Transit Company nor the ODT acted expeditiously, and riders were still waiting for implementation of the new line as winter arrived in 1943.[61]

Gasoline and tire rationing affected how workers got to work. Other forms of rationing and economic controls materially altered the way in which Milwaukeeans lived. As soon as war came, the public expressed its uncertainty over wartime controls by engaging in buying sprees. Rumored shortages of woolens, canned goods, nylon and rayon stockings, rugs, and items

containing steel, silk, or rubber created a "hoarding boom" during the week
ending January 17, 1942, and sent department store sales in Milwaukee to a
level 49 percent above the same period in 1941. Nationally, consumer buying
increased 45 percent during this period. Likewise, low sugar supplies and the
prospect of rationing brought a rush on honey and a 20 percent increase in
price.

With a few exceptions, rationing progressively became tighter as the war
continued, encompassing products that people not only enjoyed but considered necessities. Rationing of commercially processed fruits and vegetables and
of meats touched everyone. In preparation for the beginning of processed fruit
and vegetable rationing on March 1, 1943, the federal government issued War
Ration Book 2 (Book 1, issued earlier, covered specific commodities such as
sugar and coffee) to young and old alike containing blue stamps for fruits and
vegetables and red stamps for planned meat rationing. To receive their allotment of ration books, families and single persons completed a form declaring
their existing supplies of processed fruits and vegetables. Each person was allowed five cans or jars weighing eight ounces (twenty cans for a family of four).
On registration day, stamps were removed from the ration book for supplies in
excess of that limit.

A person with five or fewer cans at the time Ration Book 2 was issued was
allowed forty-eight points per month (192 points for a family of four). Purchase
of processed fruits and vegetables required the exchange not only of money,
but of ration stamps. In 1943 purchase of a twenty-ounce can of peas required
sixteen points, and a twenty-ounce can of corn required fourteen points. The
consumer needed twenty-one ration points to buy a thirty-ounce can of
peaches and fifteen points for a quart of grape juice. A purchase required exchange of blue stamps totaling the exact point value for the commodities being
purchased. The system made no provision for the grocer to give change in
points to the consumer. Rationing complicated every trip to the store, placed a
premium on the use of unrationed fresh produce, and gave new meaning to
planting a spring victory garden.[62]

Consumers used the red ration stamps in War Ration Book 2 when the
government implemented rationing for beef, pork, lamb, mutton, butter,
cheese, and edible fats on March 29, 1943. Families were allocated sixteen
points per person per week (sixty-four points per week for a family of four) for
these products. The most popular cuts, such as steak, pork chops, veal loin
chops, lamb loin chops, sliced ham, and bacon, required eight points per
pound. The consumer paid four to six points for stew meat, five points for
hamburger (made of scraps), and four points for spare ribs during the initial
months of rationing. By buying generally cheaper cuts of meat, the consumer
could reach the government's anticipated weekly consumption level of approximately two pounds of meat, four and a half ounces of butter, and two ounces
of cheese per person. Unlike processed fruits and vegetables, red point rationing allowed consumers to receive ration change when their coupons did
not match exactly the points required for a purchase. In addition, consumers

were allowed to accumulate unused points for up to a month before they expired. As a consequence, the judicious consumer could conserve points for several weeks by buying cheap meat and then splurge at the end of the month. According to Harold B. Rowe, in charge of food rationing for the OPA, "The meat ration probably will be more than many low income families will be able to afford, although less than the average purchasers of middle or high income families."[63]

For Americans accustomed to limits based only on buying power, rationing imposed new uncertainties. Each new stage in the control process tended to create a consumer purchasing rush. Only the implementation of canned goods rationing seemed to escape the consumer panic that preceded rationing of butter, coffee, and shoes. During the fall of 1942 many retailers responded to a plea by the local Retail Grocers Association and actively limited consumer purchases of canned goods. One grocer told a *Milwaukee Journal* reporter that he had been limiting purchases of canned goods to only two cans of a given item at a time. Announcement of canned goods rationing prompted this unnamed grocer to cut his self-imposed limit to only one can per item. Due to such voluntary practices by grocers, consumers may have felt that a last-minute buying spree would provide little in the way of extra supplies. By contrast, the announcement of shoe rationing early in 1943 sparked a run on many apparel products as consumers tried to "outguess the next rationing order." Sales in many Milwaukee stores briefly doubled the normal rate. Despite an adequate supply, people stocked up on clothing, furniture, mattresses, china, and glassware. Any item made of wool (clothing, rugs, blankets) was considered particularly valuable.

March 1943 brought new orders to ration meat and dairy products, and consumers again rushed to the stores. When they depleted the meat supply, Milwaukeeans hurried to hoard cheese. At the same time, a rumor started a run on soap, which was never in short supply nor scheduled for rationing. The next rush came in late summer, when the government announced its intention to devalue gasoline coupons. A coupon once worth four gallons of gasoline soon would purchase only three gallons, and Milwaukeeans flocked to gas stations to fill their cars and any available canisters with fuel. Nine months later the city witnessed a new kind of buying spree as the government removed most meats from rationing. Heavy buying soon caused scarcity, and many consumers complained that the end of rationing made it harder to buy meat than when the commodity was controlled. The reintroduction of rationing for canned vegetables several weeks later brought another rush, as did the tightening of controls on meats at the end of 1944.[64]

Although few if any Milwaukeeans went unclothed or unfed, this general reaction to rationing symbolized forces that simultaneously brought a sense of participation to the average citizen and reflected the tensions of wartime society. Rationing demanded small, relatively painless sacrifices that gave citizens a common bond with their neighbors and with soldiers on the front. Most people grumbled about rationing but willingly accepted the need for these restrictions. At the same time, debate over what needed to be rationed, how the program should be administered, and how scarce supplies best could be distributed reflected the tensions of wartime society. Nothing brought this into clearer focus than the problems that plagued meat rationing. Despite attempts to encourage use of alternative protein sources, Wisconsinites remained wedded to red meat as a fundamental part of the diet. The supply of red ration points never seemed to stretch far enough to meet consumer perceptions of the amount of meat, cheese, and butter necessary for an adequate diet.

Based on a survey taken at the A. O. Smith plant in the fall of 1943, the Smith Steel Workers union called for a more equitable distribution of red points on items necessary to maintain a healthy diet for workers. The union deplored the fact that purchase of a pound of butter required sixteen points and that both dinner and luncheon meats had to be taken out of red points as well. The union charged that the red point allotment was inadequate for workers engaging in the rigors of war production. Their survey indicated that 63 percent of the workers did not have butter in their lunches, and 43 percent had no meat or cheese. Not only did the union want more red points, it also insisted that the allotment be based on need as well. Presumably, under this proposal, a war production worker would merit more red points than a sedentary file clerk. District 10 of the International Association of Machinists proposed a similar plan.[65]

To make matters worse, consumers had to contend with periodic shortages at the retail level. The problem was particularly severe as the war ended in Europe. In March the government announced a 12 percent cut in the civilian allotment; concurrently, Milwaukee suffered from a severe meat shortage that continued into the summer. As customers clamored for more meat, butchers and grocers tried their best to distribute existing supplies among regular patrons. In some cases, the supply was so short that butchers closed their shops several days a week and took jobs in war plants. By the middle of April, little more than sausage could be found in many Milwaukee shops. Reflecting the situation, Claude Keim, recording secretary for UAW-CIO Local 75, urged Hy Cohen, the local CIO labor coordinator for the OPA, to use his influence to remedy the crisis. Keim emphasized that the problem was much worse than official reports indicated and that the shortage was causing unrest among workers.[66]

The problem was further compounded by the emphasis Americans placed on such commodities as meat and butter. Many Milwaukeeans considered red meat, served twice a day, to be an essential component of a healthy diet. In June 1945 Milwaukee labor representatives warned OPA officials of an impending "hunger strike" if the government failed to provide adequate food supplies for war workers. They complained that workers not only had difficulty getting fresh cuts of meat, but could not even find luncheon meats. George Hanner, chairman of the Smith Steel Workers OPA committee, warned that workers "can't keep up their strength on peanut butter and jelly sandwiches." Less than a week later the *Labor Press* editorialized, "America is largely a meat-eating group. When the supply dwindles to a mere pound a week, and most of that liver, brains, pig's feet and sausage, there is bound to be a reaction." In concluding its remarks, the paper called for controls to "put meat, and sugar, on our tables, and give workers decent lunches."[67]

In an attempt to better understand the local situation, the OPA Labor Advisory Committee in Milwaukee began a series of discussions aimed at pinpointing the problem and finding solutions. Labor representatives maintained that the shortage of meat arose, in part, from supplies siphoned off to the black market.[68]

The problem was real. By March 1945 sales above ceiling price or without ration points were on the rise, and Milwaukee officials began a crackdown on local black market meat trading. News of tightening domestic supplies as the government allocated meat to feed liberated Europe went hand in hand with news of six restaurants and meat markets under investigation for illegal sales. Most of the establishments were under suspicion for sale of farm-slaughtered meat that was both uninspected and outside the ration system. By the end of March an additional thirteen establishments were under investigation for OPA ration system violations.[69]

In addition to problems with the black market, the Labor Advisory Committee alleged that packinghouse warehouses contained an adequate supply of meat that was being withheld from the market because of low price ceilings allowed by the government. In response, representatives of the War Food Administration and the OPA asserted that they lacked the authority to force the distribution of supplies. Thus, the advisory committee was left with the frustration of believing that an adequate supply of meat existed although no one seemed to have the power to bring it to the people.[70]

The advisory committee found the ration point system equally frustrating. Members concluded that the United States produced enough meat to allot 3.2 pounds a week to every civilian, after taking military needs into consideration. Nonetheless, the point system allowed only 1.6 pounds a week. With red meat commanding ten points a pound for good cuts, and with the current allotment of fifty points a month, the committee argued that the average consumer could not even buy the government's minimal allotment. To buy 1.6 pounds of meat would have required sixty-four points a month, based on the labor advisory committee's figures. Meeting the additional need for cheese and butter would have required ninety-two red points a month, or 84 percent more than the existing allotment of points.

The difficulty of making ration points stretch to cover meat, cheese, and butter was particularly troubling in the Dairy State. The Wisconsin dairy industry promoted butter consumption as a basic part of a nutritional diet. The Dean of the College of Agriculture, Chris L. Christensen, told readers of the 1942 edition of *Wisconsin Labor* that butter was one of the best natural sources for vitamins A and D. In addition, Dean Christensen reported on the "butterfat growth factor," a recently discovered substance contained in butter and believed to be critical for normal growth in young animals. The OPA Labor Advisory Committee worried that poor nutrition threatened to produce an entire generation of weak, undernourished, and sickly children. Despite this publicity, military and Allied needs required a cut in the domestic butter supply. Consumers in Wisconsin watched as the ration points needed to purchase a pound of butter steadily rose until a purchase required 24 points early in 1945. For all practical purposes, butter was unavailable to the average purchaser.[71]

Despite criticism from labor representatives, organized labor provided the OPA with strong support. Both labor federations accepted rationing as the only reasonable way to allocate scarce consumer goods equitably, and they cooperated as much as possible with rationing's agent, the OPA. Likewise, they accepted the price ceiling system as an essential part of the fight to control the cost of living.[72]

Americans adjusted in a variety of different ways to the shortages imposed by the war. Agnes Zeidler, wife of Socialist leader and future Milwaukee Mayor Frank Zeidler, still remembered the shortages years later. She told an interviewer:

> Sometimes you couldn't get eggs. Sometimes you couldn't get butter. There were all kinds of things that you couldn't get, that you had to use something else of. What I disliked intensely was the margarine that I had to color in order for it to look as though it was fit to eat. When I was a young girl, I remember that my mother used to render lard and we would help her cut it into cubes and we would spread it on bread and salt it. And it was a treat. But that margarine never looked like that or tasted like it either.[73]

Rose Kaminski typified many young mothers during the war. She took a war job as a crane operator at Harnischfeger Corporation, maker of heavy equipment. By early 1944 her husband was in the navy and she was raising an infant daughter alone. Having grown up in Milwaukee, she coped with the war effort and rationing through existing neighborhood and kinship relations. She ate her main meal in the factory cafeteria because she could eat without spending ration points. "I always worried about my daughter getting the proper food," she recalled. She learned from the women's matron that she could buy leftover soup from the cafeteria at the end of the day.

> I would bring home soup for my daughter and, of course, in that quart jar that would be enough for myself and her. We'd have a nice meal out of it and then you'd be saving stamps too. So, you would have stamps for other food. And you never felt that you were depriving anybody because this would be extra, over and above, that they wouldn't use. It would be wasted otherwise, and it was good. So, I did that. That was very nice and it saved me a lot of time in cooking, too, and it helped.

Living near family also helped Milwaukeeans adjust to wartime rationing. When visiting her mother on weekends, Kaminski and her sisters would pool their meat ration points so the family could have a roast. Within a few blocks of home were her butcher and grocer. These merchants knew Rose Kaminski as a regular customer and would make sure she was well served.

> There was the small grocery store and there was a butcher and a drug store on the corner. So you know all those people over the years, personally, and your butcher would know his old customers, and not people that just came because they were trying to get something special from him. He would kind of cater to his regular customers because he knew who was working in the war plants, and the grocery men did too. So that part of it was not too bad. You didn't always get what you wanted, you had to take what they had on hand.[74]

Dorothy Keating lived on Vliet Street near Shuster's Department Store and has similar memories of coping with rationing through neighborhood support. She recalled a neighborhood center where people would gather to drink coffee, visit, and trade ration coupons. She also recalled a local butcher who sold horse meat:

> It was like hamburger and they were using that during the war in place of hamburger because the beef was going to the service people, to the army. When you'd go in there [to the neighborhood center] they'd say "Oh, so and so is having horse meat today, which would be hamburger. So be careful, tell him you don't want his horse meat, that you want regular hamburger." But you had to pay more and then you had to have a [ration] coupon.[75]

In numerous other ways Americans adjusted to the little stresses of life brought on by rationing, housing shortages, transit problems and the constant worry brought by loved ones in harm's way. The stress of war tempered people's attitudes about the war effort, and their roles in it. The record of support for bond drives, war relief campaigns, and civil defense in Milwaukee clearly illustrated the rational way in which Americans chose to support the war. Most elected activities that bore a direct relationship to their lives and to the war effort.

Although unity and cooperation characterized one side of home front life, the war carried with it the seeds of social tension. For the sake of the war effort, people in Milwaukee, as in other communities across the country, lived with the daily problems of cramped housing, poor transportation facilities, and rationing. Workers experienced the paradox of unparalleled prosperity combined with shortages that prevented them from exercising their new economic freedom. Many of the most significant home front activities were designed to alleviate these problems, but nothing could remove the tension created as the war imposed changes in living conditions on the people of America.

Likewise, there was no guarantee that the changes would be reversed with the return of world peace. Milwaukee labor could look to a future brightened by economic gains made during the war and by the knowledge that they had played a significant role in making the weapons and matériel that won the war. Nonetheless, many workers, and their labor leaders, must have reflected that they had played the same role during the First World War—only to be disappointed by renewed employer hostility in the 1920s. Would the end of the war bring prosperity or a return to industrial strife and widespread unemployment? No one knew the answer.

CHAPTER THREE

THE STRUGGLE
FOR ECONOMIC SECURITY

On November 3, 1943, Milwaukee's laborers and garbage collectors began the city's longest wartime strike, a thirty-one-day walkout over wages. The city workers feared that their monthly salary was falling behind inflation. The city used work rules, suspensions, and legal challenges to fight the union. Municipal officials received regular assistance from the *Milwaukee Journal,* which railed against the union's attack on government. Local 2 of the American Federation of State, County and Municipal Employees' Union fought back with rising piles of noxious garbage.

The city had the law on its side, and on November 8 sent strikers notices reading: "[Y]ou have been absent from your employment for a period of three successive days without leave and without notice, and you are therefore no longer in the service of the city of Milwaukee." This approach to dismissal placed the strikers in an awkward position. Because the laborers had left their jobs voluntarily, the city maintained that they had quit. Federal War Manpower Commission rules prevented war plants from hiring such "job skippers" for two months after they left their jobs. Not only were they out of work; they were also prohibited from seeking employment elsewhere.

The strikers, on the other hand, had garbage on their side. As the strike dragged on, piles of noisome refuse littered the city. A picket line around the city incinerator prevented independent haulers from disposing of their loads. The situation worsened day by day, and the health department instructed residents to burn perishable garbage. Many residents began this practice during the early days of the strike, although, as one citizen told a *Milwaukee Journal* reporter, "It makes an awful odor." The Thanksgiving holiday only compounded the problem. Garbage barrels were full to overflowing throughout the city, and unsanitary conditions were becoming an increasing problem as dogs, cats, rats, and other animals rummaged in the refuse.

Unlike private citizens who had little recourse, many Milwaukee business concerns relied on private haulers for refuse removal. They felt the impact of the strike more slowly. Even so, private haulers soon found it difficult to remove garbage. Many of these haulers were local farmers who picked up refuse, separated the vegetable matter for their pigs, and delivered the remaining material to the city incinerator. With pickets around the incinerator, these haulers had no place to dump their loads. George Shephard was the operator of the Beloit Hog Farm in West Allis. In violation of health code, he began storing refuse on his farm. He told a *Journal* reporter: "I've got a big pile of the stuff on my farm now. . . . I've got no place to put it. I'm not going to go down to the incinerator while this strike is on. No, sir! Not me." Frank Sansone was not a farmer and did not have the options open to Shephard. He serviced twenty-six stores and eight restaurants. When interviewed by a *Journal* reporter on November 17, he was still carrying a load of garbage picked up on November 9. Sansone told the reporter "I've gone down to the incinerator plant a number of times, and the strikers have warned me not to go through. . . . After all, if I do, who knows what'll happen to my truck that night—or the tires." To demonstrate the problem, Sansone took the reporter to the incinerator. When stopped by pickets, Sansone asked what he was to do with his load. A striker replied, "Dump it in the lake, pal." "Sure, dump it in the lake," he muttered to the reporter, "and get arrested by health officers."[1]

Ultimately, the union accepted a city offer of a $15 monthly raise to base salaries of $115 and a promise of 200 hours of overtime in 1944. Unfortunately, the solution was only temporary as workers continued to struggle for postwar economic security.

At its core, wartime industrial conflict represented a struggle for economic justice not just in the present but in the future. By referring to the past, an editorial in the *Milwaukee Labor Press* emphasized the seriousness with which labor viewed the postwar era.

> Because some men are working 48 hours a week (40 hours is standard); and because some families now have two or three persons working where only one worked before, rising prices just don't count, says Milwaukee's afternoon daily. Why, it moans, some $1,200 a year families are now actually $5,000 a year families!
>
> What kind of life did these people live when the whole family had to live on $1,200 a year? Certainly not the life that decent Americans are entitled to. And, if certain anti-labor groups had their way, those families would

be back there—in spite of longer hours and increasing profits and rising living costs.

Brother, could you spare a dime?[2]

The battle to maintain a decent standard of living began as soon as the smoke cleared from Pearl Harbor. America's workers quickly concluded that the government had frozen their wages; that price inflation, taxes, and the declining quality of consumer goods had reduced their standard of living; that corporate profits and salaries of executives had soared as a result of war production; and that workers were paying the bills for the war effort while industrialists reaped the profits. As a legion of governmental agencies imposed rationing and controls on wages and prices "for the duration," workers and their unions focused on preserving wage rates and buying power for the postwar era.

The nature of industrial conflict in Milwaukee during World War II reflected the workers' belief that wage rates needed to keep pace with inflation or they would find themselves with less real buying power in the postwar era. Although they were paid well during the war, most workers were concerned not so much with their weekly pay but with the clear pattern that basic pay rates[3] were barely keeping pace with the cost of living. Workers who experienced no improvement in their employment situation—who neither progressed into a better paying classification due to labor shortages and factory expansion, nor moved from a lower paying occupation such as retail to a better paying factory job—found that basic pay rates fell behind the rising cost of living. Workers who progressed to better paying jobs may have kept pace with inflation, but they did not experience an improvement in standard of living commensurate with moving into a job of greater economic value to society or in which greater knowledge and skill were required. Even for those fortunate enough to experience rising economic status due to overtime and improvements in classification or occupation, the postwar era held the real prospect of a declining standard of living. They assumed, with reason, that the postwar era would restore the forty-hour work week and that many individuals would be bumped back to old, lower paying jobs when soldiers returned from the war. With the end of overtime pay and wartime production, they would therefore return to basic pay rates—pay rates that had fallen behind inflation—and to lower-paying jobs.[4]

The *Milwaukee Journal* reinforced workers' fears by routinely attacking wage increases as inflationary and calling for greater worker sacrifice to win the war. Labor organizations countered that the war could be won without sacrificing living standards and crippling postwar recovery. As industrial companies built reserves to finance postwar reconversion, labor organizations insisted that workers required similar financial reserves to cushion the unemployment that would come with reconversion and to provide the buying power necessary to keep the economy afloat once consumer production resumed. Without such reserves, union leaders feared that America would be plunged into another depression.

The *Milwaukee A.F. of L. Labor Press* told its readers:

> Will Rogers once said that America had never lost a war, and never won a peace. It would be the irony of the ages if, while battling to "free the world," this nation should succeed merely in re-enslaving its workers in the old, odious chains of a few decades ago.[5]

The economic foundation of industrial conflict was plain to see. Normal grievance procedures and government agencies may have been adequate for settling many traditional disputes over contract interpretations, work rules, and plant discipline, but they proved inadequate for settling economic disputes. Any explanation of industrial conflict requires an understanding of the complicated forces acting upon workers in disputes involving wages or job security. On the one hand, America was at war, and her armed forces needed weapons. On the other hand, workers watched as their wage rates fell behind inflation and corporations seemed to reap excess profits. Workers looked toward the postwar era, remembered the depression they had just experienced, and envisioned an uncertain future. Although patriotism kept many workers on the job, economic issues could tip the balance and send them onto the picket line.

Industrial conflict during World War II stemmed largely from the failure to resolve issues related to economic and job security. These issues transcended the unity brought by war and sparked conflict among workers as diverse as AFL operating engineers, CIO auto workers, and municipal laborers. Even at companies such as A.O. Smith, where labor and management were on the best of terms, industrial conflict existed. Whether settled quietly through negotiation or conciliation or noisily after a public clash such as a strike, disputes in Milwaukee clearly illustrated the importance that workers attached to economic issues. Throughout the war, workers and their unions kept their gaze firmly fixed on the postwar era.

The federal government also was concerned about economic issues, but with a different focus than industrial workers. The federal government was more concerned about the impact of inflation and economic conflict on wartime society than with economic justice or the postwar economy. As a consequence, efforts by the OPA to control prices and the War Labor Board (WLB) to limit worker wage increases quickly came into conflict with labor's goals and interests.

As the battle of France raged during May of 1940, President Roosevelt reactivated the National Defense Advisory Commission (NDAC), originally authorized in 1916. The President appointed seven commissioners to the group, each with a different expertise in industrial and economic mobilization. Leon Henderson, an economist, member of the Securities and Exchange Commission, and later the head of the OPA, was named to head the Price Stabilization Division of the NDAC. The Stabilization Division laid the initial foundation for controlling prices through consumer education, farm subsidies, rent controls, and rationing. The division's legal staff drafted the executive orders that created the OPA as well as the Emergency Price Control Bill, which authorized the OPA to control prices. President Roosevelt signed the Emergency Price Control Act in late January 1942, confirming creation of the Office of Price Administration and authorizing the OPA to stabilize prices and rents, to prevent hoarding, profiteering and speculation, and to fix maximum prices when those prices rose or threatened to rise.[6] To carry out its control mission, the OPA reached into the daily affairs of every American. To control prices in a free market economy, the OPA not only had to establish an organizational structure comprised of volunteers in every community, but also had to deal with the complexities of pricing, supply, and distribution across a continent.

Unfortunately, the federal government implemented price controls only after the United States entered the war, and those controls never worked perfectly. As manufacturers shifted capacity from consumer goods to military supplies during 1941, and as workers gained disposable income with the end of the Great Depression, inflation rapidly increased. The Bureau of Labor Statistics' (BLS) Consumers' Price Index rose 15 percent between January 1941 and May 1942, when the government actively began to control prices on consumer goods. Price control efforts during the following year only partially subdued the sharp increase. Although initial regulation was largely successful in controlling the cost of apartments, apparel, household furnishings, and fuel, the price of food rose dramatically. This increase was due not to the failure of controls, but to the fact that many foods were not covered by those controls. The wholesale prices of controlled foods rose by only about .5 percent during 1942. By contrast, uncontrolled foods such as flour, cornmeal, lamb, poultry, eggs, butter, cheese, and many fruits and vegetables rose over 15 percent. Largely because of the rise in prices for uncontrolled foods, the Consumers' Price Index rose 7.8 percent by May 1943. This continued rise sparked a growing concern in government over the potential for runaway inflation wreaking havoc on the American economy.

Organized labor also was concerned with the failure of the OPA to adequately control prices. The *Milwaukee Labor Press* provided workers with a graphic illustration of the problems associated with price controls when it published the results of a survey of Milwaukee food and clothing prices conducted by the AFL's regional office under David Sigman. The report compared the cost of goods purchased by an average worker on March 27, 1943, with the cost of those same commodities on January 1, 1941. As the paper told its readers, the cost of food and clothing in Milwaukee had risen an average of 84.4 percent—far more than the 19 percent increase in wage rates received by Milwaukee workers. Because of the decline in quality of many goods, especially clothing, the paper considered this a conservative estimate. The price of milk, which had risen 18 percent, rose less than almost any other food item. Also on the low end of the scale, bread had gone up 22.2 percent; flour, 36.8 percent; canned green beans, 23.3 percent; and round steak, 35.4 percent. Every one of these foodstuffs had risen more than the wage increases being allowed by the WLB.

The majority of consumer items on the AFL's Milwaukee shopping list had risen substantially more than 40 percent. For example, consumers paid 60 percent more for Grade A eggs in 1943 than at the beginning of 1941. (Actually, Grade A eggs were a bargain compared to Grade B eggs, which had risen 100 percent during the same period.) Potatoes were up by 92 percent, canned peas by 100 percent, fresh peas by 135 percent, hamburger by 172 percent, peanut butter by 200 percent, and ring bologna by a whopping 252.9 percent. Clothing had risen more slowly, but such basic items as work pants rose 21.5 percent and work shirts by 41.4 percent.

This skyrocketing cost of food and clothing, accompanied by marginal wage increases could mean only one thing: a declining standard of living in the future. Workers kept pace during the war only by working longer hours and promotion to new, better paying jobs as industries expanded and as workers joined the armed forces. The BLS admitted that its Consumers' Price Index measured only selected items. David Sigman's AFL survey attempted to measure the change in cost of living based on a review of average buying patterns. The results dramatically demonstrated to workers that their buying power was declining. The rising cost of Sigman's shopping basket not only outstripped the 19 percent rise in average wage rates (adjusted to eliminate the influence of overtime pay), but even surpassed the workers' 48 percent rise in weekly earnings. Although BLS statistics based on a more selective shopping list showed an increase of only 35 percent for food and 22 percent for apparel, even these figures surpassed average wage rate increases in Milwaukee.[7]

Nor could Milwaukee's workers draw much comfort from the rollback of prices implied by President Roosevelt's Executive Order 9328 issued on April 8, 1943. Labor leaders, upset by the disparity they perceived between the cost of living and the wage increases being approved by the WLB, had been demanding a price rollback or an end to wage controls. With much fanfare, the OPA prepared new ceiling price lists for meats, dry goods, and vegetables. To reduce retail costs to the level of September 15, 1942, as demanded by organized labor, the price control agency planned to force a 10 percent cut in the cost of meats and a 30 to 40 percent cut in the cost of some vegetables by July 1, 1943. In practice, the rollback accomplished very little.

Indeed, the first published ceiling list provided little encouragement to those who compared its maximum prices with the food basket in the Milwaukee AFL survey. The ceiling covered dry goods such as flour, coffee, cereal, and bread, and dairy products such as milk, cheese, and eggs. For virtually all comparable items, the OPA posted ceilings higher than the prices registered by the AFL survey. Generally, the ceilings would have allowed price increases for cheese, flour, bread, raisins, prunes, macaroni, spaghetti, rolled oats, and Wheaties. Although the milk ceiling corresponded with the price found by the AFL, relatively few prices represented a clear rollback of earlier figures. The new ceiling mandated a price cut for butter, corn flakes, egg noodles, and chili sauce; but most other items showed mixed changes, depending on the precise brand purchased. Other ceilings published later for canned fruit and vegetables and for meats seemed to represent an attempt to actually bring about a rollback in consumer prices, but they failed to provide a clear image of rollbacks for the consumer. Ceilings for some items—such as canned wax beans, green peas, and pears—fell below the survey prices found by the AFL; but for many meats, only the ceilings on lower-grade cuts represented a reduction in March prices. For fresh vegetables, upon which consumers relied to augment rationed canned goods, ceiling prices remained unchanged. Likewise, fresh fish fell outside the rollback plan.

From a labor perspective, the proposed price "slash" was pitiful. As the *Milwaukee Labor Press* told its readers, "True to prediction, the 'price rolling' started over the weekend. But the first lists of new ceilings showed them rolling 'forward' instead of 'back.'" Even if everything went according to plan, the 10 percent reduction hoped for by the OPA hardly matched the rise in food prices noted by David Sigman. A full-page ad purchased by the UAW-CIO carried a similar message. The union ridiculed the OPA's control efforts and asserted that the OPA was incapable of controlling anything. The current rollbacks, much ballyhooed by the government, were virtually meaningless. As the auto workers' advertisement told readers of the *Milwaukee Journal,* "Headlines these days tell of new OPA 'efforts' to reduce the cost of living. Unfortunately you can't serve headlines at the dinner table."[8]

Having seen food prices climb, Milwaukee workers watched as independent grocers protested the recently established canned vegetable and fruit ceilings. Instead of selling these commodities, retailers withdrew them from their shelves, and some wholesalers refused to restock existing supplies. Each group claimed that the mark-up allowed by the OPA was so low as to prevent them from making any profit. The *Labor Press* bitterly attacked the grocers' stand, charging that the OPA ceiling already was ridiculously high. The editor suggested that Hitler probably was "tickled pink" at news of the retailers' "strike," and concluded ironically, "It might be a good idea for the worker to talk about making weekly profits, instead of weekly wages. Surely, it would be safer from attack."[9]

As the summer progressed, organized labor maintained its attack on the cost of food, but with relatively little result. The *Milwaukee Journal* expressed frustration over the lack of real progress in the war against prices. An editorial cartoon published in June showed two unhappy citizens watching as a gentleman labeled "O.P.A." held an ax marked "Price Rollback" and scratched his head. He had just chopped through the trunk of the "cost of living" tree, but the tree defied gravity and remained standing. The caption read "Yeh, but—?"[10] Without doubt, organized labor's response would have been that the "rollback" ax was too small and too feeble to have the desired effect.

The OPA and its price control efforts formed the front line of the government's campaign against inflation. Although originally created to help resolve labor disputes, the WLB became a second line of defense as it attempted to control wages. Wage increases had traditionally been a matter to be determined directly between unions and employers. America's entry into World War II brought the federal government actively into the equation. Locally, workers found themselves dealing with both the company and the government. Nationally, organized labor fought to preserve the original flexibility of the wage control system so that workers at the local level could continue to make economic gains, or at least keep pace with inflation.

Time after time, workers found themselves in conflict with the National Defense Mediation Board (DMB) and its successor, the National War Labor Board. In response to a wave of strikes in defense industries during the first months of 1941, the President created the DMB to work within the collective bargaining system to prevent work stoppages. The DMB had a tripartite structure. It and the individual panels appointed to resolve specific disputes were composed of individuals who theoretically represented the disparate interests of industry, labor, and the public. Although the board was successful during its first months, it collapsed in November 1941 when the CIO withdrew its support after the DMB refused to grant a union-shop clause to the United Mine Workers Union.[11]

President Roosevelt created the National War Labor Board on January 12, 1942, to replace the moribund Defense Mediation Board. The WLB received the old board's caseload and took new cases certified to it by the Secretary of Labor if a dispute could not be resolved by the Department of Labor's Conciliation Service. The new board was charged with resolving disputes that might disrupt war production. Although the WLB was given few guidelines about how to perform this function and still had the troublesome tripartite structure of its predecessor, America was now at war and board decisions carried more weight than had those of the DMB.[12]

Many disputes revolved around wage issues, and initially the WLB possessed the flexibility to protect workers' wage rates against inflation. The agency judged wage disputes on the basis of such factors as local wage rates, living standards, impact of raises on the war economy, and the financial standing of the company involved.[13]

But before long the WLB became part of the much larger government effort to control inflation, and it gradually lost most of its power to award wage increases. On April 27, 1942, President Roosevelt presented Congress with a seven-point anti-inflation plan calling for wage stabilization, heavy taxes on profits, a salary ceiling of $25,000 after taxes, price ceilings, rationing, farm prices set at parity, and curtailment of credit buying.

Less than two months later, the WLB issued an important decision that established the formula the board would use to achieve wage stabilization. The "Little Steel formula," as it came to be known, developed out of the settlement ordered by the WLB in a case between the United Steelworkers and the "Little Steel" companies: Bethlehem, Republic, Youngstown, and Inland. The United Steelworkers argued that pay at the Little Steel plants had fallen behind inflation. Union negotiators sought an increase of 12.5 percent in hourly rates; that is, an increase of approximately 12.5 cents in hourly rates of approximately $1 an hour. The WLB fact-finding panel investigating the case concluded that an hourly raise of 5.5 cents was appropriate for two reasons. The board awarded 3.2 percent because the cost of living had risen 15 percent between January 1, 1941, and May 1, 1942, compared with average pay increases for the steelworkers during the same period of only 11.8 percent. The board awarded an additional 2.3 percent because the dispute was submitted to the board before the President's message of April 27, and because inflation had been higher in steel towns than in the nation as a whole.[14]

The award established the precedent of granting wage increases to bring workers' wage rates into line with the cost of living as it stood on May 1, 1942; but the formula was flawed by the assumption that living costs had stopped rising appreciably within days of the President's anti-inflation message. During 1942, the WLB used the Little Steel formula as a guide in wage decisions; but the board granted higher raises when it concluded that an injustice existed in the wage structure or when workers in a plant were being paid less than similar workers in other area factories.

Unfortunately, the WLB lost most of its flexibility to grant wage increases in April 1943. Responding to rising food prices and inflationary pressures caused by rising incomes, President Roosevelt instructed the OPA and the WLB to "hold-the-line" on prices for farm products and wages paid to workers. The President instructed the WLB to limit wage increases to those allowed under the Little Steel formula or to rectify substandard pay. No longer could the board consider inequities between workers doing the same job at different plants as a justification for granting a wage increase. In recent months, most awards had been based on the inequality principle, and relatively few adjustments were left to be made under the Little Steel formula. The labor and public board members of the WLB protested that the President's order made it impossible for them to regulate wages successfully. While they awaited a new order to clarify their function, the board dismissed approximately 10,000 cases—three-fifths of its caseload—that had been submitted to remedy inequalities. As a result, workers at 200 Milwaukee companies found voluntary agreements with their employers thrown out by the board as a result of the WLB dismissal of cases. Although it was clear that raises might still be granted if workers were at a substandard pay level or had not been compensated according to the limits set by the Little Steel formula, the elimination of inequality as a criterion effectively created a freeze of wages.[15]

By April 1943, it was already clear to many workers that the WLB's Little Steel formula, which had once been viewed as a sign that the agency would protect workers' wage rates from the ravages of inflation, had become a trap that stifled attempts to keep wage rates in line with the rising cost of living.[16] Although weekly pay of industrial workers in the Milwaukee metropolitan area had increased by 50 percent since January 1941, far above the 19 percent rise in the Milwaukee Consumers' Price Index, the increase was largely the result of overtime work. Factory employees worked an average of 47.7 hours a week during March 1943, compared with 40.7 hours a week in January 1941. After adjusting for time-and-a-half pay, the average hourly rate among industrial workers rose from approximately 78 cents an hour in January 1941 to 93 cents in March 1943—an increase of 19 percent.

Even though wage rates seemingly kept pace with the Consumers' Price Index, these figures underestimate the real differences between wages and the cost of living. Not only was the real cost of goods several percent higher than indicated by the BLS because of changes in quality and the discontinuation of low-priced items, but the 19 percent increase in wages also overestimated real wage rate increases that would survive into the postwar era. The figure was skewed upward by the fact that industry experienced a dramatic increase in the number of high-paying jobs making durable goods such as iron and steel products, electrical machinery, and automotive equipment.

In January 1941, approximately 84,000 industrial employees worked in the Milwaukee metropolitan area. Of these, 66 percent were in durable goods manufacturing and 34 percent in nondurable goods. By March 1943, metropolitan Milwaukee companies employed approximately 131,000 industrial workers, 76 percent of whom made durable goods, compared with only 24 percent in nondurable production. Although the total industrial workforce had grown by 56 percent, the nondurable work force remained almost static, having risen from 28,843 to 31,377. The expansion of heavy industry during the war helped produce average hourly rate figures that kept pace with inflation. By 1943, workers making durable goods earned an average of 18 cents an hour more than their cohorts in nondurable goods.

Bowing to labor pressure to bypass or replace the Little Steel formula, Franklin Roosevelt asked the WLB to appoint a committee to study the cost of living. The committee consisted of two labor and two industrial members of the WLB, with William Davis, head of the Board, as chairman. The President's Cost of Living Committee began its work in December 1943. On January 25, 1944, R. J. Thomas (president of the CIO United Auto Workers) and George Meany (secretary-treasurer of the AFL), the two labor members, issued a report summarizing labor's view of the matter and recommended that the committee adopt the report as its own.[17] The report was, in fact, one of the war's most vigorous and cogent attacks on the government's cost-of-living figures.

After reviewing all of the available statistical information and conducting special surveys in ten cities, Thomas and Meany concluded in a published report that the cost of living had risen 43.5 percent between January 1941, and December 1943. By contrast, the BLS's Cost of Living Index showed a rise of only 23.4 percent. The two labor leaders argued that the disparity existed because the government had focused price control efforts on items that were included in the bureau's index and ignored items that were not. Because such efforts had kept prices on these items under some control, the results were skewed, and the true rise in the cost of living was grossly underestimated.

Organized labor's study of cities ranging in size from Boston and Flint to Oshkosh and Sioux Falls indicated that food items not studied by the BLS had increased approximately twice as much as those items sampled for the index. The index also failed to take into account the disappearance of cheaper consumption items, concurrent shifts toward higher-priced alternatives, quality deterioration, smaller portions served in restaurants, and higher rent in congested small cities. The labor report concluded that food prices had risen 74.2 percent compared to the 40.2 percent estimated by the BLS; that clothing was up 72.2 percent compared to 33.7 percent; rent was up 15 percent compared to 3 percent; and house furnishings had risen 62 percent compared to the BLS estimate of 27.8 percent. The Thomas-Meany report concluded, "since January 1941, living costs have risen 43.5 percent, and that there is a discrepancy of 28.5 percent between the rise in living costs and the wage adjustments allowed under the 'Little Steel' formula."[18]

The CIO and the AFL immediately disseminated the labor report as the authoritative critique of BLS methodology. The *CIO News* printed a four-page "Special Cost of Living Supplement" summarizing the report's findings; its cartoon illustrations said as much about the CIO's views as did the text. In one cartoon a grocer told an astonished customer, "Yes, Ma'am, these grade B eggs are sold for grade A prices." Another poor shopper looked sadly at shelves devoid of low-cost items in a clothing store, while the shelves containing high-cost items remained well stocked. The supplement's final cartoon portrayed a boxing ring in which the cost-of-living bruiser prepared to demolish his Little Steel formula opponent, the proverbial ninety-eight-pound weakling. A third figure labeled "Bureau of Labor Statistics" helplessly watched the fiasco.

The *Milwaukee Labor Press* also published Thomas and Meany's findings, noting that an AFL survey of Milwaukee, conducted as part of the research for the report, showed substantial increases in the price of food and clothing. Since 1941, for example, the price of canned pears had risen 44 percent; tomato soup was up 71.6 percent; Idaho potatoes, 120.3 percent; Swiss cheese, 215.1 percent; chopped beef, 101.6 percent; and summer sausage, 236.5 percent. Organized labor's message was clear: while the BLS Cost of Living Index underestimated inflation and the Little Steel formula held wage rates down, the average worker's standard of living was taking a beating.[19]

Throughout the spring of 1944, Milwaukee's labor papers kept the cost-of-living issue before their readers with regular articles emphasizing the need for reform. They contended that labor's goal was not to break the stabilization program, but rather to rectify the losses in standard of living imposed by the formula.

David Sigman, director of the regional office of the AFL, highlighted this point by citing a University of California survey that found a decent standard of living in Milwaukee currently required an average wage of $1.13 an hour, compared with the 83-cent figure used by the BLS. In April 1944, average earnings in Milwaukee were in fact $1.13 an hour. Thus, if one relied on BLS figures, Milwaukee's workers were earning a comfortable living. But if one employed the University of California figures, those same workers were on the knife-edge of poverty.[20]

In response to labor's charges, the BLS maintained that its statistics accurately measured the rise in cost of living. Faced with this stalemate, WLB chairman William Davis sought the advice of neutral specialists and appointed a "technical committee" of three statisticians to carefully weigh all the charges and countercharges. The committee's report virtually eliminated any possibility that the WLB would consent to labor's demands. The committee concluded that the cost of living had increased between 26.8 and 28.5 percent since January of 1941, compared with the increase of 23.4 percent indicated by the BLS Cost of Living Index. Much of the discrepancy between the BLS index and the findings of the technical committee stemmed from difficult-to-measure items such as changes in quality that the Bureau never really tried to measure. The technical report bolstered the public and industry members of the WLB in their determination to preserve the Little Steel formula.[21]

As the members of the WLB pursued their own goals, each side emphasized different statistics. Public members of the board relied upon average straight-time hourly earnings, statistically adjusted to discount the movement of workers into the higher-paying war industries, as the best measure of "changes in the average pay for an hour's work received by employees who have not shifted from the industry in which they were customarily employed." This measure included the effect on pay of such factors as accelerated merit increases and promotions, higher shift premiums, and wartime incentive rates. Based on such calculations, the public members of the Board believed that adjusted average straight-time earnings had increased by 36.7 percent between January 1941 and October 1944—well above the rise in living costs as measured by the BLS. Using these figures, they defended maintenance of the Little Steel formula as the foundation for wage adjustments.

These WLB members specifically rejected two measures that reflected lower wage increases. Average straight-time hourly earnings—what the BLS called "urban wage rates"—statistically discounted such factors as shift differentials, between-grade promotions, and the migration of employees who remained within a specific industry but moved to higher-paid localities. Based on "urban wage rates," wages rose 30 percent by October 1944. The public members also rejected scheduled wage rates as a measure because it took no account of increases that did not require board approval, shift premiums and "fringe" adjustments to wage schedules, or increases to women workers to compensate for equal work. Using wage rate schedules as a yardstick, wages for manufacturing employees rose only 19.7 percent between January 1941 and the fall of 1944, well below the 25.5 percent BLS estimate of the rise in the Consumers' Price Index.[22]

On the other hand, AFL members of the WLB argued that adjusted average straight-time hourly earnings reflected a form of take-home pay and did not adequately measure either the wages actually received by workers or the wage rates to which workers would return when the war ended. The AFL considered scheduled wage rates a more accurate tool upon which to base wage decisions, although the labor leaders believed that this measure probably overstated the pay increases workers actually received. The federation leaders preferred to use a figure that reflected only those increases paid to specific groups or individuals. When such adjustments were made, they estimated that wages rose by only 16 percent during the period studied by the WLB.[23]

When chairman Davis reported to the President in November 1944, he gave little credence to the charges being leveled by organized labor. As far as he was concerned, their argument had been demolished by the technical committee. Davis concluded that workers would have to accept the decline in merchandise quality and the disappearance of low-priced goods as one of the exigencies of war, to be endured temporarily for the sake of the nation.[24]

Having lost the fight over the BLS index, the labor federations mounted new assaults on the Little Steel formula. In at least one case, a Milwaukee local openly flaunted the formula as part of a concerted effort to disrupt the government's wage controls. Despite having received raises in excess of the formula's 15 percent limit, AFL Federal Labor Union 22631 at the International Harvester Company demanded a 22-cents-per-hour raise to bring wages there into line with the AFL estimate that the cost of living had risen 38 percent since the beginning of the war. The federal conciliator concluded that the case could be resolved only by forwarding it directly to the WLB.[25]

As organized labor pursued its attack on the Little Steel formula, the labor press in Milwaukee began placing an emphasis not only on the failure of wages to keep pace with inflation, but on the postwar consequences of this inequitable situation. Most reports in the *Milwaukee Labor Press* recounted the familiar tale of rising prices, falling quality, and inadequate wage rates; but such articles also contained a subtle shift in focus. By midwinter, the *CIO News* was carrying a similar theme. Where editors had earlier emphasized the difficulty with which workers met their financial responsibilities due to the rising cost of living, they now began placing greater weight on the importance of purchasing power in the postwar era.

The federations continued to remind their members that the Thomas-Meany study had found a 43.5 percent increase in the cost of living; but increasingly they used the technical committee's findings (rounded upward to 30 percent) as the basis for labor's pay argument. The AFL contrasted the rise in the cost of living with the 19 percent rise in wage rates and concluded that workers required an immediate pay increase of 11 percent. Philip Murray, president of the CIO, took this comparison one step further. He advocated a jump of 20 percent, at least 10 percent to account for inflation and another 10 percent to reward workers for improved productivity. The leaders of both federations warned that America was headed for a disaster if the government failed to allow equitable wage increases and if Congress failed to implement an equitable postwar program to assist workers as well as industry during the conversion process. As a cartoon in the *AFL Milwaukee Labor Press* suggested, a bridge was needed between wartime employment and peacetime employment.[26]

From labor's perspective, the failure of price controls and the success of wage controls made any such bridge perilous. By V-J Day, the BLS reported that its Consumers' Price Index had risen 28.1 points since January 1941. Unfortunately, as admitted by the BLS, the index actually underestimated the changes in cost of living by approximately 5 points during the war because of hidden increases caused by such factors as the declining quality of goods and the replacement of lower-grade goods with more expensive models or lines. In other words, the cost of living rose by approximately 33 points between 1941 and the end of the war.[27] In contrast, between January 1941 and August 1945, urban wage rates, one of the measures preferred by organized labor, rose only 30.9 percent.[28]

The discrepancy between the rising cost of living and wage rate increases, and concern for postwar living standards fueled many wartime industrial disputes, whether those disputes remained hidden behind the scenes or in public view on the picket line. The case files of the United States Conciliation Service provide one of the best windows through which to view the nature of industrial conflict, especially when that conflict never erupted into a public dispute.

The Conciliation Service was one of the most constructive agencies through which the government attempted to resolve industrial disputes. Dating to the 1930s, federal conciliators entered conflicts before they escalated into strikes. Early attention often resulted in rapid settlement. A survey of 109 Conciliation Service cases[29] at thirty-one of Milwaukee's most significant factories demonstrates that wage rates, working conditions, job security, union security, and contract maintenance remained points of contention between management and labor in Milwaukee despite a commitment to win the war. Over half of these disputes stemmed from economic conflict when workers demanded higher hourly wages, better shift premiums, equal pay for women, improved piece rates, and job reclassifications.

Of the remaining Conciliation Service cases surveyed, twenty-nine (27 percent) arose from contract negotiation disputes, almost all of which included wage issues. Some contract disputes centered on one or two issues such as wages, fringe benefits, union security, or dues check-off.[30] At other times, negotiations dissolved into wrangling over almost every conceivable issue in the contract.[31]

Twenty cases (18 percent) involved traditional grievances brought to the attention of the Conciliation Service. These included conflicts over the firing of a worker, obnoxious behavior of a supervisor, violation of a contract, improper use of job classification, failure to process grievances, failure to agree to a proper work schedule under Executive Order 9240, and banning of a chief steward from entering a plant.[32]

Conciliation cases at the Harley-Davidson Motor Company illustrated the dominant influence of wage-related issues on industrial conflict. The Conciliation Service helped to settle no fewer than eight disputes dealing with wage issues at Harley-Davidson. Shortly after America entered the war, the AFL Auto Workers local 209 demanded that wage rates be reviewed because of the rise in cost of living. The issue was tabled because contract negotiations were about to begin. Those negotiations quickly deadlocked, and the workers threatened to strike if they did not receive a wage increase. A compromise wage package settled the issue. Another compromise was needed in October of 1942, when a dispute arose over contract provisions for a cost-of-living increase. The Conciliation Service was back in the plant a year later to resolve a problem involving equal pay for women in the packing and shipping department. In April 1944, a conciliator was needed when contract negotiations deadlocked over wage issues. James Despins, another federal conciliator, visited the plant in February 1945 to resolve a dispute over payment of Christmas bonuses and the pay rate for employees transferred from one department to another. The bonus issue came up again three months later when contract negotiations stalled over whether the bonus was a management prerogative or a contract issue, whether the company should pay for the time stewards spent processing grievances, and whether provisions for paid holidays should remain in the contract. Finally, wage issues seemed to play a major part in a strike that began as soon as the war ended. Conciliation cases at Harley-Davidson reflected the desire to rectify specific inequalities in the plant, as well as the ongoing struggle between the company and its employees over the distribution of wartime economic prosperity.[33]

In keeping with the pattern of Conciliation Service cases, wage-related issues of some kind also lay behind the majority of strikes in wartime Milwaukee. Half of the city's sixty-five wartime strikes for which causes could be determined were brought on by some dispute over wages, and another one-sixth by disputes resulting from contract negotiations, which often included wage issues as a major component. In 1944, the year with the greatest number of strikes, for example, CIO steelworkers at the Crucible Steel Casting Company stopped work for three hours to protest the reclassification of several workers and the reduction of work hours; AFL steelworkers at the Globe Steel Tubes Company walked out briefly when they learned that their Christmas bonus would be half what they expected; CIO auto workers at the Milwaukee Foundry Equipment Company walked out twice, first when the company initiated new wage rate classifications and later when the Wisconsin Employment Relations Board ruled the earlier strike an unfair labor practice because of a no-strike clause in their contract; teamsters at the Petroleum Transport Company stopped work when the company refused to pay a wage increase granted by the WLB; and 1,750 AFL auto workers at Harley-Davidson took a one-day "holiday" to protest the way in which the company chose to apply a WLB rate range decision.[34]

Because of its role in controlling wages, the War Labor Board often became the focus of conflict. Frustration awaited Teamsters Local 360, for example, when it tried to bring pay for dry-cleaning route salesmen into line with the pay of other service trade sales drivers and to compensate those drivers for improved productivity. In November 1942, the union and the Cleaners and Dyers Association began work on a new contract, but they had made little progress by the time the contract ran out in March 1943. During the next five months, with the aid of the Conciliation Service, the parties resolved all disputed issues except wages. With negotiations stalled, the disagreement was certified to the WLB, which turned it over to the Trucking Commission.

At the heart of the dispute lay the Little Steel formula and the question of how to apply it to drivers whose pay was derived primarily from sales commissions. The union proposed that driver-salesmen receive a 10 percent ($2) increase in weekly rate and that the commission for work over $100 be increased from 8 percent to 12 percent. The raise was designed to bring the pay for dry-cleaning salesmen into line with the wages of comparable drivers in Milwaukee's laundry trade. While the Cleaners and Dyers Association argued that straight-time hourly earnings had increased more than the 15 percent allowed by the Little Steel formula, the union countered that straight-time hourly earnings could not be computed for workers with no definite hours. The Teamsters even questioned whether the Little Steel formula could be applied to such workers.

Douglas Soutar, a federal Trucking Commission examiner, ruled that the Little Steel formula could be applied, but he agreed with the union that straight-time hourly earnings could not be computed accurately in this case. Instead, he based his ruling on the average route earnings during January 1941. On that basis, he ruled that the Teamsters were entitled to a raise of $3.53 a week, and he increased the commission to 10 percent for work over $100 per week. However, when the Trucking Commission issued its directive order in November 1943, it reduced the recommended weekly raise to $3.

Having received WLB Trucking Commission sanction, the union learned that the directive could not be implemented until the OPA issued its stamp of approval as well. In exasperation, one union official stated that the union had conscientiously obeyed the no-strike pledge, despite a belief that a strike would have been effective, and had patiently cooperated with the Conciliation Service and the WLB. Now they had to wait longer. Perhaps a new contract deadline would arrive in 1944 before the government settled the dispute. "This case," the union official argued,

> is a living example of the ineffectiveness of the Commission form of Government to settle labor disputes. It also demonstrates why employees become restless, dissatisfied and at times even leave their jobs in protest of the great delay and injustice created thereby in these cases. It is often times said that "Justice delayed is justice denied."[35]

After learning of the new delay, Alois Mueller, secretary-treasurer of Local 360, implored the OPA to act promptly. The union had studied the financial resources of the companies involved and assured the OPA that the raise would require no price increases. The dry cleaners were experiencing a boom in business and profits, while their employees received little additional compensation for carrying a greater work load. As Mueller told the regional WLB, drivers often worked from 5:30 in the morning to 7:00 at night. They carried heavier loads, and 112 men were doing the work previously handled by 130 drivers. And finally, in recognition of the manpower crisis and the plight of the companies, the union was also allowing drivers to work more hours than permitted by the contract. In short, the companies were reaping unparalleled benefits from the higher productivity of the workers.

Finally, fifteen months after the workers began negotiating with the Cleaners and Dyers Association, the OPA approved the Trucking Commission directive. With the wage issue settled, Local 360 was ready to begin negotiating a new contract with the Association. Its old contract, to which the directive order applied, was set to expire in less than a month. While officials of Local 360 pushed their wage demands through the government hurdles, members of the union worked harder and stayed on the job with little or no outward manifestation of their irritation.[36]

In some cases, worker frustration with the overloaded WLB became great enough to spark a strike. Fifteen of Milwaukee's wartime work stoppages were directed not against companies but against the WLB. In a classic case of delay, forbearance, and frustration, which ultimately led to a strike as the war ended, members of Local 125 of the International Molders and Foundry Workers union and six Milwaukee foundries submitted a wage dispute to the WLB in December 1942. Nine months later, the Board issued an interim decision; but that decision could not go into effect until it was approved by the OPA or by the Director of Economic Stabilization. Out of frustration, the foundry workers requested a strike vote to force a final decision. This was primarily a strategic move; no strike actually took place. When the WLB finally granted a wage increase in March 1944, the *Milwaukee Labor Press* hailed the workers' patience.[37]

Perhaps because of their earlier experiences with government controls, Local 125 set out to break or bypass the limits on wages set by the WLB well before the ruling of March 1944. When the WLB rejected the union's request for a raise of 15 cents an hour at Nordberg Company, for example, Local 125 demanded that the company reclassify all jobs in the foundry. Such a reclassification would have bypassed the Little Steel formula, and would have given the foundry workers raises ranging from 8 cents to 42 cents an hour. Ultimately, the union settled for a company compromise proposal of 5 cents an hour.

These foundry workers showed much less patience as the war drew to a close. Irritated by WLB area rates for gray iron foundries, which they felt were too low, the members of Local 125 voted overwhelmingly to strike. On August 6, 1945, they struck six foundries. After one day, the workers returned to their jobs with assurances that the WLB would restudy the local rates. (Of course, the end of the war soon made such assurances unimportant as the no-strike pledge expired and the WLB lost much of its power to control wages.)[38]

Similar strikes protesting WLB action or inaction occurred at eight other plants organized by the AFL, and at one CIO factory. These stoppages were uniformly short, symbolic expressions of irritation with an overburdened WLB and with wage rates, which were falling behind inflation.

Frustration with slow government action could even spark work stoppages at plants otherwise free of strike activity. One such strike never received public attention in the press and never appeared in government statistics. The A. O. Smith Corporation, Milwaukee's second-largest employer, and the various AFL unions with which it bargained, prided themselves on maintaining cordial relations. Since the organization of the Smith Steelworkers' Union (Federal Labor Union 19806) in the early 1930s, all grievances had been settled without recourse to arbitration, and the company had willingly granted a union shop clause to the Smith Steelworkers. The rapid increase in the company's workforce during the war did little to alter this stable relationship. In August 1944, the federal union and eight craft unions began wage negotiations with the company. In November, A. O. Smith and its unions submitted a wage package to the WLB. Five months later, the case remained unresolved, and the workers began expressing their dissatisfaction. "As a matter of fact," an official of the Operating Engineers union wrote to a friend, "confidentially, there have been minor work stoppages at the plant, which fortunately, haven't received any publicity." The WLB finally awarded increases to the production workers, but only after another two months had passed.[39]

As if to underscore the economic foundation of industrial strife, Milwaukee's most prolonged wartime labor conflict originated as a dispute over cost-of-living bonuses for city workers—specifically, garbage workers. Throughout the war, city laborers and garbage workers chafed under what they believed were substandard wage rates that permitted them to live only slightly above a subsistence level. On five different occasions, groups of these workers struck to impress the city's Common Council with the importance of their wage demands.

During 1942 and the first months of 1943, both city and county governments came under increasing pressure to improve the wages of their employees. Not only were they losing experienced workers to war plants, but the workers themselves had begun to clamor for raises to offset the increased cost of living.[40] In May 1943, the Common Council began work on plans to improve city employee compensation in 1944; but for garbage workers, this was not moving fast enough. On May 27, frustrated by the rejection of petitions for higher pay and an increase in the work week to forty-eight hours, city garbage workers walked off their jobs.

To compensate for the rising cost of living, the Garbage Workers Association, an independent union, demanded a raise of $32.50 a month effective June 1, and another raise of $17.50 a month, effective January 1, 1944. Once these improvements were implemented, collectors would receive between $165 and $180 a month for their labors. At the time of the strike, city garbage workers were paid a base rate of between $115 and $130 a month, with cost-of-living bonuses of between $25 for lower-paid workers and $22.50 for higher-paid employees. If one looked only at the base rate—as workers often did because the bonus was temporary and fluctuated with changes in the cost of living—the differential between industrial pay and city pay was widening. Industrial base rates had risen to an average of approximately 92 cents an hour, adjusted to eliminate overtime pay, and were based on negotiated permanent pay increases, not temporary cost-of-living adjustments. The base rate for garbage workers amounted to between 72 and 81 cents an hour, and the employees had little chance for overtime work. Although the cost-of-living bonus had raised a garbage worker's pay to a range of 86 to 95 cents an hour, roughly comparable to pay in industrial concerns, the permanent increase sought by the collectors amounted to a raise of between 38 and 43 percent. This would have brought pay to a range of $1.03 to $1.12—well above the BLS Consumers' Price Index, but in line with organized labor's estimates of the real rise in the cost of living.

On the second day of the strike, Deputy Health Commissioner G. F. Burgardt warned residents that the strike posed a "serious health menace" to the city. He recommended that citizens burn their garbage or, if burning was not possible, that they bury it in their back yards. As collection cans overflowed throughout the city, the health department received relatively few complaints, and Milwaukeeans seemed to take the commissioner's advice to heart to burn or bury their refuse. One protest, however, was particularly effective at demonstrating the results of a long strike. The proprietor of a fish market called to tell Morris Oesterreich, superintendent of garbage collection, that she had attempted to take two barrels of spoiled fish to the disposal plant but was unable to cross the picket line. "I have placed the two barrels at the curb in front of my shop," she told the superintendent, "so if anyone complains over the week end you will know the reason why."[41]

After six days the garbage collectors and their allies from Teamsters Local 200 returned to their jobs after the Common Council had voted to seek statutory changes to allow city employees to work more than forty hours a week, to allow the city to pay workers time-and-a-half for such overtime, and to allow the city to make pay adjustments during the year instead of only on January 1. As a gesture of good faith, the Council also pledged to pay the men for the time they were on strike, provided they returned and promptly cleaned up the garbage that had accumulated during their absence.[42]

This happy solution to one problem only brought new ones for Milwaukee's city fathers. As June passed into July and the Council tried to fulfill its promises, Fred Schallert, business agent for the city's laborers, threatened the aldermen with another strike if they singled out one group for special treatment. The laborers, who were responsible for street cleaning and repair, had waited patiently for their wage demands to be met. Now, Schallert warned, "Some of our boys, including the street sanitation workers, are getting pretty hard to hold in line." To this threat, Mayor John L. Bohn rejoined, with perhaps a trace of hyperbole: "A strike against the municipality is a strike against the whole government—against the greater good of the nation in time of war and a direct aid to our nation's enemies." The mayor admitted that just grievances existed, but he urged patience as the city moved to rectify the problems.[43]

One drawback that complicated any attempt to meet city employees' demands was the fact that the Common Council could not act in a vacuum. Milwaukee County contained five independent taxing authorities: the city, the county, the city school board, the vocational school board, and the sewerage commission. By 1942, these bodies had begun to work in concert on issues of employee compensation through a joint "technical committee." To resolve some of the complaints and to prevent further defections to war plants, the technical committee settled on a bonus plan designed to offset increases in the cost of living. Based on an average civil service salary of $135 a month in the five taxing units, and using the June 15 BLS index as a measure of change, the technical committee proposed that a bonus of $30.64 become effective August 1, 1943, and that it be adjusted each January 1 thereafter. This was a bonus, not a wage increase, and it was designed to fall as well as rise depending on changes in the annual index each June. Based on the technical committee's recommendation, the city adopted the bonus on July 26 and the county board followed suit a day later.[44]

As the city finance committee considered the bonus proposal, city garbage workers took a one-day "holiday." They were irked when they learned that the new bonus would replace a $22–$25 bonus they had been receiving and would not be in addition to that bonus. The city had been unsuccessful in its attempt to change the state statutes governing when wage rate increases could be granted, and the garbage workers remained irritated with what they perceived as substandard wages. While the cost-of-living bonus compensated for rising prices, it could not alter what the garbage workers considered a subsistence pay rate. All the bonus could do was prevent the workers from being swamped by inflation. Shortly after the garbage collectors' "holiday," the city approved the $30.64 bonus recommended by the technical committee. Having received an increase in their bonus of between $5.64 and $8.14 a month, instead of the $50 raise requested in the spring, the garbage collectors remained dissatisfied. Nonetheless, they decided not to strike again. Instead, they submitted a new proposal to the city requesting that base wages be increased from the existing range of $115 to $130 a month to a uniform rate of $140.[45]

Milwaukee's garbage collectors displayed their annoyance for all to see; but, as Fred Schallert had warned in July, the city's street cleaning, construction, and repair workers were also unhappy with their wage rates. The city paid street cleaners a base rate of only $115 a month, electrical service workers $120 a month, and street construction and repair workers $140 a month. In October 1943, members of the American Federation of State, County and Municipal Employees' union (AFSCME) Local 2 voted to strike if the city failed to raise the base rate to a uniform $140 a month, in addition to the $30.64 cost-of-living bonus to go into effect in August. Representatives of the international union, the Wisconsin Federation of Labor, and the Milwaukee Federated Trades Council opposed the local's strike threat but strongly supported its demands for rate improvements. On Saturday, October 23, after receiving word that their demands would not be met, the members of Local 2 reaffirmed their desire to strike and gave the city a week to reconsider. Meeting in an adjoining room, the garbage workers voted to follow the same course as the AFL union.[46]

As the union deadline approached, a special committee of the city finance committee proposed a $15 a month raise for workers earning $115 a month. Although this would have raised the pay for over 90 percent of the city's laborers, the compromise proved to be too little and too late. On November 3, 1943, some 750 laborers and garbage collectors failed to show up for work. Thus began Milwaukee's longest wartime strike.

In the succeeding weeks, the unions assigned workers to maintain emergency services, but the strike paralyzed routine garbage collection, ash removal, street cleaning, and street repair work. The city maintained its offer of $15 a month and the unions continued to demand a $25 increase to the monthly base of $115.

As the garbage piles grew, a special committee of aldermen met with union representatives in an attempt to settle the dispute while the strike dragged into its third week. On November 19, the *Journal* announced, "Council Capitulates!" Milwaukee's principal daily newspaper opposed any solution other than a complete rejection of the union's demands; editorially, the strike was represented as a direct threat to democracy. After all, if municipal workers could strike and win their demands, then government would be run by unions and not by representatives of the people. The *Journal* viewed such a development as intolerable.[47]

The special committee's meeting with strike representatives marked the beginning of a search for a rational way to end the strike. As the city negotiated, it also intensified measures to combat the strike. It continued to block attempts by laborers to secure statements of availability (which would have allowed them to find alternative employment during the strike), and the city openly hinted that it would take action to resume suspended services if the strike did not end soon. After the strikers rejected an offer to pay time-and-a-half for overtime up to 200 hours worked during 1944, Mayor Bohn promised police protection for anyone wishing to take garbage to the city incinerator and called a meeting of the nonpartisan aldermen (twenty out of twenty-seven aldermen fell into this category) to discuss replacement of the striking workers. The seven aldermen not invited to this caucus were Progressives and Socialists who had favored reaching some accommodation with the city laborers. On December 2, in response to the city's promise of police protection, the garbage workers' union placed the incinerator under siege with a picket line of thirty-five to fifty men. The strengthened line convinced all but five of the incinerator plant workers to leave their jobs, effectively shutting down the facility.[48]

Just as most of the pronouncements on both sides seemed to point to an escalation of the conflict, the strike ended with a compromise worked out with the assistance of Arnold Zander, international president of the AFSCME, the union to which most of the strikers belonged. For all practical purposes, the city won the battle. The workers accepted the original offer, which raised salaries to $130 a month, as well as the city's compromise proposal granting overtime pay for up to 200 hours of extra work during 1944. Although it was not publicly acknowledged when the strike ended, the workers agreed to return to their jobs with the understanding that the technical committee immediately would study the basic rates paid laborers and would likely report favorably on their demands. The union also understood that an additional $5 raise would become effective January 1, 1944. With these agreements and understandings in hand, the city's sanitation and street workers returned to their jobs on December 5, 1943.[49]

The sense of relief that came with the end of the strike soon dissipated. First, 1,100 employees of county institutions, members of Local 55 of the State, County and Municipal Workers of America (CIO), called for Milwaukee County to grant similar raises. City truck drivers, members of Teamsters Local 200, quietly came to the Common Council with a pledge not to strike and a request for a raise. Equally quietly, the Council turned down the request. As the new year dawned, Milwaukee's laborers became restive again. The understanding they had with city officials proved illusory. The technical committee undertook a prolonged, detailed wage study of all workers in the county, not just the laborers, and the $5 raise turned out to be more implied than real. The mayor warned the laborers to stay at work, but 300 took a short holiday from their jobs to demonstrate their strength to the city council. Shortly thereafter, AF-SCME Local 430, which represented many of the county's employees, asked the county board for a raise of $15 a month for all employees earning less than $175 a month. The city strike was over, but the issue of substandard pay and the rising cost of living remained unsettled.[50]

The grievances of the garbage workers simmered for the rest of the war despite the increases received after their strike in 1943. On July 3, 1945, the incinerator workers and garbage collectors, who had reorganized their independent union into Local 632 of the CIO State, County and Municipal Workers union, struck to emphasize their demand that the $15 "historical differential" separating them from other laborers be reinstated. (The differential was to compensate them for work that was particularly disagreeable.) The differential had been lost in the raises granted after the 1943 strike. The stoppage lasted only one day but was repeated by incinerator operators on July 31. As the war finally drew to a close, the Milwaukee Common Council began another study of the merits of the garbage workers' demands.[51]

Milwaukee's garbage collectors and laborers vigorously pursued their demands for improvement of basic wage rates and protection against rising living costs. Disputes between the city and its workers mirrored the pattern of escalating wage demands by industrial workers. City employees, like their working colleagues in Milwaukee's factories, feared that inflated prices would become fixed when the war ended and they would be saddled with basic wage rates that had not kept pace with inflation.

While organized labor fought to protect postwar earning power, the *Milwaukee Journal,* which generally supported business positions during the war, vociferously attacked labor's drive against wage controls. The paper attributed labor's insistence on higher pay to greed and to an unwillingness to sacrifice for the war effort. For workers paying daily bills or thinking about future employment, a clear double standard existed between the way their demands for greater economic security were treated and the way similar corporate concerns were perceived. During the war, the federal government granted subsidies, low-interest loans, rapid tax write-offs for new facilities and equipment, and cost plus a fixed fee contracts to hasten production. To foster postwar conversion to a peace economy, corporations were encouraged to set financial reserves aside. Unlike a worker's savings, these reserves were subtracted from taxable income. Likewise, although workers used their extra income to pay off debts and to fulfill delayed needs for scarce consumer goods at inflated wartime prices, businesses received easy credit for expansion and, as the war ended, were able to begin purchasing facilities built by the government at a fraction of their actual value. Corporate demands for postwar financial reserves and favorable reconversion policies received sympathetic treatment by government officials and the press. It seemed clear to many observers that such measures were necessary to guarantee postwar prosperity. Maintenance of worker buying power through protection of wage rates received much less consideration, and organized labor pointed out the inconsistency.

When the *Milwaukee Journal* published an article that reported declining profits during 1943 for seventeen heavy industry groups nationally, the *Labor Press* rejoined that the reduction was based on a comparison of profits to total sales—not of profits to invested capital as had been the practice in previous years. It was more accurate, the labor paper contended, to report that before-tax profits rose $188 million in 1943 while after-tax profits were up $14 million. Indeed, the editor went on, the *Milwaukee Journal* based its criticism of the "swollen" paychecks of workers on total income, ignoring the fact that higher paychecks resulted from working longer hours—the equivalent of companies earning more money because they sold more goods. Citation of after-tax profits as an indication of the price being paid by business for the war effort also ignored the fact that after-tax figures excluded money set aside for postwar reconversion. That money was subtracted from the ledger before the calculation of taxable profits.[52]

Although the war was clearly funded by deficit spending, individual income taxes, and corporate income taxes, in that order, the *Milwaukee Journal* argued that American industries had sacrificed profits to fund the war effort. The paper continually cited figures supplied by the Securities and Exchange Commission to bolster its view that net profits had lagged far behind corporate sales. In other words, American business and industry had created a production miracle, but was reaping few of the benefits of that miracle. In a typical article, the *Journal* concluded that the war was much less than a "bowl of cherries" for Milwaukee's war producers. Faced with high taxes, soaring labor costs, and rising operating and maintenance expenses, Milwaukee's industrialists viewed the future with trepidation. Not only did they expect reconversion to be expensive, but the government's renegotiation act, under which federal officials could renegotiate contracts if they deemed profits to be too excessive, also made it difficult to estimate what resources might be available until after the government had taken its additional slice. Using as examples the A. O. Smith Corporation, Cutler-Hammer, Inc., and the Harnischfeger Corporation, the paper's business editor, Ralph Werner, argued that large inventories, new loans, collapsing prices, and uncertain markets made for an uncertain future. He also noted ominously that corporate executives worried "that the postwar period may be capitalism's last chance to prove itself. If jobs aren't available for all the persons who want them they see appetite upsetting visions of communism or some other isms."[53]

The *Milwaukee Journal* often turned its analysis of the plight of business into a critique of labor's demand for higher wages. In one editorial, the paper reported that North American Aviation had a net profit after taxes and expenses of $7.37 million during fiscal 1942–1943. "That's a big sum," the *Journal* admitted. "It possibly may look like 'excessive profit,' or an inordinately high 'take,' to workers earning $1,000 or $2,000, or $5,000 yearly." Nonetheless, the paper told its readers that this profit amounted to a mere 2.91 percent of the company's sales of $253.23 million for the same period. The *Journal* asked pointedly if a fine craftsman making a $253 piece of furniture would feel "overpaid if he received $7 net for his work."[54]

In a later editorial, the *Journal* made a more direct analogy as it attacked labor's attempts to "smash wage ceilings and the 'Little Steel' formula." A recent study of forty companies doing war work had indicated that between 1940 and 1942, production had risen 81 percent, wages were up 96 percent, and taxes had soared 193 percent; but profits had fallen 17 percent and dividends 20 percent. Despite these unfavorable statistics, the *Journal* reminded its readers that no stockholders had gone on strike to demand higher dividends. The conclusion was inescapable: the government had held profits down and it should do the same for wages.[55]

In fact, the picture was not as bleak as Ralph Werner or his paper portrayed. Without question, the federal government taxed corporate profits heavily during the war. Indeed, most comparisons between the net profit after income taxes in 1941 and the same figures for 1944 or 1945 showed skyrocketing production and sales, but a decline in net profits. Therefore, by looking only at profit after taxes, corporations and newspapers such as the *Milwaukee Journal* could argue that industry had borne the financial brunt of the war, while workers' wages soared.

But such comparisons often were fallacious, for they dealt only with wartime figures and ignored the future impact of exemptions to the excess profits tax. To be sure, the government taxed corporations more heavily during the war than during the defense crisis that preceded it. The Revenue Act of 1941 imposed a graduated taxation system which siphoned off no more than 60 percent of excess profits. In contrast, the Revenue Act of 1942 raised the tax to a flat rate of 90 percent. Comparisons made during the war ignored the Revenue Act's postwar refund provision, which lowered the tax rate to 81 percent. An additional relief provision cut the net tax rate to 72 percent for a small number of companies that owed approximately 40 percent of the total tax liabilities.

Comparisons between corporations and individuals also ignored the fact that individual taxpayers paid a greater share of the war's costs than did corporations. In 1944, for example, individuals paid nearly $20 billion in federal income taxes while corporate tax liabilities amounted to $14 billion. Likewise, comparisons seldom addressed the fact that sharply rising payroll figures were influenced by improved worker productivity, longer working hours, and grow-

ing numbers of industrial workers. For the worker, these factors were comparable to the production and sales figures cited when arguing that corporations
were overburdened by war taxes. Taxes took a much larger portion of corporate
income than of individual income, but the total annual net profits after taxes
still averaged $8.625 billion during each of the war years. It was specious to
argue, as Ralph Werner of the *Milwaukee Journal* did, that the war had worked
a hardship on business.[56]

As the national statistics suggested, war taxes cut into the profits of many
Milwaukee companies. In reports to the Securities and Exchange Commission,
the Harnischfeger Corporation showed a 32 percent jump in net profits after
income taxes between 1941 and 1942. By the end of 1944, the company's net
had fallen 44 percent below the 1941 figure. The Chain Belt Company reported
a more moderate change; its net profit after income taxes fell 1 percent in 1942
and 10 percent in 1944 when compared with figures for 1941. This decline was
relatively mild compared with International Harvester Company, whose after-
tax profit plummeted 13 percent during the first year of war and continued to
fall until it was 17 percent lower in 1944 than in 1941. In 1944, Bucyrus-Erie
Company recorded a decline of 21 percent, and Briggs and Stratton Corporation's after-tax profits fell 19 percent when compared with 1941.

Yet such comparisons oversimplified the impact of the war on Milwaukee
companies, just as they did on the national level. In preparation for the postwar
era, all but one of these Milwaukee companies amassed sizable cash reserves to
soften the blow of reconversion. International Harvester showed a net profit of
$25 to $30 million after taxes during each of the war years, and put $2.5 million
into its postwar reserve during each year America was at war. In 1941, it reserved over $5 million for postwar use. The Chain Belt Company reported only
$829,000 in after-tax profits during 1944, but was able to set aside $337,000 for
postwar contingencies. Similarly, Harnischfeger set aside sums equaling 30 to
112 percent of its after-tax profits during the war years. Bucyrus-Erie followed a
slightly more modest course. Only Briggs and Stratton failed to set any money
aside for reconversion.

None of these companies lost money during the war, and none was threatened with financial extinction. The net worth of each company rose steadily,
and by the beginning of 1945 the net worth of each ranged from 11 percent
higher than in 1941 (Bucyrus-Erie) to 43 percent higher (Harnischfeger).
Yet, as the war drew to a close, the *Milwaukee Journal*'s reporting on these
companies emphasized the relative decline in profits they were suffering compared to previous years. Commentary on postwar reserves, corporate optimism
for postwar production, and net worth tended to appear at the end of such
articles.[57]

The *Journal* followed the same pattern when reporting about companies
such as A. O. Smith and Cutler-Hammer. Ralph Werner had used A. O. Smith
and Cutler-Hammer as examples of the plight faced by Milwaukee companies;
but A. O. Smith showed a net profit after taxes for 1944 that was almost 60
percent higher than the company's profit in 1941, and Cutler-Hammer in-

creased its net profit level by almost 17 percent. Cutler-Hammer's net worth grew by a modest 22 percent between 1941 and 1945; A. O. Smith's grew by more than 69 percent in roughly the same period. Although neither company established a sizable postwar financial reserve, they could hardly be said to have suffered at the hands of government taxation and rising labor costs as the *Journal*'s business editor contended.[58]

Some of the *Journal*'s articles seemed to contradict the image of the long-suffering corporations. After an exhaustive study of corporations listed on the national stock exchanges, the *Journal* reported, the Securities and Exchange Commission concluded that corporate working capital rose 63 percent by 1945 and provided a firm foundation upon which to finance postwar reconversion. The SEC attributed this healthy rise to the retention of profits after taxes and dividends, and to the fact that government construction of plant facilities lessened the expenditure of private capital for expansion and modernization. Much of the resulting surplus was held in cash, and the SEC expected that private capital was more than adequate to finance conversion to civilian production after the war.[59]

When placed alongside the struggles of workers to secure a standard of living that would not be eroded when the war was over, corporations seemed to have reserved for themselves a comfortable position from which to expand in the postwar era. The *American Federationist* typified organized labor's critique of corporate wealth built upon wartime production when it told its readers: "Profits are supposed to be the reward for the risk capital takes. Capital is risking much less in this war period than ever before in history. It has an assured market for everything it can produce. Much of the production is on a guaranteed cost-plus-a-profit basis." The paper charged corporations with building large postwar financial reserves to avoid paying the excess profits tax and to avoid the public outcry that would arise if they distributed huge profits in the form of dividends.[60]

This was the side of business labor saw and resented. Far from the sense of unity that characterized so many aspects of life on the home front, the debate over who profited from the war revealed the underlying tension regarding economic issues that could not be quieted by patriotic fervor or devotion to the war effort. Corporate net profits after taxes did not keep pace with the rate of sales, as the *Journal* often pointed out—but neither did wage rates keep pace with inflation and productivity. Like corporate profits, the workers' take-home pay skyrocketed; but ever-greater amounts went to taxes, living expenses, and war bonds. Many workers looked at their employers' profits and saw profiteering. They read in the labor press about the unequal sacrifice being expected of them, and the proof was all too plain as wage rates fell behind inflation.[61]

Throughout the wartime years, the basic disagreement among government, management, and labor over what statistical measuring tools best conveyed the realities of wages and profits, costs and income, gains and losses led the contending parties to different conclusions about the relationship between real income and the cost of living. Organized labor recognized that the substantial earnings of workers during the war derived from working long hours at high-paying war jobs—a temporary condition. The end of the war would mark an end to the long work week, and many workers would soon return to prewar occupations. When this happened, it held the prospect of workers returning to basic wage rates that had not kept pace with inflation and that could no longer be supplemented with overtime pay.[62]

Government officials were concerned primarily with gauging and controlling inflationary pressures during the war itself. Business and industrial managers were concerned primarily with low-cost production and building a base for postwar profits. Labor leaders were concerned with basic economic justice for American workers and with the need to provide a consumer foundation for the postwar economy.

Given the incompatible goals of labor, management, and the government in controlling wages and fighting inflation, and given organized labor's focus on the postwar era, industrial conflict was almost inevitable despite wartime unity. The perennial tension between worker and employer over economic issues worsened as the war progressed and eventually manifested itself in strikes, work stoppages, and many more subtle industrial conflicts.

Wisconsin National Guardsmen occupy the E. P. Allis Reliance Works on May 5, 1886. Governor Rusk ordered militia troops to fire on striking Milwaukee workers, who had been agitating for the eight-hour day. By the end of the day five people were dead, including three protestors and two by-standers.

Workers take a break outside the Milwaukee Harvester Works, c. 1910. Milwaukee was one of the most industrialized cities in America at that time.

WHS Archives Lot 561; WHi(X3)28834

People, wagons, and streetcars shared Milwaukee's busy streets in 1908. This view is at North Third and Grand Avenue looking east.

An early twentieth-century forge shop at Allis-Chalmers.

West Allis Historical Society

WHS Archives CF 6803; WHi(X3)33738

Milwaukee women make and repair clothing for relief families as part of a Wisconsin work relief project during the Great Depression.

WHS Archives/*Milwaukee Journal* photo

At the Seaman Body Corporation, Socialist Milwaukee Mayor Daniel Hoan speaks to a crowd of workers in support of a strike for union recognition, March 20, 1934.

"Union Gift to Soldiers": Local 1131, representing workers at the Louis Allis Company in Milwaukee, presented thirty radios to the USO in the summer of 1942. The workers used flags and a portrait of FDR to symbolize their loyalty and patriotism.

The Wisconsin state CIO board in 1943. Harold Christoffel, the controversial leader of UAW Local 248 at Allis-Chalmers, stands in the center.

"Soldiers without Guns": heroic figures on the home front.

Elizabeth Little, age thirty and mother of two, sprays gasoline trailer tanks for the U.S. Army Air Corps at the Heil Company.

"I can do as much work as any man, and I can do it just as well or better," boasted Theresa Langolf to a *Milwaukee Journal* reporter in 1944. At the time Langolf was a nineteen-year-old welder making army tanks at Milwaukee's Chain Belt Company. She was the first woman in Wisconsin to pass the army's test for armor-plate welding; her first test weld was perfect.

CIO organizers during the Greenebaum union organizing drive of 1942.

In the face of strong CIO organizing, AFL unions in Milwaukee maintained their strength with traditional crafts and at major factories such as International Harvester, Harley-Davidson, and A. O. Smith. AFL President William Green (seated, third from left) posed with Wisconsin union leaders when he attended the 1943 convention of the Wisconsin State Federation of Labor in Milwaukee.

Although people claimed to be following OPA restrictions, Milwaukee had a flourishing black market for meat during World War II. In this *Milwaukee Journal* photograph, Lawrence P. Dwyer, OPA investigator, stands beside pails of blood and the carcasses of freshly slaughtered black-market pigs and a cow. Deputy sheriffs seized the farmer, William H. Beck, and two helpers in May 1945.

The Office of Price Administration urged home-front consumers to fight inflation by curbing their spending habits. In 1942 the OPA froze the current retail price of food as a maximum, or ceiling. Price controls were generally successful, but the cost of living still outstripped wage rate increases.

The Victory Kidines (kid marines) collected five thousand pounds of scrap in West Allis in July 1944.

CIO News Wisconsin Edition, September 14, 1942; WHS Microfilm P42448

As this political cartoon attests, many Wisconsin workers and farmers believed that they bore the brunt of wartime sacrifices while industrialists became fat on government contracts.

CIO News Local 248 Edition, January 31, 1944; WHS Microfilm P35004

The government and organized labor disagreed on the rate of inflation and its impact on workers' cost of living.

Interior of the Nordberg Manufacturing Company.

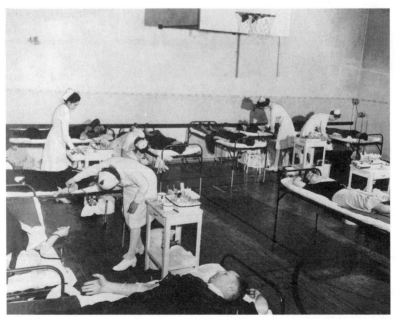

Milwaukee Red Cross nurses draw blood for the war effort, January 1943.

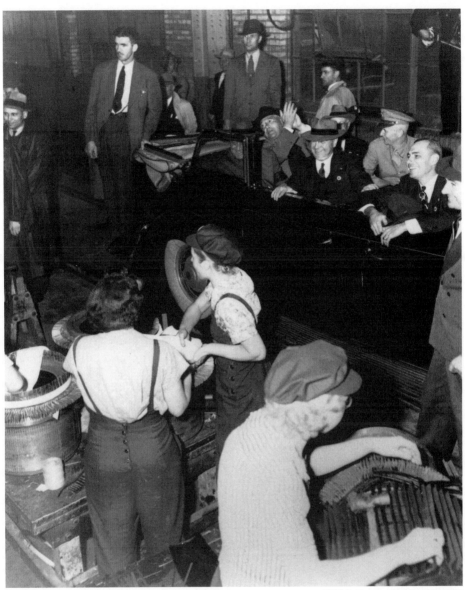

FDR visits the Allis-Chalmers plant in Milwaukee on September 19, 1942. Governor Julius Heil applauds the workers for their efforts and patriotism.

Wisconsin AFL-CIO

Jean Richter, a three-year-veteran coil winder at the Louis Allis plant, does war work in the fall of 1942.

U.S. Army-Navy "E" Ward presentation at the main plant of the Cutler Hammer Company, 1943. The "E" stood for "excellence." The federal government gave these awards to companies that met government contracts on time and produced quality war matériel.

Wisconsin AFL-CIO

R. J. Thomas, vice president of the CIO autoworkers and of the CIO, joined thousands on picket lines outside the Allis-Chalmers plant on November 25, 1946. Workers and unions sacrificed to help make the production miracle possible during World War II, but all too often they received little recognition of their efforts in postwar labor disputes.

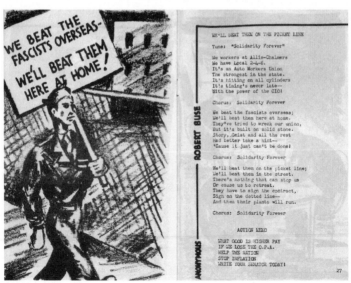

West Allis Historical Society

The workers of Allis-Chalmers went out on strike right after the war in order to win the wages and respect they felt they deserved. This is a page from their 1946 strike songbook, entitled *The Pavement Trail*.

CHAPTER FOUR

WORKER MILITANCY AND WARTIME INDUSTRIAL CONFLICT

"The men in the brass foundry call him 'Big Bill.'

"But Bill Zastrow, steward of the Brass Foundry workers, is more than big. He's a 100% Union guy and a real example for every steward in the Union." Zastrow helped build his union during the 1930s and sustain it during World War II. When United Auto Workers Local 248 (CIO) at the West Allis plant of the Allis-Chalmers Corporation wanted to publicize the work of stewards in the *CIO News*, the union focused on Bill Zastrow as the epitome of a stalwart union man: "rough," "tough," and "a 100% union." As a shop steward in the brass foundry he was a militant, prepared to stop work when necessary to protect his union against incursions by other labor organizations, to take vigorous steps when a foundry worker strayed from the union fold, and to use the grievance/arbitration system to gain new authority on the shop floor.

As the newspaper told its readers, he worked in the foundry for fifteen years, and "many of those years were spent without any union to protect him and the rest of the boys. Bill never forgot what it was to work there without a union. And he never let any of the other guys forget it either." Zastrow would tell new workers and members waffling on their support of the union "Look it; we got a 100 per cent department here. Every guy is in the union. We made a lot of changes around here with the union and we intend to keep them. We got a lot more work to do. You better join up with the rest of us. We don't like no hitchhikers in this place."

For Local 248, "Big Bill" Zastrow represented the ideal union member and steward, always willing to defend the interests of his union and his fellow workers in the face of hostile management. The *CIO News* told its readers:

> He's always on the job, using the steward's job and his union grievance structure to protect the men. No matter what goes wrong, Bill is right there to see that justice is done and the men get a fair shake. Wage adjustments, working conditions, a tough foreman—no matter what it may be—Bill wades in, with his 100 per cent department in back of him and the whole union in back of that department.
>
> That's what convinces the men in the brass foundry. They see the union, through Bill, really doing a job, protecting them every day, fighting for their rights. And they can understand that such things can't be done unless they stand 100 per cent solid with Bill and the union.[1]

The struggle was perpetual. Through the first half of the twentieth century, workers at Allis-Chalmers—maker of turbines, electrical generators, pumps, and tractors—fought a never-ending battle for union recognition and protection. If economic issues sparked many disputes, the militancy of individual workers and their unions provided the fuel necessary to do battle with management despite the constraints imposed by wartime unity. The struggle at Allis-Chalmers captured three important elements influencing wartime industrial conflict: the militancy of individual workers, competitive challenges from other unions, and attacks on the union by hostile management. In many other Milwaukee factories during the war, workers engaged in similar struggles to defend their rights and their unions.

Wartime industrial conflict had many faces. It was the challenge to new piece rates; confrontation over work rule interpretation or the foreman's authority on the shop floor; slowdowns to defend against piece rate speed-ups; strikes to protect wage rates; competition with other unions in jurisdictional disputes; and perpetual organizing in the face of employer unwillingness to recognize the union's right to exist. At the heart of industrial conflict was the willingness of workers to take direct action in defense of their economic interests and their unions. Worker militancy manifested itself in a variety of ways: individuals and unions engaged in strikes and slowdowns when mechanisms for conflict resolution proved inadequate; unions fought jurisdictional battles when existing unions failed to meet worker needs or when an outside union attempted to displace a recognized bargaining agent; and some unions were forced to engage in a continuous struggle for recognition or existence when faced with hostile and recalcitrant management.

The war united Americans in a common cause, but that unity did not compel them to act in unison nor to drop all other interests and concerns influencing their lives. Workers and unions, managers and companies adapted to wartime conditions. They mobilized, focused their energies, and produced the supplies necessary to fight the war. But they also fought to protect what was best for themselves as workers, unions, managers, and companies. The future world for which everyone fought was being determined not only on the battle-field but also on the shop floor, in the boardroom, and at the conference table.

Wartime industrial conflict stemmed from fundamental concerns of work-ers and unions, which patriotism and national unity could not supplant. The war did not alter the fact that workers valued and fought for economic security and control over the workplace, nor that unions fought for the interests of their members and for self-preservation against attacks from other unions and from employers. The breach between labor (workers and unions) seeking its own goals and industry (managers and companies) seeking to control the workplace and to maximize profits guaranteed that industrial conflict would continue throughout the war. Industrial peace required a sense of common in-terest between labor and management. All too often, such a common interest did not exist.

The factory worker of 1940 lived in a complex world of conflicting alle-giances. Workers and unions were by no means immune to the feelings of pa-triotism that stirred the rest of the American people. Work stoppages during November 1941 consumed .24 percent of the available work time but dropped to a mere .07 percent in December. Whereas 271 strikes involving 227,000 workers began in November, only 143 strikes involving 29,000 workers began during December. This sharp decline illustrated the impact of the war upon factory workers and their unions, but it was only the most obvious sign of the urgency and seriousness with which America's workers viewed the outbreak of the war.[2]

Following the attack on Pearl Harbor, Philip Murray and William Green, presidents of the Congress of Industrial Organizations (CIO) and the Ameri-can Federation of Labor (AFL), respectively, wasted little time before calling for an end to work stoppages in defense plants. In a national radio address sev-eral hours after the United States officially entered the war, Murray said that his members would "do their utmost to defend our country. . . ." A few hours later, Allan S. Haywood, CIO director of organization, reminded another radio audience of the thousands of CIO members serving in the armed forces, and of the millions willingly serving in the production army. In the days that followed, international and local unions alike flooded CIO headquarters with statements of support for the war effort and their commitment to all-out pro-duction.

William Green likewise declared the AFL's support for the war effort, and called for an end to work stoppages in defense plants. The federation's mem-bers clearly supported Green's response to the Japanese attack. Telegrams and letters streamed into the federation office from union locals and central labor unions throughout the country, pledging support for the war effort.

The leaders of America's two major labor federations quickly committed their members to abide by a no-strike pledge. They did so with the full knowl-edge that such a commitment was necessary to preserve the labor movement;

but they also understood that the pledge would be difficult to enforce if mechanisms for resolving legitimate grievances failed to work properly or in a timely fashion.[3]

To foster the kind of cooperative relationship necessary for industrial peace, President Roosevelt called some of the major leaders of labor and business together for a conference on December 17, 1941. The President's labor-management conference began its deliberations in the hope of formulating a program to assure continuous production during the war. Six representatives of the CIO, six representatives of the AFL, and twelve business executives attended the conference. Although they agreed on a no-strike, no-lockout policy and on the need for a war labor board, the conference deadlocked over the closed shop issue. Organized labor had long argued that industrial peace depended, in part, on union stability. The best way to ensure stability was to guarantee full union membership by requiring, as a provision of the contract, that no one work in the plant without joining the union. Company managers often opposed such provisions on the grounds that they infringed on the individual worker's right of free association. Business leaders preferred an open shop with no requirement of union membership. The labor delegates also insisted that disputes involving the closed shop should be placed within the labor board's jurisdiction, but industry delegates feared that decisions by a government agency would rob management of an important prerogative. The industry representatives demanded that existing conditions be frozen and that such disputes be excluded from the board's supervision.

The President settled the matter by accepting the three points of agreement: the no-strike, no-lockout policy; peaceful settlement of disputes; and creation of a new War Labor Board (WLB) to settle all conflicts that could not be resolved by other means. The labor delegates were pleased with the final outcome, but the industry representatives were shocked. They expected the President to hear their arguments before making such a move. This he had not done.

In these darkest days of the war, when victory was distant and tenuous, representatives of labor and management could not reach an amicable agreement. The industrial members of the conference believed that the open shop was a fundamental principle in a free society. Organized labor, having committed itself to the war effort, viewed WLB jurisdiction over closed shop disputes as essential to union security. Without the strike weapon as a means of defense, the labor representatives looked to government adjudication to protect local unions from destruction at the hands of hostile employers.[4]

During the defense crisis of 1941, as the United States was preparing for war, strikes reached a level comparable only to the peak years of 1917, 1920, and 1937. CIO and AFL organizing activities, communist militancy prior to the German invasion of Russia, and coal strikes combined to produce 4,288 strikes during 1941. These work stoppages involved 1,860,621 workers and cost industry 28,424,857 man-days of idleness. During the first year of the war, strikes fell by 31 percent, involved 64 percent fewer workers, and cost 82 percent less idleness. In other words, there were fewer strikes, they were short, and they involved a comparatively small number of workers. As workers became increasingly concerned about the rising cost of living and their postwar wage rates, strike activity escalated. By 1944 there were 16 percent more strikes than in 1941, involving almost as many workers. Nonetheless, the war and rapid government intervention contained the strikes to such an extent that they resulted in only 38 percent of the idleness recorded in 1941.[5]

Unfortunately, as unions increasingly relied upon government for assistance to settle disputes and prevent conflicts from developing into strikes, the agencies to which they turned often proved inadequate for the task. Workers became impatient and disillusioned with WLB delays, with stalled contract negotiations, and with the apparent failure of their wage rates to keep pace with inflation. The rising number of strikes illustrated the frustration they felt. It also demonstrated that workers on the shop floor still sought to control their own destinies, and that union leaders still sought to protect the rights of labor and the power of their organizations. Nonetheless, the strike remained a weapon of last resort to which workers turned when more acceptable means failed to resolve an industrial dispute.

Milwaukee's unions abided by the no-strike pledge as best as they could, but that pledge was never considered holy writ. Strikes usually were settled quickly by negotiation, conciliation, mediation, or arbitration. When necessary, the leaders of an international union or of the CIO or AFL applied pressure to urge strikers back to their jobs. In Milwaukee, unlike the pattern in locals of the Detroit auto workers and the Akron rubber workers,[6] such pressure was seldom applied with enough force to crush a strike. It did not need to be applied in such a manner. The average Milwaukee strike was a short, spontaneous, local affair that neither threatened the war effort nor challenged the authority of the parent union. A strike by one of Milwaukee's unions may have brought negative publicity to the labor movement and sharp rebukes from union leaders, but a locally focused strike seldom initiated the takeover of a local by a parent union or the ousting of strike leaders by officials with greater power.

In fact, most industrial conflict never entered the public arena in the form of a strike. Instead, it was resolved quietly within the normal collective bargaining and grievance process, or through the aid of a government conflict resolution agency. The Conciliation Service was one of the first agencies likely to be contacted when a dispute reached an impasse, and it assisted in resolving many such conflicts without public strife. When, for example, the Heil Company hired eighteen new employees while thirty-two workers remained on layoff, the Steelworkers' local cried foul. The case was adjudicated with the aid of the Conciliation Service and the company agreed to pay damages to the aggrieved workers.[7] At the Nordberg Manufacturing Company, members of Molders and Foundry Workers Local 125 threatened to walk out if the company did not fire Alex Fedorwicz, who had been involved in several altercations with fellow workers. Company officials refused to take action, claiming that the underlying cause of worker discontent was the fact that Fedorwicz was a "pace setter"—meaning he worked too fast. The Nordberg management would not countenance such efforts to control production and undermine managerial control. Whatever the cause, tempers cooled after a federal conciliator convinced the union to forget the fight that sparked the dispute.[8] Workers at Globe-Union, Inc., maker of batteries and switches, fought with the company for over seven months in 1943 and 1944 about piece rates. In disgust, the affected workers undertook a six-week slowdown. Only intercession by a Conciliation Service official prevented a strike.[9]

When the Conciliation Service could not solve a problem, it often certified the dispute to the WLB for resolution. Many workers saw this process as a bureaucratic mire that led only to endless wrangling. Still, most workers stayed on the job despite endless delays, frustration, and defeat.

The course of a dispute between the AFL Operating Engineers and the United States Rubber Company, operators of the Milwaukee Ordnance Plant, provides an excellent example of a union waiting patiently for a decision and being defeated by delays. During the fall of 1942 the Milwaukee Federated Trades Council (FTC) and the United Rubber Workers of America each launched organizing drives at the newly constructed facility. In April 1943, the National Labor Relations Board (NLRB) conducted an election in which the workers chose Federal Labor Union 23359 and fourteen AFL craft unions to represent them.[10]

Immediately, Operating Engineers Local 311 began negotiating a contract to cover powerhouse, sewage treatment, water treatment, and utility workers. Negotiations soon bogged down over questions pertaining to union security, wages, vacations, seniority, and overtime. With the aid of the Conciliation Service, the parties settled their disagreement regarding vacations and overtime, but they could not reach agreement on the other issues. The rubber company refused to force workers to join a union, and the Operating Engineers feared their position as bargaining agent was being jeopardized by disparaging remarks from low-level company officials and by wartime wage controls that made it difficult for the union to act visibly on the workers' behalf. With these shackles in place, Local 311 worried that existing delinquency in the payment of dues might escalate until the union found itself bargaining for all of the employees under its jurisdiction while only a small portion paid for the service.

The union pointed to numerous examples of inter- and intra-plant inequalities to defend its demand for a ten-cent-an-hour raise. On seniority, the company continued to insist that it needed a six-month probationary period to determine whether an employee was fit for a job. The union proposed a three-month probationary period—two months longer than in most of its other contracts—and insisted that many of the employees under its jurisdiction came to the company already trained and certified with a city stationary engineer's license.

With these issues unresolved, the case went to the WLB in September 1943. A little over two months later, the regional WLB granted Local 311 a standard maintenance-of-membership clause and a clause specifying a three-month probationary period. The board did not approve the union's wage demands. It concluded that wages conformed to local practice and that no inter-plant inequality existed. The WLB panel declined to rule on the issue of intra-plant inequalities until after the Wage Administration Agency ruled on an earlier wage application upon which the Operating Engineers' case was based. In May 1944, well over a year after the union began bargaining, the regional WLB issued a directive order denying any general wage increase. By that time a wage increase was irrelevant; the Milwaukee Ordnance Plant had closed, its services no longer necessary to the war effort. After waiting patiently, the union had failed to get satisfaction on the one issue that would have benefited the workers most directly and that would have demonstrated the value of the union most clearly.[11]

Despite patriotism and the efforts of federal dispute resolution agencies, workers did strike. The Bureau of Labor Statistics identified eighty-eight strikes in Milwaukee between the beginning of 1942 and the end of 1945. Perhaps as many as twenty of these occurred after the war ended. As on the national level, the number of work hours lost due to strikes peaked in 1943 and then declined in 1944 despite a sixfold increase in the number of work stoppages.[12] Over half of the sixty-two local strikes that occurred during the war and could be studied in any detail lasted a day or less. (See Graph 1.) Only 13

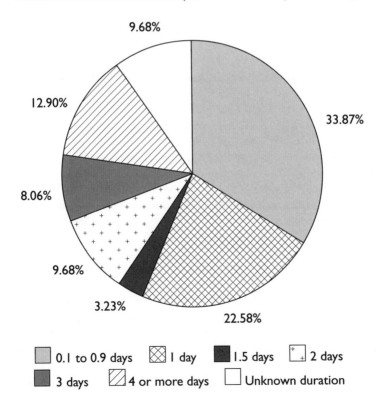

GRAPH I
Duration of Strikes in Milwaukee (December 1941–September 1945)

9.68%

12.90%

33.87%

8.06%

9.68%

3.23%

22.58%

0.1 to 0.9 days	1 day	1.5 days	2 days
3 days	4 or more days	Unknown duration	

percent of the strikes lasted longer than three days. This record was a tribute to the patriotism of workers, even when they were on strike, and to union leaders who promptly acted to cajole, persuade, and convince workers to return to their jobs.

Only eight of the Milwaukee strikes for which the duration could be determined lasted four or more days. The longest strike actually was a prewar conflict. AFL structural steel workers had been on strike since October 1941 protesting use of non-union Works Progress Administration employees on the new National Guard air base at Mitchell Field. The conflict had stopped work on aircraft hangers for the facility. Structural steel workers agreed to return to their jobs on December 18, 1941, after Secretary of War Henry Stimson issued a direct appeal to the workers. The month-long municipal strike of 1943 was the city's second-longest stoppage. The third-longest strike lasted twelve days. It occurred when workers at William Grede's Smith Steel Division unsuccessfully tried to end a collective bargaining stalemate with the company's owner, who fended off union recognition at every turn. Both AFL and CIO unions were represented in the remaining six strikes that lasted four or more days. These disputes involved contract negotiations, grievances, and wage issues.

Milwaukee's strike record was not unusual when compared with the most strike-prone cities in the United States and with cities having a comparable number of wage earners.[13] Detroit, New York, Philadelphia, and Pittsburgh each had at least fifty strikes a year, according to the BLS. Milwaukee had thirty-seven strikes in 1944, but only eight in 1942 and six in 1943. Of the cities studied for this comparison, only Dearborn (five strikes in 1942) had fewer strikes than Milwaukee during the first two years of the war. When the data are adjusted to eliminate city size as a bias influencing the strike statistics (see Graphs 2 and 3), Milwaukee had thirty strikes per 50,000 wage earners in 1944 and 18.7 strikes per 50,000 wage earners in 1945. This placed the city well behind Detroit and Pittsburgh for those years, but ahead of New York and Philadelphia. Similarly, although Milwaukee had a very low strike rate for 1942 and 1943 when compared with six cities having a comparable number of wage earners (Baltimore, Boston, Cincinnati, Dearborn, Los Angeles, and Newark), it had slightly more strikes per 50,000 wage earners than any of those cities except Cincinnati in 1944 and slightly fewer than four out of the six cities in 1945.

When one measures the severity of strikes by comparing man days idle per worker involved (see Graphs 4 and 5), Milwaukee's record was both much better and much worse than other cities, depending on the year.

Of the ten cities used for comparison, only Detroit and Dearborn had lower relative levels of strike idleness than Milwaukee in 1942 and none of the ten cities had a lower level in 1944. In contrast, Milwaukee had a higher relative level of idleness than any of the other ten comparison cities in 1943 (when it only had six strikes), and in 1945. Probably because of the protracted municipal dispute in 1943, Milwaukee registered almost twice as much relative idleness as Boston and almost four times as much as Detroit. In 1945, only Philadelphia approximated Milwaukee's level of strike idleness, although a 192-day postwar

GRAPH 2

Milwaukee Strike Record Compared to the Record
of the Most Strike-Prone Cities (January 1942–September 1945)

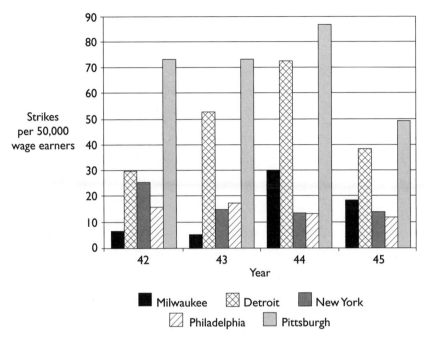

strike at Geuder, Paeschke and Frey, a manufacturer of metal and enameled kitchenware, probably skewed Milwaukee's record.

Workers struck when they were left with the choice between walking off the job or capitulating on an issue they perceived to be significant—but only after the normal grievance-and-negotiation process and the government's conflict-resolution agencies had failed to resolve the dispute. The source of disputes lay within traditional areas of industrial conflict: the preservation of wage scales, the negotiation of contracts, and the handling of grievances.[14] (See Graph 6.)

The first two categories accounted for well over half of Milwaukee's strikes for which causes can be identified. Approximately nineteen (one-third) of the city's work stoppages involved non-wage grievance issues. Such grievances included, for example, the demand that an employer reinstate a fired worker, that a company transfer an oppressive supervisor, that new work rules undercut established working conditions, that a company failed to process grievances, and that seniority rights had been violated. Few grievance-related strikes involved issues that threatened the existence of the union, but they represented attempts by workers and their unions to maintain control over the workplace.[15]

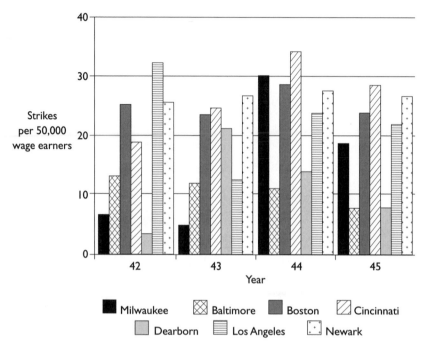

GRAPH 3

Milwaukee Strike Record Compared to Cities
with Comparable Number of Wage Earners (January 1942–September 1945)

    In typical Milwaukee disputes, workers at the Milwaukee Foundry Equip-
ment Company, Harley-Davidson, Geuder, Paeschke and Frey, and Ampco
Metal disrupted production over wage issues when wartime conflict resolution
systems failed. Simply put, patriotism, union leaders, and government agencies
limited the extent to which conflict interfered with production, but economic
issues, combined with long settlement delays and wartime tensions, could push
workers to take actions to defend their interests, even if those actions had a
negative impact on the war effort. At the Milwaukee Foundry Equipment
Company workers struck over rate classification despite pressure from the
union to return to work immediately. At Harley-Davidson, women workers
took a "holiday" in protest over equal pay issues. A protracted dispute over
time study and piece rates resulted in at least one slowdown, three short strikes,
and numerous smaller disputes between Fabricated Metal Workers Local 19340
(an AFL federal labor union) and Geuder, Paeschke and Frey.
    Not all disputes resulted in strikes. The Employees' Mutual Benefit Asso-
ciation and management at Ampco Metal fought throughout the war over
piece rates and production limits. The company fired a steward for usurping a

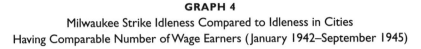

GRAPH 4

Milwaukee Strike Idleness Compared to Idleness in Cities
Having Comparable Number of Wage Earners (January 1942–September 1945)

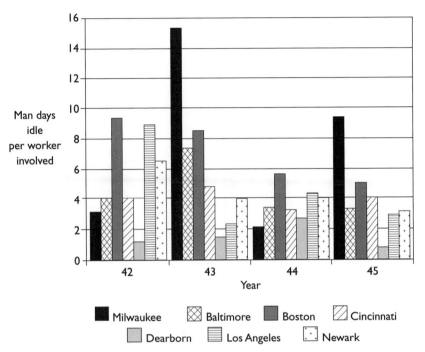

management prerogative when he encouraged a worker to stay within established production limits. In a later case, the union expelled a worker (tantamount to firing the worker because union membership was required for employment at Ampco) for exceeding the company's production limits and thereby threatening the established piece rates. These disputes were settled only through lengthy arbitration. At their core, all of these disputes revealed the willingness of workers and unions to take direct action in defense of economic interests.

In the summer of 1944, when the CIO auto workers at the Milwaukee Foundry Equipment Company struck to protest an Employment Relations Board ruling that they had engaged in an unfair labor practice, they were really demonstrating their frustration with problems over rate classifications. Under a WLB directive, the rate classification dispute was to have been settled by arbitration, but the company and the union could not agree on the arbitration procedure. The unfair labor practice ruling triggered a spontaneous strike that lasted at least a week despite intervention by Walter Cappel, international representative for the United Auto Workers Union. Beginning on the first day of the strike, Cappel urged the workers to return to their jobs. As the Conciliation Service entered the case, it was clear that the quasi-judicial mechanisms for

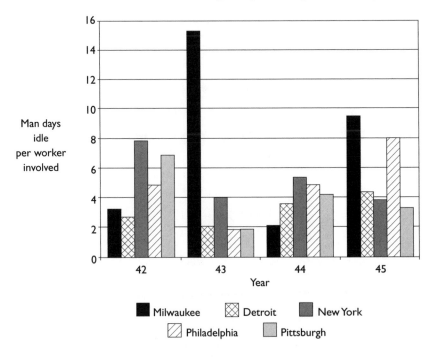

GRAPH 5
Milwaukee Strike Idleness Compared to Idleness
in the Most Strike-Prone Cities (January 1942–September 1945)

Milwaukee   Detroit   New York
Philadelphia   Pittsburgh

handling disputes had broken down and that the workers had taken matters into their own hands to force a resolution of the problem.[16]

Women in the prepacking department at the Harley-Davidson Motor Company (members of AFL auto workers Local 209) demonstrated a similar willingness to force the resolution of a nagging wage problem by refusing to work. In November of 1943 the Conciliation Service came to the plant to settle a dispute involving women in Department 19. Harley-Davidson had formed Department 19 to dip motorcycle parts in wax (to protect them against corrosion) and then pack the parts for shipment overseas. The company previously limited packing and shipping work to men in a different department; the new department was staffed entirely with women. In a move designed to protect male positions from being undercut by the newly hired female workers,[17] the union demanded equal pay for the women in Department 19, as well as improvements in the base rate for women workers. Union officials contended that women packers did work equal to that of their male counterparts or, in the case of the waxing operation, more difficult than the work expected of men. The starting rate for men at Harley-Davidson was 79 cents an hour. Women earned an hourly starting rate of only 55 cents with raises of 2.5 cents an hour

GRAPH 6
Causes of Strikes in Milwaukee (December 1941–September 1945)

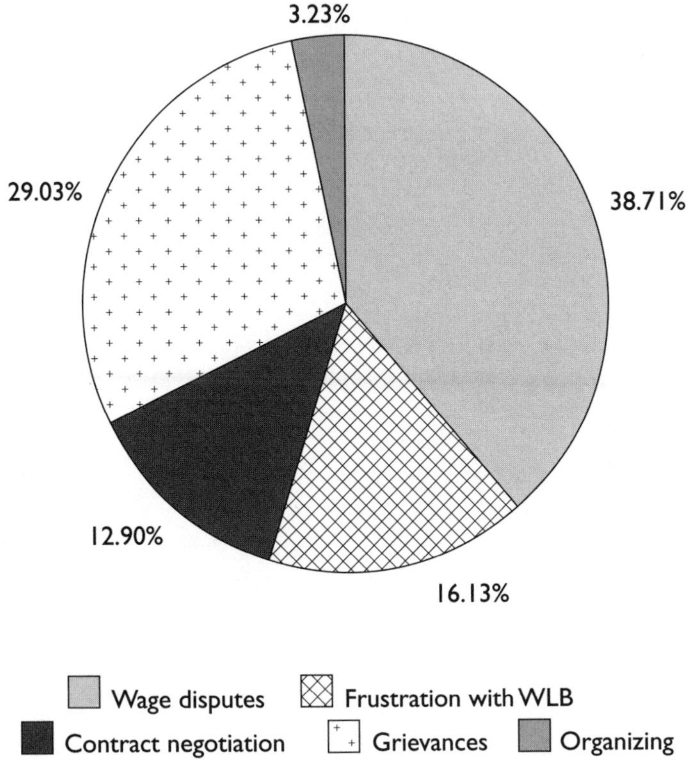

3.23%

29.03%

38.71%

12.90%

16.13%

▢ Wage disputes   ▨ Frustration with WLB
■ Contract negotiation   ⊞ Grievances   ▨ Organizing

every three months for a year. A woman with one year's service earned 65 cents an hour. Based on this scale, women in Department 19 worked within a rate range of 55 cents to 65 cents an hour in November 1943.

Despite the semblance of demanding equal pay, the union actually demanded only an increase in the base rate of 10 cents an hour for women in Department 19, which would have boosted the lowest-paid women to 65 cents an hour. A woman earning 65 cents an hour prior to the raise would earn 75 cents an hour after the raise. In effect, this process would create a new range for women in Department 19 of 65 cents to 75 cents an hour. The Conciliation Service arranged a compromise with the company that left the base rate at 55 cents an hour but accelerated the schedule for raises so that the women reached 66 cents an hour after only three months. After evaluating the work being done in the department, Harley-Davidson also agreed to a new rate range of 66 to 79 cents an hour. The compromise was forwarded to the WLB for approval.

Seven months later, the board finally issued its ruling, granting a rate range of 65 to 78 cents an hour—but without making an adjustment in the existing process that brought new women workers to 65 cents an hour after four 2.5-cent increases. With approval in hand, the company and the union disagreed over how to implement the new rate range. In stark contrast to the agreement worked out by the Conciliation Service the previous fall, the company now insisted that the WLB had approved only the new rate range but had not approved any increases above the minimum of 65 cents an hour. The company maintained that all women workers in Department 19 should be placed at 65 cents an hour regardless of their previous rate, and that subsequent raises should be based on merit. The union contended that the WLB ruling allowed a 10-cent raise, placing the women within the rate range in keeping with their previous position. This interpretation meant that the highest-paid women in Department 19 should receive 75 cents an hour. The union agreed that the remaining 3 cents an hour (bringing a worker to the top of the range of 78 cents) could be reserved for merit increases.

Faced with further delays, the women in Department 19 wanted to strike. They stayed on the job on June 6, 1944, only at the behest of the union bargaining committee, which spent the day in discussions with management officials. That evening, despite the welcome news that the Allies had landed in Normandy, the bargaining committee decided to call a "work holiday" for the following day. Technically this "holiday" was not a strike. Under an unusual contract clause, the union could call a one-day work stoppage in the event of a serious controversy with the company; but the "holiday" did not have the same force as a strike. As Leonard Hackert, president of the union, told a reporter:

> We told the men, when they reported to work Wednesday morning, that no one had to stay out of the plant. We said the women were determined not to go to work until something was done about the rates and the others could do what they wanted to about it. They decided on their own not to work.

The workers went back to their jobs the following day, after Harley-Davidson agreed to grant an immediate 5-cent raise to workers in Department 19 (bringing workers at 55 cents up to 60 cents an hour, workers at 62 cents up to 67 cents, and so forth), with additional raises to await approval of the WLB. The WLB settled the issue the day after the June 7 "holiday" by accepting Local 209's interpretation. The 125 women in Department 19 received the full 10-cents raise negotiated in November of 1943, maintaining the old rate relationships between women in the department and reserving the remaining 3 cents for merit raises.

In a sense, the union sanctioned this job action by calling a "work holiday," but it was the militancy of the women of the prepacking department whose refusal to work brought the conflict to a head. For these women, the issue of the dispute was economic justice. For the union and the company, however, another set of issues took precedence. The company insisted on implementing the new rates in a manner that would have based future raises within a given rate schedule upon the subjective judgment of management as to the merit of the employees involved. Such a system would have made it difficult for workers to judge the fairness of raises and, from their perspective, could be viewed as a move toward greater management control of the workplace. In contrast, the union advocated maintaining a system based on seniority, a system that could be judged objectively, as well as a system that would have maintained existing differences between workers.[18]

A work stoppage could be brought on by a dispute over wages, contract interpretation and negotiation, or concern for a mistreated worker. Nonetheless, the causes of any particular strike often lay as much with the cumulative effect of several events as with any one incident. The history of industrial relations at Geuder, Paeschke and Frey typified the complex forces acting upon Milwaukee workers who struck during World War II.

Members of Fabricated Metal Workers Local 19340 struck in May 1944 to protest production standards that were set so high that inexperienced employees working on piece rate received less than the minimum wage set by the contract.[19] Behind this event was a history of conflict over time study methods and piece rates. Relations between the company and the union seemed cordial during the defense crisis, and the company frequently sought the union's "advice, consent and suggestions on matters pertaining to defense work."[20] The relationship soured in the spring of 1942 when company managers refused to discuss several grievances and walked out of a meeting with union representatives. As Walter Norbeck, business representative for Local 19340, told William Green, relations had become "very strained." The existing wage agreement failed to establish clearly the accepted piece rates for many operations and resulted in numerous disagreements between company and union officials. After intervening, AFL organizer David Sigman optimistically reported to William Green that the problem would be resolved in the new contract currently being negotiated.[21]

Unfortunately, Sigman's optimism was premature. Contract negotiations deadlocked in June and the union requested assistance from the Conciliation Service. When conciliator R. G. MacDonald took the case, he found both sides intransigent. The union continued to demand a wage increase while the company insisted that such a raise would force it to reduce the labor force to 25 percent of its normal level. After a month and a half of further negotiations, both parties accepted MacDonald's suggestion and referred the matter to an arbitrator. Two months later, in September, the arbitrator ruled that a raise of 3.5 cents an hour was in order because of inflation. He also suggested that two union-management committees be established to study and fix piece rates and to study improvement of working conditions. Both parties accepted the pay increase, but the company balked at the precedent of joint union-management decision-making regarding piece rates and working conditions. This portion of the arbitrator's recommendations struck at managerial control over the workplace, and the company would not yield on this issue of joint committees.[22]

At the same time, workers at Geuder, Paeschke and Frey remained discontented over piece rates. They often complained that rates set by the company were too "tight" and that delays in meeting requests for the retiming of jobs were demoralizing the work force. When the company changed the production methods used to produce baking pans for the quartermaster corps, the workers deliberately cut production in half. R. G. MacDonald was called to end the slowdown and obtained an agreement between the company and the union to accept the findings of a Conciliation Service expert who would set a fair piece rate for the operation. However, before the Conciliation Service technician reported, the two parties negotiated a mutually acceptable piece rate in March 1943.[23]

The negotiating skills that brought an agreement in March failed to resolve other general concerns over piece work rates and worker participation in time studies. After an arbitrator settled another rate dispute in August, the union decided to take matters into its own hands. It was clear that workers at Geuder, Paeschke and Frey did not trust management to conduct fair time studies. They wanted to participate in the process of timing jobs and in the establishment of bonuses for day-rate employees who assisted piece workers. Based on the assumption that "a knowledge of time-study would assure fair time and rate schedules by the company," Fabricated Metal Workers Local 19340 organized a series of time-study classes for its members.[24]

Rate disputes seemed to abate for a time, but the old conflict arose again in May 1944, when the company renewed production of twenty-five-pound lead kegs after a lapse of many months. The rate for the job was to be the same as when the kegs were produced earlier. The union protested that the old rate was set using experienced workers and that the current, less experienced work force would not be able to produce at the same rate. The company made two adjustments, which the Fabricated Metal Workers felt were inadequate; but management refused to change the rate further. In protest, the workers cut production to almost nothing, and Geuder, Paeschke and Frey retaliated by implementing a policy of paying piece workers only for the material they actually produced without regard for the minimum hourly pay set by the contract. Tensions already were high in the plant due to a series of unresolved grievances, and when several workers received only $19.06 for a forty-eight-hour week, employees in the paint pail department spontaneously quit work. The work stoppage quickly spread to the rest of the plant. The one-day strike ended when Major James P. Holmes, a federal conciliator, negotiated an arrangement whereby

> The Union General Committee agreed to co-operate in securing productive capacity on disputed piece rate jobs at least sufficient to enable the employees to earn the minimum rates, or more, and to continue such cooperation even where the Company pursued the new policy of paying only what the employee actually earned, but reserving the right to carry the matter through the Grievance Procedure.

It was a pragmatic solution. The company got a promise from the union to help maintain production, but with no benchmark against which to measure that cooperation. The union accepted the possibility that the company might pay workers on a slowdown only for the work actually done. Nonetheless, the union reserved the right to grieve such actions and thereby refused to sanction the company's right to cut pay unilaterally.[25]

The solution settled the precise cause of the strike, but it did little to ease the hard feelings that had developed between the company and its work force. Two other strikes occurred at Geuder, Paeschke and Frey as the war drew to a close; both were quite predictable, given past events. As Germany collapsed, employees in one department spontaneously started an unauthorized strike to protest several disciplinary discharges that appeared to be part of a calculated effort by the company to remove "troublesome" employees. The walkout quickly spread through the plant. On several earlier occasions the company had fired workers under circumstances the union found unacceptable. In one case, management even refused to divulge the precise charges or the source of their information. In another case, the company took disciplinary action against a woman who had allegedly led a one-hour sitdown strike. In each of these situations, the union found itself forced to take the issues to an arbitrator. The new firings in 1945 fit an established pattern, and the workers had had enough of delays and legalistic solutions.[26]

Similarly, almost immediately after the war ended, the Fabricated Metal Workers union began a 192-day strike as they sought an acceptable contract with the company. The pattern was all too familiar. Earlier contract negotiation disputes had been resolved through arbitration or the WLB. The 1942–1943 contract expired on June 30, 1943. Union and company representatives began negotiating the new contract on June 11 but came to no agreement. Negotiations remained at an impasse even after Maj. Holmes of the Conciliation Service met with the parties several times in July, and the dispute was certified to the WLB.

When the WLB panel reported in November 1943, it was clear that the establishment of piece rates and union participation in time studies remained the major stumbling blocks obstructing the negotiations. Taking full advantage of its control over information, the company steadfastly refused to provide the union with the formulas used to set rates. Management officials also argued that the time study process was too complicated for the union to be able to supply an individual competent enough to participate in the process. Perhaps because they feared the loss of managerial control, the company had no intention of providing their union opponents with information on piece-rate formulas and time-study methods, the two most significant sources of worker discontent at Geuder, Paeschke and Frey. The WLB panel failed to solve these basic issues of conflict and the dispute was still unresolved a year after the 1942–1943 contract ran out. In trying to bring the conflict to an end, H. Herman Rauch, an arbitrator from the Wisconsin Industrial Commission, clearly stated the problem and outlined its impact on the company's workers. He lectured the company:

> One of the major complaints voiced by the Union related to the current vagueness of the expected earning rates of piece workers. There is no way

of telling when an employee on a particular job is achieving what can reasonably be expected from such operation. The Union had no knowledge and does not seem to be able to find out with any degree of accuracy how the Company reaches its conclusions on the matter. . . . The lack of proper information on so vital a point caused suspicion and discontent. Consequently, grievances on rates have been abnormally numerous and bitter. . . .

There can be no doubt that the Union and each employee have a right to know precisely what wage rate applies and how it is determined. Such knowledge is indispensable in the case of an incentive system where the "will to work" is the key to increased production.[27]

With a certain sense of exasperation, Herman Rauch returned to this case in October of 1944 and helped the parties negotiate an interim rate schedule that could be used to determine the back pay due workers under the 1943–1944 contract, for which negotiations were still underway. Ironically, that contract had expired on June 30, 1944. With the new rate schedule in hand, the old contract was finally completed, and negotiations began on the contract for 1944–1945.[28]

This new round of negotiations immediately bogged down as the parties argued, in the words of conciliator J. J. O'Brien, over "practically every sentence of the contract." The dispute went to the WLB for settlement, where it remained when the contract officially ran out at the end of June 1945.[29]

With the 1944–1945 contract dispute awaiting settlement by the WLB, negotiations on the 1945–1946 contract stalled, once again, on virtually every major issue. The workers were fed up with delays in negotiations, an accumulation of unresolved grievances, and the company's failure to implement both an equal pay for equal work clause from the 1943–1944 contract and the interim piece-rate schedule that had been negotiated with the help of Herman Rauch in October 1944. As the United States made final preparations for the atomic bombing of Japan, the frustrated workers at Geuder, Paeschke and Frey requested a strike vote as required by the Smith-Connally Act. William Green immediately informed the local that the AFL would not sanction a strike as long as the nation was still at war, and he urged the union to abide by the no-strike pledge.

Soon after the Japanese capitulated in September 1945, the union asked again for AFL support. Green instructed Jacob F. Friedrick, the AFL organizer in Milwaukee, to try to resolve the conflict. Friedrick found negotiations blocked by company officials unwilling to compromise on any of the issues in dispute. On September 8 the NLRB conducted a strike vote. The workers voted 350 to 23 in favor of a work stoppage. After another round of fruitless negotiations, the membership again voted to stop work. Thus, after a long prologue, one of Milwaukee's first and most protracted postwar strikes began on September 12, 1945.[30]

In contrast to the impression often given by the daily press in its coverage of strikes, Local 19340 was not a power-hungry organization hell-bent on dominating either the metalworkers or the company. The strikes stemmed from the union's and the workers' desire to protect wage rates from being undercut by the company, from the desire to protect employees from discriminatory firings, and from the frustrations of wartime industrial relations. The strikes that occurred during the war need never have happened. There existed governmental machinery to settle all such disputes; but that machinery never worked perfectly. It could not always relieve pent-up worker frustration, nor did it always work swiftly. When the workers at Geuder, Paeschke and Frey engaged in a slowdown or went on strike, it was not because of caprice. Such actions represented an institutional response by the union to the need to protect the rights of its members, and a personal response by workers as they tried to exert control over their lives and futures. The years of conflicts and of delays took their toll. Agreements had not been kept, expectations had not been met, grievances had not been resolved, negotiations had been stalled, and disputes had festered over time-study methods and the setting of piece rates. Slowdowns and strikes remained weapons of last resort, but they were weapons that workers were willing to use when the quasi-judicial conflict-resolution system failed.

At a company like Ampco Metal, Inc., conflict with management over economic issues could lead workers to take direct action to protect themselves. During the prewar and early war years the Ampco Metal company and the Employees' Mutual Benefit Association, an independent union, had maintained a good-faith relationship. Disagreements sometimes occurred, as they did in any industrial setting, but they were handled routinely through the grievance procedure. For example, on one occasion in 1943, the company and union submitted four grievances to the Wisconsin Employment Relations Board. Before the board could act on two of these disputes, both dealing with claims for back pay, the parties reached settlements. The other two cases dealt with a worker discharge and with the payment of the third shift premium to employees starting work at 4:00 in the afternoon, both of which the arbitrator settled in the union's favor. Another case in 1943 nullified the closed-shop clause in the Ampco contract because it had never been ratified by the workers as required by Wisconsin law. A referendum shortly thereafter fulfilled the legal requirement, and the closed shop clause could once again be enforced by the union and the company. If anything, these arbitration cases demonstrated to the union that it was secure and that it could deal with Ampco on a reasonable basis.[31]

But during 1944, this good-faith relationship degenerated into one of distrust. The union feared that the company was trying to cut the piece rate, and the company charged the union with an organized attempt to limit production. Management officials made several technological changes in production equipment and methods during 1944 and, as a consequence, they retimed some of the jobs in the plant in order "to maintain the relationship between earnings and effort."[32] These changes smacked of a wage cut to the workers at Ampco and gave way to the fear that once workers reached a certain unspecified income level, the company would retime the job and review the rate. The employees' discontent with this situation boiled to the surface when a steward, Edward Mesarich, was fired for threatening a worker with suspension from the union unless that worker stayed within the company's established production limits. Under the closed-shop clause, suspension from the union would have forced the company to fire the hardworking employee.

Although the employee in question charged that Mesarich had told him specifically to hold down production because his performance was detrimental to the other workers in the department, the Employees' Mutual Benefit Association argued that the steward was defending the company's own limits. Far from doing anything disruptive, the union argued, Mesarich had simply warned Albert Vail to operate within established machine speed and feed rates set by the time study or risk company discipline for abusing his machine. Rather than try to prove its charges against Mesarich in the hearing, the company discharged the steward for usurping a function of management—something Ampco could not countenance. Its employees had to know that they answered to company supervisors and not to union stewards. As one might expect given the company's defense, the arbitrator concluded that Ampco had not proven its case against Mesarich and reinstated the steward. Nonetheless, as a warning to other workers who might try to limit production, the arbitrator refused to grant Mesarich any back pay for the time he was without work.[33]

Despite the arbitrator's admonition, the Mesarich case did little to settle the larger piece-rate dispute between Ampco and the employee association. In December 1944 the union expelled Leroy Gilbertson for behavior unbecoming a union member. He had ignored direct instructions from the union to abide by established production standards designed to protect the quality of production and the maintenance of machinery. As Gilbertson stated at the arbitration hearing, he believed he had been moved from the first to the second shift because of union favoritism for another employee, and he therefore had set out consciously to break the established production ceiling. When the union warned him that he was breaking the ceiling in violation of the contract, Gilbertson informed the union board that he had no intention of abiding by the ceiling agreement, that he did not like the union, and that he had no confidence in what it could do. Thus challenged, the union board believed it had no alternative but to expel Gilbertson.

Ampco immediately charged that the union was attempting to limit production and refused to fire Gilbertson. Ampco officials took a much more aggressive stance than in the Mesarich case and told the arbitrator, "The union expelled Gilbertson because it deems limited production by the employees to be necessary to 'the general welfare of fellow workers, or to the Union as a whole.'" Such an attitude violated the letter and the spirit of the contract, the company argued, and it delivered a poignant warning:

> Think of the effect upon a worker in any all-union shop plant if he should learn that even in war time, and with the country crying out for more and more production of war products, in light of the acute manpower shortage

of which the country is so painfully aware, his refusal to arbitrarily limit his production will bring about expulsion from the Union and loss of his job.[34]

The union's defense clearly outlined the origins of the employees' fear that any extra production would result in an immediate retiming of a job with an accompanying reduction in the piece rate. Near the end of 1943 the company restudied propeller cone production, on which Gilbertson worked, and proposed cutting the rate from 14 cents to 11 cents. The union argued that some workers were neglecting their machines and tools, causing numerous production delays for workers on following shifts, and that average production never exceeded eighty-six cones per operator per eight-hour shift. When the company proposed to cut the piece rate, all of its operators applied for transfers to other jobs. In January 1944 the company and the union came to an agreement specifically designed to increase production. The rate was frozen at 14 cents and a production ceiling of ninety-five pieces per eight-hour shift was set for the duration of the war. Almost immediately morale improved and production soon reached the ceiling level. The company responded by proposing a new ceiling of 105 pieces; but the union refused to raise the ceiling in the belief that the change would only bring a return to old work patterns.

In another arrangement designed to increase production, the two parties agreed that when a worker developed a way to improve production, the benefit would be split in half between the company and the workers, resulting in faster, more profitable production for Ampco and higher wages for workers on that operation. After receiving WLB approval for this agreement, however, the company decided that it had given up too much and convinced the labor board to rescind its sanction, a move that convinced the union that Ampco was no longer prepared to deal with its workers in good faith.

The Gilbertson case only heightened the union's concern. Ampco's refusal to fire Gilbertson, combined with repeated changes in piece rates elsewhere in the plant, served to promote the kind of production limits the company wanted to avoid. The company's time-study engineer openly admitted that high earnings on the part of an operator were a "red light" indicating to the management that the job needed retiming—hardly an attitude designed to instill confidence or good feelings among the workers. The Employees' Mutual Benefit Association summarized its views when it told the arbitrators,

> The Company seems incapable of comprehending that the fear of piece rate cuts on the part of operators is to blame for production hold-backs. The Union is just as anxious as the Company to eliminate this fear and open the way to unrestricted production. Both the Company and the operators would profit from it. The Union, however, is powerless so long as the Company adheres to its present piece rate policy.[35]

The arbitration board upheld the company's refusal to fire Gilbertson on the grounds that expulsion by the union constituted an attempt to prevent individuals from performing to the best of their ability as stipulated in the contract. In an attached explanatory opinion, L. E. Gooding, chairman of the arbitration board, questioned why the union took the most severe action available instead of filing a grievance asking the company to discipline Gilbertson for violating the ceiling. Although he refused to blame the company for the workers' fear of wage cuts, Gooding acknowledged that such fears existed and that the company acted in an "underhanded" manner when it withdrew from the piece-rate compromise after WLB approval. He concluded by urging the parties to return to their earlier good-faith relationship.[36]

That good-faith relationship had succumbed to the traditional industrial conflict between management's desire to produce as efficiently and cheaply as possible and the workers' desire to protect their wage rates. When the company retimed jobs, it reinforced the workers' fear that they would be working harder and earning less. Members of the Employees' Mutual Benefit Association took direct action to protect themselves and to enforce limits on production. The war effort—encompassing patriotism, self-sacrifice, and good will—became a secondary consideration in this conflict.

It would be difficult to overestimate the significance of wage-related issues in labor-management conflict during World War II. Nonetheless, issues related to union security also influenced industrial relations as unions sought to protect themselves from company interference and from attacks by other unions. Many government agencies dealt with labor relations issues, but a local union could not afford to allow these agencies to replace the collective bargaining process. Neither the Conciliation Service, the WLB, nor the NLRB were likely to play a significant role in a conflict unless a deadlock had already been reached. Long before that time, most disputes were resolved through the normal functioning of the collective bargaining system. When a dispute could not be solved quietly, government agencies tried to protect the rights of each party under the law and to mediate or impose a solution without an interruption of production. These activities ultimately gave meaning to labor legislation that had recognized organized labor's right to exist; but the local union still bore the responsibility for ensuring that the company followed the contract, that workers' rights were not violated, and that members continued in good standing.

Measures such as the WLB's maintenance-of-membership awards could protect a union from direct attacks, but the WLB could not stop conflicts that arose out of the workers' desire to be represented by another bargaining agent or the unions' desire to expand its membership through organizing. The WLB and similar conflict-resolution agencies created a quasi-judicial setting within which unions could operate, but they did not replace the need of workers and unions to protect their own interests.

Jurisdictional disputes, which the Milwaukee press portrayed to the public as irrational squabbles, often developed out of such needs. They marked one of the boundaries beyond which organized labor would not go in the name of the war effort. American corporations continued to advertise, seek new markets, and develop new products for the postwar era. Similarly, unions refused to stand idle while competing organizations raided their membership and stripped them of their power. The principal distinction between corporations—which funneled resources into maintaining a share of the market—and unions—which continued to organize—was that union competition frequently caused noisy, visible, public conflict, while corporate competition did not. Just as companies saw no reason to stagnate or cease competing with their rivals in the marketplace, unions continued to attract new members and to fend off challenges from other unions. The NLRB conducted approximately 3,762 certification elections and cross-checks during the war years. Over half the disputes that came to the Board's attention were direct confrontations between unions of the rival labor federations. Most such disputes were settled through the normal functioning of the NLRB, resulting in little or no lost work time.[37]

Jurisdictional conflicts in Milwaukee consisted almost exclusively of fights between two or more AFL international unions or between an international affiliated with the AFL and an international affiliated with the CIO. The Milwaukee CIO, dominated by the auto and steel unions, suffered relatively little from internal strife. Disputes arose from the basic right of workers to be represented by the union of their choice and from the refusal of unions to give up the right to organize during the war.

Thus, when the Firemen and Oilers union tried to raid members of the Pulp and Sulphite local at Hummel and Downing, the paper union fought back. Struggles between the AFL and CIO Auto Workers at Wisconsin Motor Corporation; between the Amalgamated Clothing Workers (CIO) and the United Leather Workers (AFL) at J. Laskin and Sons; and between the Operating Engineers (AFL), the Brotherhood of Firemen and Oilers (AFL), and the United Auto Workers (CIO) at Seaman Body all reflected ongoing competition between unions, as well as the willingness of workers to defend their unions or shift allegiance when necessary to protect their interests.

The Wisconsin Employment Relations Board upheld the right to be represented by a union of one's choice when, in 1944, it ordered an election at the Hummel and Downing Company, a paper manufacturer. For many years the International Brotherhood of Pulp, Sulphite and Paper Mill Workers represented the paper company's carpenters, millwrights, pipe fitters, machinists, electricians, welders, and plant oilers, but these maintenance employees had become disillusioned because their wage rates had fallen behind those of metal workers in war plants. As a consequence, Local 125 of the Firemen and Oilers union petitioned the Employment Relations Board to order an election so that the maintenance workers could decide whether to form a separate bargaining unit.

When the board held a hearing on the petition, the Pulp and Sulphite union's principal organizer in Milwaukee, Valeria Brodzinski, argued that the Firemen and Oilers had no jurisdiction over the Hummel and Downing maintenance employees. Pulp and Sulphite locals all over Wisconsin had represented maintenance workers for many years, and, in Brodzinski's opinion, establishing a separate bargaining unit would only create disunity and hamper production. In response, the Firemen and Oilers' representative maintained that no jurisdictional dispute existed, that this was simply a case of disgruntled workers who wished to form their own bargaining unit.

After the hearing, the Wisconsin Employment Relations Board ruled that the state employment peace act protected the right of employees "having common interests" to "determine for themselves whether they desired to constitute themselves a collective bargaining unit. . . ." The legislature felt this right was basic enough that it stripped the board of discretion when ruling on such cases. It was a matter for the employees to decide, and the board thereupon ordered an election. The Firemen and Oilers union won by a landslide.[38]

The Employment Relations Board believed that the workers had a basic right to decide whether they should be represented by the Pulp, Sulphite and Paper Mill Workers union or by Local 125 of the Firemen and Oilers union. Likewise, the workers themselves believed they were being served poorly by the existing local and that they had a right to choose a different bargaining agent. The Firemen and Oilers agreed. For the Pulp and Sulphite union, the employment board's decision and the results of the subsequent election constituted a dangerous precedent. The union could not be expected to greet the loss of forty-six employees at Hummel and Downing with enthusiasm, nor could it be expected to accept passively this threat to its jurisdiction. If the Hummel and Downing case developed into a trend, the Pulp, Sulphite and Paper Mill Workers union stood to lose members in locals all over Wisconsin.

Conflicts between unions affiliated with the AFL and those allied with the CIO underscored the clash of organizational goals behind many jurisdictional disputes. When George Kiebler, regional director for the UAW-AFL, realized that the CIO auto workers' union was trying to take over Local 283 at the Wisconsin Motor Corporation, he moved quickly to investigate. What he found was a local being wooed by promises of higher wages and local officials who showed no interest in combating the CIO raid. With authorization from the international he suspended all of Local 283's officers, took over as temporary administrator, and appointed a forty-member committee to run the local pending a trial of the officers.

However, while Kiebler complained about the raid, officials for the United Automobile, Aircraft and Agricultural Implement Workers union argued that they had simply responded to an internal movement initiated by the members of Local 283. The takeover bid received little or no opposition from within the local. Despite Kiebler's drastic action and the arrival of an organizer sent by the international, the battle was lost. The CIO already had the allegiance of over half the local's 700 members. Five days after Kiebler suspended the officers of Local 283, they held a meeting at which the 376 attendees voted unanimously to affiliate with the CIO. By that time, as many as 500 employees of the Wisconsin Motor Corporation may have signed cards indicating their preference for the CIO, and in March of 1943 the local formally affiliated with the United Automobile, Aircraft and Agricultural Implement Workers of America.[39]

Workers clearly were willing to act on their own behalf when their union failed to act in a manner they found acceptable. Fed up with delays in negotiations on their demand for higher pay, workers at the J. Laskin and Sons tannery struck just five and a half months after America entered the war. The job action was one of Milwaukee's first wartime strikes, and the leadership of the CIO Amalgamated Clothing Workers' (ACW) union moved swiftly to make good on its no-strike pledge. As A. G. Piepenhagen, manager of the Milwaukee joint board of the ACW, told reporters,

> They got a little excited . . . and took things in their own hands. But the union made them go back. We not only have a contract which does not permit walkouts of this sort but the plant is working 100% on war production. I told them they would have to go back. It's just a matter of getting together.[40]

The Laskin workers "took things in their own hands" again one year later when they voted to leave the CIO union and affiliate with the AFL United Leather Workers' union. They were displeased because the ACW joint board had renewed the union's closed-shop contract with the tannery despite objections from the local's leaders. When the company complied with a request from the ACW joint board to fire seven leaders of the new AFL local, five of whom were leaders of the old ACW local, the Laskin workers struck a second time.

Despite pleas by the fired workers, the strikers stayed away from work for three days until the WLB promised to adjudicate the case. Members of the Leather Workers' union voted to contribute an hour's pay a week to support their fired leaders while the case was pending before the WLB. A month after the strike, the NLRB held an election in the tannery and the workers voted 319 to 59 to join the AFL. The company soon rehired the fired employees.[41]

Local 815 of the International Longshoremen's Association (ILA) was considerably more successful at smashing a CIO threat. The dispute began when two longshoremen openly began organizing for the CIO. At a special meeting on March 30, 1942, members voted overwhelmingly to expel the local's vice-president, a member of the executive board, and five other members for disloyalty to the ILA and for attempting to disrupt the local. The members reaffirmed this decision a month later after holding a formal trial. In the weeks that followed, the local purged itself of members who expressed sympathy with the CIO, disrupted union meetings, or held "communistic" views. Apparently, the local's vice-president was considered a member of this faction because he too was expelled although no evidence indicated a tie with the CIO. Instead, he was removed for failing to give due regard to the union, for using obscene language when dealing with employers, for promoting slowdowns, and for obstructing work. Because, in this instance, the local moved quickly to protect itself and to eliminate all of the visible CIO sympathizers, no formal jurisdictional dispute developed.[42]

A formal dispute did arise, however, when Local 311 of the Operating Engineers sought to establish a separate bargaining unit for powerhouse workers at the Seaman Body plant where UAW-CIO Local 75 had exclusive bargaining rights. Ultimately, three unions (the International Brotherhood of Firemen and Oilers also sought bargaining rights) became locked in combat over nine workers.

The Operating Engineers and Local 75 of the auto workers fought a similar battle prior to the attack on Pearl Harbor. In that case, the powerhouse workers voted unanimously for the auto workers' union. Ten months later Werner Schaefer, business agent for Engineers Local 311, again requested that his union be allowed to negotiate on behalf of the boiler room employees, many of whom already belonged to the local. Officials at Nash-Kelvinator Corporation, parent company for the Seaman Body plant, indicated their willingness to negotiate, but requested that the Operating Engineers seek NLRB recognition for these workers as a separate bargaining unit to avoid a violation of the CIO's exclusive bargaining rights in the plant. Shortly after the NLRB ordered an election, the International Brotherhood of Fireman and Oilers, with whom the Operating Engineers had a long-standing jurisdictional feud, also requested recognition, and was placed on the ballot. Thus the dispute developed into a classic conflict between the two labor federations and between two AFL unions, although the Firemen and Oilers seemed to be a minor third party in the conflict.

Warren Schaefer perceived the election as an opportunity for the AFL to strike a major blow against the rebellious CIO. As he told one of his supporters, "This case is quite important in our opinion because if we can win, it will be the first plant in which we have been able to win against the CIO in an election." Schaefer knew that his union did not hold a majority in the powerhouse when the election campaign began, and he relied upon existing friends and members of the Operating Engineers who were already employed by Seaman Body to establish enough support for the Operating Engineers to win the election. Ultimately the election drive failed, and UAW-CIO Local 75 maintained control over the nine powerhouse workers by a five-to-four vote.[43]

Jurisdictional disputes represented a competitive challenge that unions could not ignore. Similarly, there remained too many signs of business hostility for labor to relax its organizing activity. National figures such as Thurman Arnold, Eddie Rickenbacker, and Admiral Emory S. Land criticized labor's disloyalty to the war effort, its greedy pursuit of wage increases, its violation of the no-strike pledge, and its illegal tactics.[44] In Milwaukee, the daily papers focused on labor's faults and called for legislation to curb labor's supposed abuses of power. The National Small Business Men's Association sent letters to Milwaukee employers soliciting membership in the organization and attacking the Wagner Act (which placed the authority of the federal government behind unionization), the forty-hour week, and the closed shop. The Milwaukee Association of Commerce urged its members to lobby for the Smith Labor Bill, which, unlike the "pro-union" Wagner Act, was "drawn to give protection to all three groups [labor, business, and the public] of our citizenship." As World War II progressed, such attacks on organized labor continued, with no clear evidence that prewar gains sacrificed for the duration of the war would be restored when the conflict was over.[45] Given these dark clouds on the horizon, organized labor could not afford to become complacent, despite high weekly earnings and burgeoning union membership.

Indeed, for some unions in Milwaukee, organizing became a way of life as they fought recalcitrant employers who still considered collective bargaining to be a violation of their entrepreneurial rights. Because of employer intransigence, workers at J. Greenebaum Tanning Company and at foundries operated by William Grede never really progressed beyond the organizing stage. At Allis-Chalmers, talented and aggressive leadership founded UAW Local 248 (CIO), but relations between the company and the union can be characterized best as a perpetual struggle for control of the shop floor. Although war raged in Europe and Asia, workers never lost sight of the importance of their unions and were willing to fight for their rights even if such actions impeded the war effort.

On August 5, 1942, the employees of J. Greenebaum Tanning Company voted 568 to 278 for the CIO International Fur and Leather Workers Union. Contract negotiations began a month later but immediately stalled over the issues of wages, security, equal pay, and working conditions. Major James Holmes, the Conciliation Service mediator appointed to break the deadlock, found the company intransigent and, fearing that a work stoppage might be imminent, quickly urged that the dispute be certified to the WLB. Ten months later, the WLB granted maintenance of membership to the union, but denied the union's request for a wage increase because raises already granted Greenebaum workers exceeded the 15 percent limit set by the WLB. Instead of a general wage increase, the WLB instructed the two parties to negotiate a pay plan that would eliminate intra-plant inequalities. For all practical purposes, the WLB action gave the workers a contract; but the company continued to stall on wage negotiations. At the end of 1943 the WLB again addressed the matter and, in time for Independence Day 1944, ordered that the old contract be carried over and that the company begin negotiating with the union. With this order in hand, the management of the tannery found a new way to avoid meeting with the union. The old contract required that they bargain with Local 260, but the old local had merged with another Fur and Leather workers local, becoming Local 47. Seizing upon this technicality, the Greenebaum Tannery argued that there was no certified agent with whom they could bargain legitimately. Not until December 1944—more than two years after the union won its election—did the Greenebaum company finally agree to carry over the old contract with its union security clauses intact and begin negotiating.

It had been a long battle, and the union had progressed only slightly beyond the stage of organizing the plant. It had little to show for its efforts other than what the WLB had granted. The company refused to enter into a productive labor-management relationship and insisted on operating its affairs as if there had been no war. At the Greenebaum tannery, the union and the workers paid more heed to the war effort and stayed on the job as the WLB slowly adjudicated their cases. It was the company's intransigence that prevented the union from moving beyond simple self-preservation to greater labor-management co-operation on behalf of the war effort.[46]

Although the experience at Greenebaum may have been frustrating to the workers, it could not compare with the treatment received by workers at William Grede's foundries in Milwaukee. Grede was an old-fashioned industrialist who refused to acknowledge that the Wagner Act gave workers the right to organize. Locals of the Steelworkers' Organizing Committee in his plants found it almost impossible to get recognition from management representatives. Grede was so successful in his opposition to the union that the steelworkers never progressed much beyond the stage of running organizing campaigns.

In December 1942 William Grede purchased the Smith Steel Foundry, where United Steelworkers Local 1300 had a valid contract. Grede immediately fired all the employees, offering to rehire them with the understanding that they were now dealing with a new management that had no contract with the union—a procedure upheld by the WLB. According to W. O. Sonnemann, a CIO attorney, "The position Mr. Grede has taken . . . is that when he took over Smith Steel all he bought was the buildings and machines." For the remainder of the war, the workers in this plant tried to negotiate a contract. Grede's inimitable negotiating style permitted him to meet with union officials and to avoid any direct action to destroy the union, while at the same time avoiding any action that might legitimate the union. Plainly put, Grede tied union negotiators into semantic knots. When discussing establishment of a grievance procedure, for example, he asked union officials, "Well, what is a grievance?" Grede immediately accepted the union's definition of a grievance as an "unsatisfied complaint," and then turned the definition against the union. If a grievance was an "unsatisfied complaint," he argued, there was no need for a steward to present an employee's complaint because a complaint was not a grievance until it was rejected by the company. Of course, any procedure that sidestepped the union steward was completely unacceptable to the union, so around and around went the debates. As James Holmes commented to his superiors in the Conciliation Service, a union representative told him "after you have argued for several years on such trivial matters, it is impossible to think clearly."

Frustrated by such tactics, workers at Smith Steel struck on July 25, 1944, to protest company delays in contract negotiations. On May 3 of that year the union had been certified as the bargaining agent, and contract discussions had been stalled ever since. Fed up with non-coercive methods, the workers struck. Despite pressure from the international union, the steelworkers refused to return to their jobs. After eight days, Local 1568 at the Milwaukee Steel Foundry (another Grede division) joined the strike, having become equally impatient with Grede for his refusal to abide by a WLB directive that gave the union maintenance of membership, voluntary check-off, and grievance procedures. The company's president argued that the labor board had gone beyond its jurisdiction in ordering implementation of these standard contract features. The members of Local 1300 and Local 1568 returned to work on August 7 after the parties agreed to negotiate the issues.

Seven months later, nothing had changed for the Smith Steel Foundry workers. Grede continued his delaying tactics; virtually the entire contract remained unsettled. James Holmes seemed exasperated with the company's behavior and again certified this case to the WLB. Despite the lack of progress, the union agreed to wait for a labor board decision, and the workers stayed on the job. As the war drew to a close, the steelworkers in Grede's plants were only one step beyond organizing. They were still trying to develop a stable relationship with an employer who refused to accept the union's right to exist.[47]

Most Milwaukee disputes, like their national counterparts, were settled quietly through negotiation, mediation, and arbitration. Nonetheless, as the Grede example demonstrated, there were times when negotiation failed. The strikes in Grede's foundries represented the culmination of a series of events throughout which the workers showed great forbearance. Far from representing a workers' grab for power and monetary gain, the strikes in Grede's foundries represented another side of the tensions that existed between labor and management in wartime as well as peacetime.

Strikes were only the most obvious signs of the ongoing struggle between labor and management. They highlighted the colliding interests of labor and management. On the other hand, the absence of a strike seldom meant the absence of conflict. At the Grede foundries, the steelworkers struck despite the war and the opposition of their international. Had there been no strikes, however, the conflict still would have existed between Grede and his workers, just as it would have existed between the management of most factories and their employees. This fact was illustrated most poignantly by the relationship between Allis-Chalmers and UAW Local 248, one of Milwaukee's most militant unions. Throughout the war, the leaders of Local 248 maintained steady pressure on management in a prolonged battle for control of the hearts and minds of the workers at Allis-Chalmers. Yet the union never went on strike during the war. The war simply presented a new setting for an old struggle.

Unionization at Allis-Chalmers was always a struggle. In 1901, 1906, and 1916 the company fought unions over control of production on the shop floor, a theme that was to be played over and over again in the next forty-five years. The International Association of Machinists (IAM) initiated a national strike on May 20, 1901, to protect against mechanization of the workplace and erosion of craft standards. Allis-Chalmers machinists joined the walkout. The company threatened to fire striking workers and secured an injunction against strike activities. Workers gradually returned and by late July the union had lost the battle.

In 1906 the company's skilled molders participated in an International Molders' Union strike in protest of growing mechanization and in favor of a nine-hour day. The company hired detectives to police the plant, secured court injunctions against picketing, intimidated workers, and hired unskilled labor to run newly installed molding machines. The strike collapsed, and with it the power of the Molders' Union at the West Allis plant. The drama was replayed in 1916 when 1,200 members of the IAM struck and demanded an eight-hour day with no pay reduction. As had been true in the past, other employees at Allis-Chalmers stayed on the job during this dispute. After eight weeks, machinists returned to work and the strike died. The company made no concessions and maintained an open shop.[48]

Harold Story, Allis Chalmers' vice president for industrial relations and leading strategist in all labor disputes during the 1930s and 1940s, expressed the company's attitude toward its workers, labor relations, and unions when he told a legislative committee, "The company organization has many of the characteristics of the family unit. Management stands in the position of parent." To his way of thinking, it was "just as unfair for a labor union . . . to interfere with the relations of that employer's industrial family group as it is for a total stranger to mix into the affairs of an actual family unit."[49] Rather than being representatives and advocates for workers, Story viewed unions as interlopers with no rightful place at Allis-Chalmers.

When the National Industrial Recovery Act recognized and encouraged union organizing, the company created the West Allis Works Council to represent the workers and avoid establishment of a real union. The move reflected a new gambit through which the company could maintain managerial control over the workplace. In the words of Harold Story:

> The Works Council . . . contained our outstanding, mature, skilled men. They were men whom we knew, who on account of their closeness to management, could bargain effectively [and could] effectively attain all that the Company could afford to offer at that time.[50]

In other words, the union was a tool for maintaining management's definition of the rule of law in the workplace.

During the same period, a group of AFL unions began organizing the plant. They received polite treatment from the company, the right to present grievances to management, and a unilateral company expression of its willingness to bargain with any legally constituted union in the context of an open shop. In a factory increasingly devoted to mass production and in the face of continued corporate hostility, craft union organizers found it difficult to recruit workers. Although organizing drives in 1934 failed, several pockets of skilled workers committed to union representation formed within Allis-Chalmers. Led by such dynamic leaders as Harold Christoffel, future president of Local 248, these groups became the incubators from which came militant representatives elected to the Works Council in 1934. As John Blair, a local communist organizer, recalled, "Allis-Chalmers had established a company union. The progressive people in the plant ran for the posts of representatives on the company union. When elected, they exposed the set-up by making real demands in behalf of the workers."[51] The company council dominated by non-union workers was thereby transformed into a body dominated by union members and prepared to do battle with management.

When the AFL sought to form a federal labor union at Allis-Chalmers in 1936, the craft leaders who had been frustrated in their earlier drives to organize skilled workers and who had made the Works Council a forum for workers' concerns urged skilled craftsmen to join this new AFL industrial union. Federal Labor Union 20136 soon enrolled approximately 2,000 members, drawn from the ranks of skilled and unskilled alike.

The size of this local and the fact that it was absorbing craft workers posed a serious threat to the old craft unions. Milwaukee's AFL leaders balked at the precedent of allowing craft workers to abandon their old unions in favor of an industrial organization, and they feared that the local's representatives might dominate the Federated Trades Council. The FTC refused to seat delegates from Allis-Chalmers on the grounds that they were skilled workers who belonged in craft unions. As a result, FLU 20136 reconstituted itself as Local 248 of the UAW-CIO, an action that marked the beginning of open conflict in Milwaukee between the fledgling CIO and the FTC.

In May the company recognized Local 248 as the bargaining agent for its members and a year later as the exclusive agent in the plant. The first contract granted the union little more than a grievance procedure—and even this provision left seniority and discharge cases in the hands of the company and outside the grievance system. The system was weakened further by a clause that encouraged workers to bypass the union committeeman and take grievances personally to the foreman. A secret supplement to the agreement gave the company the right to recognize other unions at the expense of Local 248's jurisdiction if the competing unions possessed the ability to close the plant. Allis-Chalmers had given up as little as possible to the union, but development of a written contract with a grievance procedure marked the first time workers at Allis-Chalmers had an official channel through which to express the daily concerns of the shop floor.[52]

Between the signing of the first contract and America's entry into World War II, Local 248 negotiated annual agreements and engaged in two strikes, both of which centered on the questions of union security and the union's presence on the shop floor. Management officials clearly wanted to promote union fragmentation as a way to weaken the CIO local and wanted to limit shop-floor activities, especially grievance handling, as a way to weaken the union's most visible presence in the plant. Throughout the prewar period the company steadfastly refused to grant any type of security clause to Local 248. Instead, company representatives gave union officials verbal assurances that they would not countenance any employee actions that might undermine the union. Allis-Chalmers agreed to protect Local 248 from open subversion, but it would do nothing to prevent workers from leaving the local or to make union maintenance easier.

The company's promise not to undermine Local 248 was cold comfort to union leaders. Although the local received 78 percent of the votes in the NLRB representation election in 1938, it faced repeated challenges from the AFL, from dissidents within the UAW, and from independent unions. In the most blatant attack, the AFL mounted a Wisconsin organizing drive with Local 248 as one of its main targets. The drive against the UAW local was unsuccessful, but one episode during the fight sheds considerable light on the company's real goal in refusing to sign a contractual security agreement. In October 1940 David Sigman, a representative for AFL president William Green, met with Harold Story to discuss AFL organizing plans. Story expressed the company's willingness to cooperate with the AFL should the campaign succeed. Sigman opened the organizing drive the following day. Clearly, Allis-Chalmers wanted to avoid any contractual agreement that would bind it to the militant unionism of Harold Christoffel and UAW Local 248.

The union initiated a twenty-six day strike when the company encouraged anti-UAW workers interested in establishing an Independent Union. The matter was complicated after the strike began when the IAM volunteered to represent those workers in the plant who were eligible for IAM membership. Local 248 insisted on a closed shop or union shop to protect against future attacks by rival unions. Fearing erosion of managerial prerogatives, the company refused. The strike ended with a compromise. The union did not get the security it sought. Instead, it got a strengthened grievance procedure and improved vacations. The company also promised to provide detailed piece rate information and to negotiate wages.

A seventy-six day strike began on January 22, 1941 and caught national attention amidst charges that the union was impeding defense production. Once again, this strike revolved around Local 248's desire for protection from raids by the AFL and independent unions. After two separate meetings in Washington, the parties reached an agreement providing for an impartial referee "to decide questions of activity which constituted 'undermining the union' and resulted in disrupting shop discipline." Although they had not gained the desired union security clause, the referee system provided a new tool with which to battle management and defend the union.[53]

Wartime contract negotiations at Allis-Chalmers reflected the animosity that developed before 1942. Apparently having concluded from its earlier battles with management that no security clause would be granted voluntarily, the union virtually bypassed collective bargaining on a new contract in 1942, and the case went to the WLB. The company opposed granting any maintenance of membership clause under which union members would be required to remain members for the life of the contract, and the WLB panel agreed because of Local 248's "irresponsible" behavior. The National WLB, disregarding its panel's report, granted a standard maintenance of membership clause to the union. Although the board believed that Local 248 had been "highly irresponsible," it acknowledged that the company had to share the blame. The WLB granted the security clause in the hope that it would help to improve relations between the warring parties.[54]

Only a revolution in labor relations could have eased the tension at Allis-Chalmers. Union leaders learned to use whatever tools were at their disposal in this battle to protect the organization and its members. In the late 1930s Local 248 used brief work stoppages and departmental sit-down strikes to win disputes with the company. These methods enabled workers to force action on their grievances and the union to demonstrate its ability to work on behalf of its members. The binding arbitration of grievances imposed by management on the union in 1941 established a rule of law on the shop floor. Local 248 turned the grievance arbitration system into a blessing during World War II as the union tried to adhere to the CIO's no-strike policy.

The grievance system became a weapon with which to bludgeon the company in what both sides perceived as a battle for the hearts and minds of the workers. While Allis-Chalmers refused to grant any concession that might make the union feel more secure, stewards and committeemen actively pursued grievances to demonstrate the local's value to the work force. Indeed, both the union and the company carefully guarded and nurtured their prestige with the workers and reacted negatively when they thought their respective images had been damaged. Although one WLB panel criticized the union for overloading the grievance system with petty complaints, actually nothing could have been further from the truth. The grievance system had become a major battleground on which the company and union fought for control of the work force.[55]

Local 248 used a well organized shop steward system to implement the union's approach to industrial democracy. Harold Christoffel described the importance of stewards in the following fashion:

> Any grievance in the shop is taken care of by the steward structure. In other words, the real union work is done in the shop by the stewards. That is one of the differences between industrial and craft unions. Industrial unionism depends upon the democratic set-up of the stewards to represent the workers and the craft unions are represented by the business agents.[56]

As "Big Bill" Zastrow illustrated, stewards served as a committed cadre of union activists ready not only to represent and defend the interests of workers in the West Allis plant, but also to implement the union's well organized use of the grievance and arbitration system as a weapon in their battle with management. Although Allis-Chalmers officials considered a majority of grievances to be specious, the grievance process provided a venue through which workers expressed dissatisfaction. By carefully screening grievances and pressing those that had significant implications for the union's power or workers' rights, Local 248 undermined managerial control, reinforced the image of the union's power, and established new legal precedents. In this manner Local 248 mounted regular challenges designed to expand union authority and limit that of the company. Company officials watched in dismay as the time they spent processing grievances skyrocketed from 220.5 hours in 1939 to 3,172.6 in 1944. Although the union often lost its appeals, it won often enough to make inroads into dearly held management prerogatives.[57]

At least as early as February 1943, officials at Allis-Chalmers expressed concern about the erosion of managerial authority through concessions to Local

248. Company attorney Harold Story and Lee Hill, wartime vice-president for industrial relations, were the chief architects of Allis-Chalmers' labor relations policy. To a business friend, Story wondered if his refusal to compromise his beliefs on company authority to run the plant was a sign of becoming old-fashioned. He feared that the appeasement of labor would result in the "eventual disintegration of management control." A short time later, he commiserated with a colleague about the problems inherent in using mediation panels to settle labor disputes. Because of "union agitators" on mediation panels, he said, "matters in mediation proceed on the theory of a compromise always in favor of the union." Instead, he wanted Allis-Chalmers to be known on the East Coast as a poor compromiser when the company knew it was right.[58]

Lee Hill shared Story's views. In numerous pronouncements during the war, he inveighed against labor's preemption of managerial prerogatives. Hill told the Society for the Advancement of Management in Milwaukee that mutual consent clauses in contracts give "the union or the employee a veto on management action;" that strict adherence to seniority in decisions of layoff, transfer, promotion, and job assignment ran counter to the principle of giving preference to the most able individual; that joint committees were "another device of the unions to limit the rights of management;" and that acceptance of binding arbitration, "especially in the hands of an aggressive union, or one bent on harassing tactics, would in effect substitute the referee for the board of directors and the management."[59]

By 1945 the corporate leaders of Allis-Chalmers clearly believed that their ability to manage was being eroded by the referee arbitration system as it was being used by Local 248. In a brief before the WLB, the company stated that the local's major objective in negotiations since 1942 had been "the strait jacketing of shop management." Labor's demand in 1945 that the referee's power be extended to any controversy struck company officials as the realization of their worst fears. The company brief to the WLB stated their concern:

> The union demands that the Referee have jurisdiction over "*any controversy* between the parties, or between the Company and the employees."
>
> The achievement of this demand would pervert the comprehensive arbitration system which has been an integral part of the collective bargaining relationship between the parties . . . into an instrumentality of positive usurpation of management control of essential management functions.[60]

The struggle for power and influence extended to the Allis-Chalmers labor-management committee, one of the joint committees so abhorred by Lee Hill. Elsewhere in industry, labor-management committees represented one of the most positive developments in industrial relations; but at Allis-Chalmers it became a platform on which to do battle for control of the workplace. Although the contending parties formed a labor-management committee in March 1942, the group's activities reflected the tension between labor and management rather than any sense of cooperation. The company remained antago-

nistic toward any suggestion that might reflect favorably on the union or in-
fringe on its perception of managerial prerogative. For its part, the union used
the labor-management committee to highlight issues that would improve its
position in the struggle with Allis-Chalmers.

At one time, the company used production "scoreboards" based on production tonnage as a motivational tool. When union representatives suggested
that production scoreboards be implemented again, the company refused on
the grounds that such boards failed to adequately reflect production trends.
Local 248 then proposed using scoreboards based on the dollar value of production, or progress on specific products, or in specific departments, or on the
general rise and fall of production. The company turned down every alternative
plan the union proposed. With a sense of exasperation, the union asked why all
of its scoreboard proposals were unacceptable to the company. The *CIO News*
suggested that the company's opposition to scoreboards came from not want-
ing workers to know which departments were doing well and which were
doing poorly. Company officials probably disagreed with this assessment, but
it came very close to the mark. During the defense crisis and the first year of the
war, the union had been very critical of lagging production in certain departments and had used this criticism as a rhetorical weapon against the company.
Allis-Chalmers was unlikely to agree to any proposal that might provide more
ammunition for the union's attacks on the company's production effort. Likewise, when union representatives proposed revitalizing the committee structure in 1945 to include greater joint activities to curb absenteeism, cure production bottlenecks, and solve safety problems, Allis-Chalmers showed no interest.
Even when local 248 proposed that the labor-management committee implement an on-the-job hot food program, the idea received scant attention from
the company. Cooperative programs, especially on issues such as production
bottlenecks, were anathema to company officials who already believed they had
conceded too much managerial control to the union.[61]

The labor-management committee at Allis-Chalmers illustrated the limits
of national unity during the war. Prewar industrial relations formed the foundation upon which labor and management built their wartime relationship. When
interaction between a union and a company involved the normal range of suspicion, hostility, and conflicting interests inherent in industrial relations, national
unity and patriotism could bring workers and managers together in a successful
labor-management committee. No amount of cooperative spirit, however,
could surmount a long, bitter tradition of hostile interaction. Prewar relations
between Allis-Chalmers and Local 248 degenerated to the point where each side
viewed every aspect of labor relations as a life-and-death struggle. By 1942, no
amount of wartime good will could bring the labor-management committee to
life. The committee at Allis-Chalmers became little more than a new tool with
which the two parties did battle. Despite adherence to the rhetoric of national
unity, the committee was trapped in the past.

Unions could not afford to forget the past and the struggles that had been
necessary to build the strength of organized labor and protect workers' rights.

Most Americans willingly sacrificed for the national defense, but for industrial workers the future was too uncertain to assume blithely that all would be well in the postwar era. The war changed many aspects of workers' lives, but it did not alter the basic relationship between employers, workers, and unions. Nor did the war change the basic nature of industrial conflict. Often disputes were settled in a more legalistic fashion than before the war, but the disputes still existed. Workers fought for those issues that remained so significant that conflict surfaced despite wartime unity. Stewards continued to file grievances when companies violated contracts, disciplined workers unfairly, or unilaterally changed working conditions. When legalistic methods of resolving problems seemed to fail, workers took extralegal measures to protect their rights. Despite pressure from regional and national labor leaders, Milwaukee workers and unions struck when they perceived a threat to their union, security, or wage rates. Although some disputes made their way to government agencies or into public view, many other daily conflicts remained hidden from sight. The slow-down at Ampco and the flood of grievances at Allis-Chalmers provide brief glimpses of the many subtle ways in which workers continued to fight for control over the workplace.

The war altered many aspects of home-front life, but Americans could neither forget the past nor ignore the future. This perspective influenced not only industrial cooperation and conflict, but also the ways in which unions and male industrial workers responded to women in the workplace. The war did not bring women into factories for the first time. Ever since the industrial revolution women had filled factory jobs. Nonetheless, the war brought women into new jobs—jobs once held exclusively by men. With memories of women being used to undercut male wage rates and with ongoing concern for postwar employment, male workers and their unions grudgingly accepted women into new employment realm as a patriotic necessity, but they did so with the same desire to protect past gains as they did in their ongoing conflict with employers.

CHAPTER FIVE

THE RESPONSE
TO WOMEN WORKERS

In one of the best-publicized appeals to the glamour of war work, the Hearst Press, embodied in the *Milwaukee Sentinel,* organized a hunt for "Miss Victory," the ideal woman war worker. The *Sentinel* described candidates for "Miss Victory" in language that made factory work seem both glamorous and patriotic. In one of its earliest articles on the "Miss Victory" campaign, the *Sentinel* told readers that "life in a typical Wisconsin factory is far from dreary or uninteresting, according to women production workers." The paper described one of these women as

> A slim, blond girl who used to be a fashion model before the shortage of male help landed her, with thousands of others, in a job amid the humming machines of wartime production, took a healthy bite from a red skinned apple she had in her lunch box. She looked up, displaying unusual gold flecked gray eyes that gleamed with vitality. To a question she retorted: 'Me bored? In all this activity, when we're helping to make history with every spin of the wheel?'[1]

When the newspaper described Mildred McAllister, a turret lathe operator who later became the finalist from Wisconsin, the *Sentinel*'s message was unmistakable:

Bronze dust glittered in her dark hair as she bent over her machine in the new defense plant at Ampco Metals, Inc. Two encircled shavings caught to a wisp of hair like an earring. The smile on her face was as buoyant as a debutante's.

It was a smile of victory, repeated again and again on the faces of nearly 300 women turning out airplane parts in Ampco shops. One of them may be 'Miss Victory of Wisconsin,' picked to typify the spirit and skill that women factory hands are putting into the effort to lick the Axis.

Mildred McAllister had, in fact, been a commercial artist before the war. Other Ampco candidates included a food demonstrator, a stenographer, a Ziegfield girl, a soldier's wife, and a corset model. The emphasis on glamour said more about perceptions of women and how to recruit them for the work-force than it said about real women. All of the contestants joined the industrial workforce because of the war effort.[2]

Seldom, if ever, were women motivated by the "glamour" of factory work. Instead, they left home, lower-paying jobs, and non-factory employment out of a sense of patriotism, a need for employment, or a desire for higher pay. When asked about her first impressions of Allis-Chalmers, Dorothy Keating re-sponded,

> It's so big I'm going to get lost in here. It's just immense. . . . The ceilings were so high because they had these gigantic great big turbines and if you can imagine, one would be almost as big as these apartments here and that went into a submarine. . . . It was scary at first but because you knew you were doing something for your country I guess you forgot all about that. You just went to work. . . . I put my heart into it and really worked hard. Well, I liked making the money [laughs].[3]

Early in the war, Rose Kaminski worked briefly as a machine operator for a supercharger plant run by General Electric. An experienced machinist did the setup work and she simply operated a machine. She had been employed for less than eight months when the plant closed.

> I didn't work there very long and the thing I remember the most about it is that we replaced the men at that time. We ran a machine shop, and men came in and set up the machines and we were like little robots. We just picked up the pieces and then inserted pieces in the milling ma-chines and in the presses and in the threading machines and counted them and put them in bins. You really felt like a machine, working a ma-chine. It was not really fulfilling in the sense that you were really doing something or accomplishing something because you did not know the ins and outs.

Looking for a new job after the plant closed, Rose Kaminski was deter-mined not to be a "robot." After her stint as a machine operator, she returned to homemaking until 1943, when she responded to the call for more women workers in Milwaukee's war plants.

> [T]hey were asking for women to volunteer and they were hiring at . . . the old Rex Chain Belt Company and they had an ordnance plant. My husband was in the service then and I decided, OK, I'm going to go to work. And I needed that money because the little pay that you got from the government was very little. . . . I went in to apply for work as an inspector. I thought, oh well, this is going to be a little bit more meaningful—inspection work. I won't be a robot.

In addition to inspectors, Chain Belt Company was hiring crane operators. Crane operators were responsible for positioning a grinder in a howitzer barrel as part of the rifling process and then loading the barrel on a flatcar for shipment. Her stepfather had been a crane operator, and this was a job Rose Kaminski wanted to do.

> So he took several of us and walked into the factory and here was this great big ordnance plant with machines all lined up in rows . . . and great big gun barrels. They were making great big Howitzer barrels for the guns. Overhead were the cranes and he showed us what we'd have to do. . . . Well, I was running one in three days. It just came to me, I loved it, there was no problem, it was not difficult and here I thought you can see the gun barrels, you know that it's part of the war. It wasn't like at the other place where you had piddly little pieces and you didn't know where it belonged. This seemed like part of it. You were doing something. You were accomplishing something.

Early in 1944 Rose and several other women decided to seek employment at the Harnischfeger Corporation, maker of heavy cranes and excavating and earth moving equipment, within walking distance of her home.

> [W]e went together to apply for work. Because in numbers there's a little strength and you need a little moral support. You're not used to looking for a job and you didn't know what you were getting into; you were afraid at that time. We were not as bold as we are now. . . . We were taken into the shop and shown where we would work. Of course, at the ordnance plant everything was new, it was just a new government building. Everything was clean, everything was nice. It was a machine shop; it was not dirty; it was not smoky. Well, we walked into this building where we were supposed to work. The cranes were, oh my, about 30 feet up in the air compared to maybe about 15–20 feet in the machine shop. It was a difference and there was nothing but welding, and smoke, and dirt. I said, "oh no, I don't think I choose to work in this building—no." The gentleman who eventually was my boss, said, "Rose, we need you, we really, really need you ladies. Give it a chance."

After two weeks Rose Kaminski had learned the job and felt so well respected for her work that she stayed until March 1946, when she was laid off to make room for a returning veteran.[4]

As the military drew more and more men into service, massive industrial recruitment campaigns progressively targeted single women, then married women without small children, then even mothers of young children. Wartime industrial production required this infusion of new employees. Mildred McAllister, Dorothy Keating, and Rose Kaminski were committed to the war effort and were valued for the work they performed. Nonetheless, they and many other similar women workers threatened the established order. Their record influx into heavy industry and the skilled crafts during World War II not only called into question cherished views of women's roles, but also raised questions about the economic security of men in the postwar era. The reaction of male workers and of unions to the presence of women in new roles, and to issues of importance to these women, reflected the complex intertwining of social and economic concerns. The resulting interplay of issues, feelings, and beliefs created another facet of industrial conflict characterized by a general desire to protect the seniority rights, the earning power, and the job security of male workers. The experiences of working women, especially those with families, shed light on the history of the home front, the special role women played in winning the war, and the role of women in the workplace and in society.

During the "defense crisis" of 1941, astute observers in government, labor, and industry recognized that women formed a labor reserve upon which the nation would have to draw if it were to reach its full potential as a military power. Rapid expansion of both industry and the armed forces guaranteed that new workers would have to be recruited to maintain war production. The exigencies of the war dictated that women move from the home, from non-industrial jobs, and from "women's" jobs in factories into the industrial workforce and into jobs once performed exclusively by men. Massive recruiting campaigns, registration drives, and media publicity encouraged women to leave the home and non-essential employment to join the ranks of the industrial army. Yet few of these women were new to the paid labor force; most of them, and even many of the housewives, had worked prior to marriage. They now returned to work out of patriotism, familial loyalty, and economic need.[5]

The largest demand for women often came from companies that had recently expanded their production capacity, but some Milwaukee firms simply continued a practice begun a generation earlier, during the First World War. For example, Briggs and Stratton Corporation, Cutler-Hammer, Inc., and Globe-Union, Inc. each maintained a comparatively large female workforce in the years between the wars and recruited new women workers as male employees entered the armed forces. Likewise, they looked upon married women who had worked in Milwaukee's hosiery and textile mills as likely recruits for war plants because of their easy adaptability to the factory regimen. The War Manpower Commission (WMC) placed a special emphasis on trying to entice former workers back into the labor force in the hope that these former workers would be able to reestablish old work patterns with the least disruption to production.

In the spring of 1942 Allis-Chalmers Manufacturing Company conducted its first hiring campaign on a mass scale after putting new production facilities into operation and recruiting approximately 2,000 women workers. The opening of U.S. Rubber's ordnance plant created a demand for several thousand more women. Milwaukee's second-largest employer, A. O. Smith Company, hired its first female factory employees during the late summer, by which time it was abundantly clear that women workers were vital to the local war effort. The employment of married women was actively promoted as early as March 1942, but for most employers and government officials, this implied women without children below the age of fourteen. Few people advocated the recruitment of mothers with young children.[6]

When the first women arrived on the shop floor or took jobs once reserved for men, they immediately became the objects of attention and scrutiny. Although male workers occasionally greeted such intrusions with open hostility, more commonly they reacted with a mixture of suspicion, questioning acceptance, and apprehension. As the war progressed women won the respect, sometimes grudgingly given, of their male co-workers; but even those men who accepted women on the factory floor continued to wonder what such changes would mean when the war was over.[7]

Union policies on issues important to women members reflected the uncertain future and the lack of women's power within organized labor. More often than not, when unions fought for equal pay or for a single, plant-wide seniority list, the reasons for such a fight related more to protecting men's jobs and pay rates than to achieving just treatment for women. Conventional wisdom held that women were best suited for repetitive tasks requiring fine hand coordination, that they were temporary workers, and that they could not be trained fast enough to be considered skilled. Such beliefs reinforced the tendency to discount women workers and to view their needs as unimportant. Likewise, the belief that a wife's or mother's first responsibility was to serve her family reinforced the notion that women were temporary workers serving for the duration of the war. Union leaders, social welfare specialists, and government officials generally reacted unfavorably to any hint that many working women neither desired to return to their old jobs nor to a purely nurturing role once the Axis powers were defeated. Such a trend threatened not only the jobs of male workers and returning veterans, they believed, but also undermined the very foundations of society. The attitudes of union leaders and workers alike stemmed from this mixture of cultural norms and fears about the future. The exigencies of war paved the way for women to be accepted in new roles, but such acceptance was only temporary. The reaction to mothers who took jobs, in particular, underscored the superficial nature of war-born social change.[8]

Approximately 6.5 million American women entered the labor force during World War II. Of this number, 2.5 million new women workers joined the ranks of industrial labor. The influx of women workers more than tripled the number of female union members from 800,000 in 1940 to 3 million in 1944. Nonetheless, women seldom exerted influence within their unions in proportion to their numbers. Instead, they generally held minor offices and were assigned to organizing and steward duties only where the majority of the workers were women. In some cases this gender stereotyping extended to relegating women to traditional clerical and social duties within the union. Plainly put, more often than not, women took notes and made coffee.[9]

By 1944 national conventions of both labor federations committed organized labor to recruiting women and encouraging their active participation in union affairs. Such a commitment was badly needed. It also was hard to implement. When the Women's Bureau studied women and unions in the Midwest, survey workers learned that over half the union locals had no women members before the war. In only four cases had women been members of the union for at least ten years. In addition, they did not share positions of power in proportion to their numbers, although there appeared to be a relationship between the number of female union members and the existence of at least one female officer. Only four unions had a woman president, and the same number reported the election of a woman vice president. Out of seventy-five women serving as officers of local unions, forty-one served as financial secretary, recording secretary, or trustee; eight served on the union executive board; nine were delegates to city or state bodies. The remaining nine were sprinkled among the positions of guide (four), sergeant at arms (two), business manager (one), shop chairman (one), and division chairman (one). In fact, when it came to negotiating new contracts or settling grievances, women union members held pitifully little power.[10]

The pattern was no different outside the Midwest. It was ironic, for example, that the International Ladies Garment Workers Union had only one woman on its executive board despite the fact that 75 percent of its members were women. Some national unions, such as the CIO auto workers and electrical workers, established programs to encourage leadership development among female members, but making leadership a reality at the local level was much more difficult. To some extent women faced male hostility, but primarily they faced an institution and a set of cultural values that contained little sympathy for women's issues. What was more, the double duty women faced as homemakers and workers made it difficult for them to be active union members. Issues unique to women seldom received much attention, either because they were unimportant to, threatening to, or misunderstood by the male majority. Establishing a common seniority system, for example, would have helped to secure women's job rights; but it would also have reduced the security of male workers. Likewise, UAW Vice President Richard T. Frankensteen rejected the child-care issue because he could see it only in terms of the battle with management and not in terms of women's needs. Frankensteen denounced company day-care centers as a threat to the hearts and minds of future generations of workers. He asked the 1942 CIO national convention rhetorically,

> What better way is there for a paternalistic company to control the destinies of their workers than to set up child training centers, to open up

nursery schools and allow these women to place their children there, and
then training those children on the basis they want them trained upon?[11]

The lack of power possessed by women workers and the importance of social stereotypes in limiting their advancement in the workforce were reflected
in the implementation of contract provisions such as equal pay for equal work
and the elimination of discriminatory job-classification procedures and seniority lists. Both labor federations actively supported the concept of equal pay for
equal work, but that fact guaranteed little for women at the local level. In six of
the midwestern plants reporting to the Women's Bureau, women were relegated to women's jobs. In eighty factories they performed some of the jobs
held by men, and union contracts guaranteed men and women the same rates
in 70 percent of these cases. Unfortunately, contract language often meant
much less than it implied. In practice, women seldom received merit increases
or promotions equal to their male counterparts. The transfer of a woman to a
man's job often included alterations in the job to accommodate the supposed
mechanical deficiencies or physical weaknesses of the new worker. Because of
such changes company officials, union leaders, and male and female workers
alike often concluded that the work was not equal to that done by men and did
not warrant equal pay. The existence of women's jobs and separate women's
departments also weakened the equal-pay principle. Women on such jobs seldom received pay comparable to their equally skilled male counterparts. Finally, women tended to remain in lower-paying jobs longer than did equally inexperienced male workers.

As in the case of equal pay, the Women's Bureau found that international
unions strongly favored the elimination of discriminatory seniority provisions
and the enforcement of existing contract clauses that provided equitable seniority for women. In 80 percent of the contracts they studied, the Bureau's
agents found clauses protecting men and women equally. Nonetheless, seniority lists did not guarantee that workers would be promoted based on that seniority, nor did they protect women from being laid off as companies curtailed
war production. The best seniority clause could not protect workers who entered factories as replacements for young men drafted into the armed forces,
nor could it protect female workers whose "women's jobs" were discontinued.
When the war ended, when servicemen returned, when production slack-
ened—when that day came, the future of many women workers remained un-
clear and largely undefended by their unions. At least thirteen of the contracts
reviewed by the Women's Bureau made no pretense of equal seniority protection for men and women. Separate seniority lists based on gender offered little
protection for women workers, even if they had worked before the war. Under
such contracts, companies could lay off women while employing male workers
of lower seniority and not violate the union agreement.[12]

The Bureau's survey, which included factories in Milwaukee, reflected an
underlying fear of the future on the part of men and women alike. Neither
knew what would happen when the war was over, and much of the relationship

between women and organized labor should be viewed, and understood, in the light of this uncertainty. Although some union leaders defended equal pay for equal work on principle, more often it was defended as a measure to protect men's jobs and wage scales. Similarly, many unionists supported full seniority rights for women to prevent employers from replacing highly paid men with less senior women at a lower rate. Others denied women equal treatment as a means of protecting the jobs of male breadwinners and returning servicemen in the postwar era. All of these actions emphasized the protection of men's jobs and wage rates. The role played by women activists within unions depended less on women's issues than on working within boundaries defined by class unity and male perspectives.[13]

When the Women's Bureau surveyed unions in Wisconsin, it picked eighteen Milwaukee locals: ten from the AFL and eight from the CIO. The selection included Milwaukee's largest employers as well as several shops employing less than 200 workers. It included locals that went out of their way to assist women and protect their jobs and ones that looked forward to the day when women would return home "where they belonged." The eighteen surveys convey the impression that many locals only reluctantly accepted the advancement of women onto the shop floor and into men's jobs. Only a handful of this group actively supported the demand for equal pay and seniority protection, and fewer yet admitted women to the inner circle of union leadership. In these regards, there was little difference between organizations affiliated with the AFL and those identified with the CIO.

Women comprised at least 50 percent of the workers in four AFL plants and in five CIO plants. Their numbers, however, did not assure power within the union. At Milwaukee's Globe-Union company, manufacturer of batteries and electrical switches, membership in AFL United Auto Workers local 322 consisted of 1,587 women and 500 men. This overwhelming numerical superiority seemed to assure a more equitable distribution of power than in most other locals. Although men held the presidency and vice presidency, women held the positions of recording secretary, financial secretary, and chief steward. Half the stewards were women, and they also were represented on the bargaining committee.

This power was an illusion. The union had a credible record of defending the principle of equal pay when the company tried to place women on men's jobs at a lower rate, but such disputes were relatively rare. Most jobs at Globe-Union were women's jobs, and relatively few women had ever been shifted to men's duties. Women's jobs always carried a lower rate than any of the men's jobs, and promotion was based on managerial prerogative rather than seniority. Seniority at the plant was maintained separately by gender, and the contract actually specified that all men's jobs taken over by women during the war would revert to men after the emergency. If a job had been altered technologically to such an extent that it was now considered a women's job, it was exempted from this provision. The contract also specified different starting rates for inexperienced men and women.

At Globe-Union, women possessed the numerical superiority necessary to dominate the union, but they did not do so. The union worked for equal pay but made little headway when it came to issues such as comparable pay, seniority, and starting pay. Indeed, union leaders may never have tried to alter these discriminatory practices. When questioned by Women's Bureau agents, both male and female union officials at Globe-Union agreed that the union was respected by its members for its stand on equal pay and for vigorously pursuing grievances. No one seemed to believe or was willing publicly to challenge discriminatory practices in the contract and in the plant.[14]

The picture was even bleaker for women at Briggs and Stratton, where 550 men and 1,150 women belonged to AFL United Auto Workers Local 232. The union had no women officers, no women on the bargaining/grievance committee, and only one female steward. Inexperienced men and women started work with a seventeen-cent differential, which narrowed to fifteen cents after three months. Many of the jobs in the plant were listed by gender, and the women's jobs inevitably carried a lower rate than the men's jobs. The union had fought for equal pay with little success. Two factors seemed to influence affairs in the plant. The union, despite representing 83 percent of the employees, was unable to influence basic economic conditions in the factory. The company steadfastly refused to implement a classification system. It set job rates at will, placed new employees wherever it chose, and seldom upgraded any employee. The union seemed to be impotent when it came to solving these problems. Yet even if the union had been powerful, it might not have acted to solve issues such as lower pay on women's jobs; nor was it likely to have encouraged greater female participation in union affairs. Several local leaders were ambivalent about their female constituents. Clifford Matchey, union financial secretary, favored the elimination of separate jobs for women; but he acknowledged to the Women's Bureau agent, "Men fear women will drive them from the plants." The union's president, Clarence Erhman, felt that women were unsuited for some of the jobs at Briggs and Stratton. Both he and Matchey argued that the election of a woman to union office would only result in jealousy on the part of other women in the plant. That, they claimed, had been their experience with the one female steward.[15]

In the CIO locals women fared little better. At the Fulton Company women comprised 63 percent of the workforce, and everyone belonged to Automobile, Aircraft and Agricultural Implement Workers Local 335. Two women, one of whom was the chairman, sat with seven men on the board of trustees and negotiated contracts, resolved grievances, and handled the general business of the union. Two women and one man served as stewards. Nonetheless, seniority lists were arranged by gender, inexperienced workers started at different pay rates based on gender, and relatively few women worked on men's jobs because the union opposed transfers. Both the contract and company practice clearly demonstrated the problem posed by separate job classifications based on gender. Because so few women worked in the male sector, equal pay never really became much of an issue, and the company always paid assembly workers (almost exclusively women) less than machine operators (almost exclusively men), with little regard for the skill of the job. When women worked in the machine shop they did lighter jobs than men and received a base rate of fifty-four cents an hour. Men received base rates ranging from seventy-two cents to seventy-nine cents. The union's president made it clear to the Women's Bureau that single women would be employed after the war just as they had been employed before the war, but married women would work only in special cases of need. In the Bureau agent's words, union president Robert Schmidt believed "that there won't be enough jobs and the men should be employed in most cases." Schmidt clearly perceived married women as a threat to his primary constituency, male union members.[16]

Likewise, at Master Lock Company all of the 150 female and fifty-six of seventy-five male employees belonged to Local 469 of the CIO auto workers union. Despite their numerical disadvantage, men held all the major offices and positions on the bargaining and grievance committees. Women received discriminatory wages, and the local's leaders showed no interest in promoting equal pay. As the Women's Bureau surveyor reported,

> Bargaining Committee members are all men and the men interviewed said that they believed that the men had more [financial] responsibility so should have higher rates. This seems [to be the] reason that [the] union did not try to get higher rates for women and equal pay in cases where the work performed is same as that men had done.[17]

Men and women alike in this local believed that the union had secured the same seniority rights for both sexes, but the Women's Bureau interviewer saw a different pattern in the plant. Few women worked at positions that by local practice were considered men's jobs, and the union seemed to be cooperating with the company in an effort to formally classify jobs by gender.

Women received little support from their unions in factories where they held a majority of the jobs. In factories where they were a minority, issues such as equal pay and seniority became enmeshed in the larger scope of labor-management relations. At Harley-Davidson Motor Company, for example, women comprised 17 percent of the labor force and were represented by the AFL auto workers. At A. O. Smith they comprised 20 percent of the workforce and were represented by the AFL Federal Labor Union 19806. In both cases they held no positions of power, equal pay did not exist, and union officials expected relatively few women to be working for these companies after the war. Felix Reisdorf, financial secretary and chief operating officer for the federal union at A. O. Smith, told the agent of the Women's Bureau that women should be laid off after the war regardless of seniority. He was contemplating establishing separate seniority lists for men and women but "didn't have the nerve to suggest it." For all practical purposes, postwar layoffs were likely to solve his dilemma, since no women had worked in the plant before the war and the government guaranteed the right of servicemen to return to their old jobs.

Reisdorf seemed to epitomize the lethargy with which Local 19806 approached women's issues. Women workers expressed frustration because the union was doing little on their behalf. Female informants questioned the union's commitment to women members and the fact that women were both unclassified and paid less than men in the plant. Not only were they a minority in the union, but the organization exhibited little interest in their needs.[18]

Women in Local 409 of the United Automobile, Aircraft and Agricultural Implement Workers of America (L. J. Mueller Furnace Company, manufacturer of heating equipment for the army) and in Local 75 of the UAWA (Seaman Body, a subsidiary of Nash-Kelvinator that manufactured aviation engine parts) faced many of the same problems as their sisters in the AFL. They comprised only 8 percent of the workforce at Seaman Body and 25 percent at Mueller Furnace. Men held all of the significant offices and a disproportionate number of stewards' positions. In neither case did women receive equal pay for doing men's jobs, nor did inexperienced workers receive the same entry rate. Many workers at Seaman Body spent the first two years of the war working at other plants while on layoff as the company haltingly converted to war production. As a consequence, the union was deeply concerned about protecting the jobs of its male members, and the company tended to feed the union's insecurity. Repeatedly, managers at Seaman Body tried to place women on men's jobs, and then to reclassify those positions as women's jobs at a lower rate of pay. The plant maintained separate seniority lists for men and women, so any reclassification of this type inherently undercut the number of positions and the pay rate of men. At Mueller Furnace, women faced a variation on this theme. Ironically, the union's demand for equal pay and the company's intransigence kept women at lower-paying jobs throughout the war. Whenever the company upgraded a woman, it set a lower rate for her than was normally paid to male workers on that job. The union protested all such changes and demanded equal pay. In response, the company downgraded the female employee to her old job. Nonetheless, women workers interviewed by Women's Bureau agents agreed that the union was providing them with protection and that union leaders had worked conscientiously to solve their grievances. Indeed, during negotiations in 1945, company bargainers had proposed establishment of separate seniority lists arranged by gender. Union negotiators refused.[19]

Women at Allis-Chalmers became the victims of an even more fundamental dispute between a union and a company. Since its founding in 1937, United Automobile, Aircraft and Agricultural Implement Workers of America (CIO) Local 248 and Allis-Chalmers had been locked in almost constant struggle. Each side believed that its basic existence and prerogatives were at stake. Both on principle and because of its struggle with the company, officials of Local 248 vigorously encouraged women to become active union members. Likewise, Allis-Chalmers seldom gave in to any union demand without a fight, fearing that the union would use such a sign of weakness to promote the strength of the union. When women first worked on men's jobs, Local 248 demanded equal pay, but the company refused. They met similar resistance while negotiating contracts in 1943. The War Labor Board resolved the issue by approving the company's existing policy of paying women 82.6 percent of the male rate when working at a man's job. (Allis-Chalmers arrived at this formula by dividing the minimum women's incentive rate by the minimum men's incentive rate.) Judging the comparability of men's and women's work remained a prerogative reserved by management and a position from which they would not budge. When negotiations began in 1944, the union again demanded equal pay for equal work. This time the company compared "the average hourly earnings of men and women workers doing the same work and paid identical incentive rates." The company concluded that women were 87 percent as productive as men. Based on this data, the company argued that Local 248's demand for equal pay actually violated the principle of equal pay for equal work since equal work was not being done. The union made little headway on this issue, although it did succeed in ensuring that women received their share of merit pay increases.[20]

Most women workers at Allis-Chalmers who were surveyed by the Women's Bureau faced a future of downgraded jobs or layoffs. Although Local 248's recording secretary, Fred McStroul, favored special seniority provisions to protect the jobs of women, the management of Allis-Chalmers was unlikely to agree. The contract specified that women hired before October 1, 1940 would be returned to their old work units after the war, while women hired after that date would remain in their existing jobs. As was likely to occur at A. O. Smith, many women hired after October 1940 expected to lose their jobs when servicemen returned.[21]

Virtually everyone accepted the principle that soldiers must be rewarded for their service, and that employers had a legal and ethical responsibility to provide them with jobs when the war was over. As Rose Kaminski told an interviewer about her experience at Harnischfeger: "We knew that we would be laid off eventually and there was no qualms about that, there was no we're going to fight for our rights or anything. We knew what we were there for. We were there to relieve the men from their duties so that they could go into the service."[22]

In plants where women had never worked before the war, this meant that female workers who entered employment during the war had little job security. Even in factories where they had worked before the war, most could expect to be transferred back to women's jobs. Union officials surveyed by the Women's Bureau were particularly adamant that married women with other means of support should be excluded from the postwar labor force. As one interviewer told her superiors, the president of International Association of Machinists Lodge 66 "felt when the war was over women who have support should stay home, keep a nice home and let the men have the jobs." In several CIO locals the impression persisted that women were working simply for pin money.[23]

The discrimination faced by women could not be solved during the few years encompassed by World War II, for discrimination in the workplace was a manifestation of a vastly larger social system that was generally accepted by men and women alike.[24] Angeline Macak, a steward and committeewoman for her local, told an interviewer from the Women's Bureau that men took it for granted that women should work for less than men. Florence Mueller, a steward for another Milwaukee union, told an interviewer that women tended to care little for the long-range future of the union or the well-being of their fellow workers. The agent paraphrased Mueller's comments, "They [women] want 'to get while the getting is good,' and don't care what happens to the job. She thought men reason more, think ahead, and stick together better."[25] Such comments routinely appeared in the Women's Bureau interviews. Few people, male or female, seemed to recognize the inconsistency of paying two inexperienced workers differently because of their gender, of maintaining "men's" and "women's" job classifications, or of paying a wage rate that kept the most skilled women below the pay of the least skilled male worker. Yet, whether the factory was organized by the CIO or the AFL, this is exactly what most women found when they went to work.[26]

The recruitment of women for war work did not signify an alteration of the belief that the appropriate place for married women was in the home. Agencies such as the WMC and the Office of War Information urged women with children to attend to their primary duty: the care of those children. The same government campaigns that encouraged women to enlist in the production army subtly but unmistakably conveyed the message that they were but temporary members of the industrial workforce.

Government advertising emphasized the patriotic contribution women could make by working in a war plant. Women were being asked to join the production effort for the temporary purpose of winning the war. A United States Employment Service (USES) poster, which exemplified one of the prevailing social attitudes about women workers, portrayed a woman in overalls. Behind her was her husband. The poster caption read, "I'm Proud . . . my husband *wants* me to do my part." Her part was to take a war job, but only for the duration of the war, and with her husband's approval.

Such government propaganda, which also portrayed war work as being as glamorous and easy as a woman's normal household tasks, demonstrated that basic attitudes toward the role of women were not changing. Unlike the masculine portrait of Rosie the Riveter, memorably painted by Norman Rockwell for *The Saturday Evening Post* in 1943, the recruitment posters distributed by the USES portrayed women war workers in fashionable dress, with well-kept hair and makeup, and a radiant smile. The message was clear: factory work was not going to transform a woman into a new being, because a woman could maintain her femininity while working in a factory.[27] The emphasis on glamour, on similarities with housework, and on the temporary nature of women's war work underscored the perception of women as a reserve labor force that did not deserve the same treatment accorded male workers.

In few cases were the subtleties and implications of sexual stereotypes as clear as in the relationship between Valeria Brodzinski and the International

Brotherhood of Pulp, Sulphite and Paper Mill Workers. When the war began, Walter Trautmann served as the union's principal Milwaukee organizer. Brodzinski worked with Trautmann, especially when women were concerned. When he was drafted in November 1942, Brodzinski became the International's organizer for the Milwaukee area.[28]

Valeria Brodzinski's activities on behalf of the union were limited more by stereotypes of her as a woman than by her own abilities. When United Mine Workers District 50 threatened to take over a Pulp and Sulphite local in Ladysmith, international vice president Raymond Richards suggested sending the union's Milwaukee organizer to rally the local, despite a belief that "it is a man's job there because those organizers of District 50 are quite tough."[29] The international president agreed, and plans were made to send a special organizer to assist Brodzinski. The union leaders never questioned her ability as an organizer; they were concerned about her physical stamina. When she became ill shortly before the campaign began, Burke told Richards, "This being a labor organizer is enough to kill the strongest man, let alone a girl or woman."[30] The Pulp and Sulphite union won the Labor Relations Board election in Ladysmith, and Richards considered sending Brodzinski to Rhinelander to stamp out another problem. She questioned such a decision on the grounds that the Rhinelander local included few women, remarking "I know how men are when a woman tries to organize them."[31]

Valeria Brodzinski had been organizing for the union long enough to understand the problems faced by women in leadership positions. As a consequence, she never felt completely comfortable with her role as the chief organizer in Milwaukee. At times, she told John Burke, being an organizer was a man's job; she could never quite overcome the feeling that it was a temporary job for her and could not understand why he kept her on the payroll. She was employed by the union because she was a good organizer. Nonetheless, when Walter Trautmann returned in the summer of 1945, Brodzinski found new reasons to express her doubts. She had been negotiating with the management of Downing Box with little to show for her effort. After three conferences she had made no progress. Trautmann attended the fourth session, and to her amazement the company negotiators were pleasant and the meeting went smoothly. Afterward she wrote to Burke: "I have now realized what Dr. Beran Wolfe meant when he wrote, 'It is still a man's world, run by men and for men.'"[32]

The issue of equal pay underscored Valeria Brodzinski's observations. Shortly after the war began, the International Brotherhood of Pulp and Sulphite Workers met with officials of the International Paper Company and established an equal-pay policy. The policy guaranteed that women who were placed on jobs normally done by men and who fulfilled all of the responsibilities normally carried out by male workers would receive the full rate for the job. For those women who did less than was expected of male workers on the same job, a new rate would be established beginning with the existing minimum women's rate. After a training period of at least a month, and after consulting the union, management would establish a maximum rate based on the work done by male employees in the same position. As a protective measure, however, the union and the company agreed that any men's jobs held by women would revert to male employees after the war.[33]

John Burke informed all locals of this policy in August 1942. It was reconfirmed periodically thereafter, and the locals in Milwaukee adhered to the policy. As the Women's Bureau found elsewhere, this union acted on the assumption that the employment of women on men's jobs was a temporary wartime phenomenon and that the most pressing need was to protect male wage rates from being undercut by women workers. Leaders of the Pulp and Sulphite Workers Union prided themselves on running a reasonable, responsible labor organization. This image was conveyed through their willingness to sanction the simplification of jobs so that women could do them during the emergency, but they carefully provided for the elimination of female workers when the war was over. The union also consistently maintained the practice of discriminatory wage rates for women's and men's jobs. Walter Trautmann and Valeria Brodzinski negotiated numerous contracts that specified a base rate differential of more than ten cents an hour between men and women. Contracts negotiated during the war seldom rectified this discrimination, for the raises granted men were often several cents an hour more than those granted women. As a consequence, the inequity tended to grow, despite increased numbers of women in the workforce.[34]

The perpetuation of wage rate discrimination and of women's jobs provided a common denominator for working women no matter whether they were employed in a large or a small shop, or were represented by the AFL or the CIO. In 1942, for example, the AFL union at International Harvester's Milwaukee plant agreed to a minimum wage of eighty-five cents for men and seventy-five cents for women. The company's CIO unions at other plants across the country agreed to the same provision.[35]

The problem clearly crossed corporate lines as well. In the spring of 1942, the National Association of Manufacturers (NAM) surveyed 550 corporate executives nationwide. Based on the responses, William Witherow, president of NAM, concluded that women were worth "equal pay for equal performance," and "that there is little difference between men and women as regards their satisfactory performance in industry." Nonetheless, Witherow suggested that there were inherent limits to female participation in factory work. The executives seemed to agree that women were unsuited for "dirty, dusty, hot or wet" jobs, that they needed help with lifting and machine setups, that they had a shorter industrial life, suffered fatigue more easily, and had a higher rate of absenteeism than men.[36] The Wisconsin Manufacturers' Association reported similar conclusions drawn by the Bureau of Employment Security, which found that women were easier to supervise than men and that employment of female workers reduced the number of accidents, the labor turnover rate, and the number of damaged tools. Based on these findings, the *Weekly Bulletin* concluded that women made good employees despite the fact that they tired more easily and exhibited more of a negative reaction to noise, dirt, and noxious fumes than did their male counterparts. When companies accommodated these perceived weaknesses, the *Bulletin* concluded, women made excellent workers.[37]

Ironically, such accommodation also made it easy to rationalize away concerns regarding equal pay. The *Milwaukee Journal* routinely aired views similar to those of the business community. On one occasion, for example, the paper cited several experts who believed that women possessed approximately half the strength, were more sensitive to criticism, tired more easily, and had less mechanical aptitude than men.[38]

Discrimination often stemmed from the perception that women were less skilled, less productive, and consequently less important than men. When female workers had no male counterparts and worked on women's jobs, the pay rate reflected the view that their jobs were less valuable to the economic activity of the company than were the jobs of male workers. Labor leaders and employers alike accepted the premise that women needed protective legislation, could not master the skills necessary to do the same jobs as men, and would return home when the war was over. On this foundation of assumptions rose an economic system in which women could achieve economic parity with men only if they competed directly with male workers, and then only if the employer failed to alter the job to meet the perceived weaknesses of women workers.

The view that women were inherently less capable than men offered the major loophole in the principle of equal pay for equal work. In practice, because of the assumptions and perceptions employers and union leaders brought to their work, almost anyone who cared to do so could find support for the view that women could not do equal work and therefore did not deserve equal pay. It need hardly be said that few companies arrived at their pay rate for women by any scientific means. When women took men's jobs, their pay often reflected negotiations between the company and the union or was determined by management alone. Seldom was any attempt made to determine the comparability between their work and that of men workers. Most companies studied by the Women's Bureau did not even undertake time studies when determining piece rates. Because of their assumption that women were weaker, less skilled, and less mechanical, many companies simplified the work or assigned a man to do "setups" (i.e., prepare work for a less skilled worker) as soon as a woman arrived on the job. Such precautions automatically precluded equal pay. In addition, few companies compared women's jobs with similar men's jobs to determine whether they were of comparable economic value to the company, and the issue of equal pay seldom arose in this context.[39]

The idea that women were little more than a reserve labor force employed for the duration of the war was one of the most persistent stereotypes that plagued female workers. Indeed, it tended to reinforce the idea that women were relatively unimportant to the postwar economy, and it muted concern for equal pay. In the face of numerous reports to the contrary, the Women's Bureau survey of Milwaukee found men and women alike who were unconcerned about equal pay because of the assumption that most women would return home after the war. When the Wisconsin State Council of the International Association of Machinists met in November of 1942, the machinists seemed to agree that women workers would not be a serious problem after the war. As the minutes recorded, "The thought was expressed that these women were willing for the time being to work in the shop but that they most certainly did not consider making this a life time [sic] condition as they were mainly interested in making a home and settling down."[40] Even in 1945, after numerous polls had reported otherwise, the leaders in Milwaukee's machinists' locals still expected women workers to leave their jobs after the emergency.[41]

This was exactly the misconception the Women's Advisory Committee of the WMC wished to contradict when it issued a strong declaration in 1943:

> The Government and industry must not assume that all women can be treated as the reserve group during war only, nor should those who wish to stay in the labor market be accused of taking men's jobs. The right of the individual woman to work must be recognized and provided for, just as the right of the individual man to work.[42]

Despite such statements, the popular image persisted that women were temporary workers who entered the labor force only for the duration. Nineteen-year-old Theresa Langolf typified this stereotype in Milwaukee. After being trained as a welder by the National Youth Administration, she took a job in the tool room of a war plant. In April 1943 she became the first woman in Wisconsin to pass the army ordnance test for armor-plate welding. Her work was so good that she quickly advanced to highly skilled piece-rate jobs. Yet despite the acclaim she received, she intended "to quit the minute the war is over." As she told a *Journal* reporter,

> When those fellows come home, most likely they will be getting married and will have families to support and I don't think it's fair if they have to stand by while girls do their jobs in the plants.[43]

From the standpoint of many policymakers, Theresa Langolf represented the ideal female worker. She was single, childless, and compliant.

During the first two and a half years of the war the WMC and the USES made little attempt to recruit mothers.[44] The manpower pool remained large enough during those years to fill Milwaukee's industrial needs, and civic leaders clearly opposed any hint that mothers should be drawn away from the home. The nurturing of future generations was considered to be too important to be traded for a short-term gain in the labor force. Indeed, in the minds of many Milwaukee union, industrial, community, and political leaders, World War II was being fought for these future generations. They feared the consequences of large numbers of married women, especially mothers with young children, entering the labor force.

For over a year after the war began, no mother with a small child could read the *Milwaukee Journal* without receiving the message that her place was in the home, serving the needs of her family. The paper conveyed this message most strongly during the fall of 1942. At that time, articles made it clear that the U.S. Department of Labor and the WMC opposed employment of such women as an unnecessary disruption of family life. Indeed, as the government found it necessary to recruit large numbers of women, the WMC amended its manual of operations to formally state that the first responsibility of mothers with young children was "to give suitable care in their own homes to their children." This view also was reflected in an article in which B. H. Thompson of the Milwaukee USES office told readers that it would be preferable to close all nonessential industries and transfer their male workers to war jobs than to employ women with children.[45]

Officials of the Wisconsin Congress of Parents and Teachers, the state's department of public welfare, and the Milwaukee Council of Social Agencies conveyed a similar message during 1942 and the early months of 1943. As far as these leaders were concerned, working mothers posed a fundamental threat to American society. Lester Brown, director of the local WMC, assured Milwaukeeans that an adequate supply of women without young children existed to meet manpower needs; Elizabeth Yerxa of the state welfare office argued that a mother's best war job was in the home.[46]

Milwaukee's social welfare agencies actively discouraged employment of mothers with small children. As Louise Root reported to the executive committee of the Milwaukee Community Fund and Council of Social Agencies:

> Industry has been contacted with a request that they not employ women with children under two, that women with children under 6 not be employed until production makes this absolutely necessary, that women with children not be employed on night shifts and that they keep us informed of the trends so that plans can be made.[47]

The message was clear: government leaders and child-care specialists alike expected mothers of young children to protect their children and to preserve the family for the future. To do otherwise, they feared, would be catastrophic for society and might result in winning the war at the expense of America's future.

The editors of the *Milwaukee Journal* reinforced the message. Frequently the paper opposed measures such as the establishment of day nurseries for the children of women who wanted to perform war work but were otherwise confined to the home with child-care duties. As far as the *Journal* was concerned, nothing should be done to encourage the movement of mothers with small children into factories. To solve the growing manpower shortage, the paper urged women with light household duties to take war jobs. Even the employment of sixteen- and seventeen-year-olds seemed preferable to mortgaging the future by recruiting mothers into the factory labor force. On New Year's Eve 1942 the *Journal* urged the community to "go slowly" in establishing nursery programs, concluding, "No nursery school can wholly replace a mother's care and no nursery school can get the housework done for a mother who spends half her waking time in a factory." A month later the *Journal* told its readers that

> there is no compelling need for women with minor children to leave their home responsibilities for war work. . . . A mother's first duty, in the absence of compelling need elsewhere, is to her young children. A housekeeper for a large family of war workers owes it to those war workers to stay home to prepare food and restful surroundings for her family.[48]

Milwaukee's principal daily simply reflected the views commonly held by government and social service officials. The negative publicity, combined with the primacy of motherhood for many women, produced gradual rather than rapid growth in the number of working mothers with child care duties. By the fall of 1944, employment officials no longer actively discouraged the employment of married women with small children. If a mother of children under the age of fourteen could "make good provisions for their care," she should consider taking a war job. The WMC feared the manpower pool was running dry.[49] As the war drew to a close, 20 percent of working women had children under the age of fourteen. Although the vast majority of working women were single or without small children, attention focused on the guardians of the future, the mothers of young children.[50] Indeed, by definition, a mother who worked outside the home was perceived as neglecting her children. In a report titled "What employment is doing to home life," the Wisconsin Federation of Business and Professional Women's Clubs concluded

> that to protect the health and well being of children, to lay the foundation for a well-balanced emotional and intellectual life for children so that they may be equipped to meet the stress of life, women with young children have a first responsibility to their family.[51]

In contrast to many dire predictions, home and family remained abiding concerns for many of the women who donned overalls to fill the void left by men entering the armed forces. The fact that approximately 3.7 million married women and mothers went to work during World War II seldom implied a rejection of their home duties. Indeed, for many women workers this fact simply meant that they worked two jobs instead of one. Far from abandoning their families, married women workers carried out their normal household chores in addition to working full shifts in factories. They prepared the meals, did the wash, went shopping, and looked after the needs of husbands and children. Unfortunately, public officials did little to ease the burden borne by working wives, a phenomenon the officials clearly viewed as temporary.[52] The reaction of social service agents, the press, union representatives and industrialists to the problems faced by many working women in Milwaukee made it clear that they expected married women, particularly with children under the age of fourteen, to return home when the war was over.

Of particular concern to policymakers was the fear that women doing two jobs could not properly nurture families. Stories in the *Milwaukee Journal* and *Milwaukee Sentinel* publicized the fact that wives and mothers across America suffered under the double burden of housework and factory work. This load could become oppressive for the woman worker. When the Chain Belt Company proposed to meet its contract commitments by implementing ten-hour work shifts six days a week, women members of United Steelworkers Local 1527 opposed the change in schedule. The women complained that such a schedule would make it impossible to conduct their household duties, and they demanded that the company hire available black women to solve its manpower shortage. In addition, they denounced a rumor—allegedly spread by the company—that they would not work with blacks.[53]

The Chain Belt workers provided a dramatic example of the problems facing women who worked two jobs, but in most cases the problem was expressed in subtler ways. Bakeries in Milwaukee, for example, noticed a 15 percent increase in sales, attributable in part to women workers who bought bread instead of baking it themselves. Other service establishments such as lunch counters and ready-made clothing stores noticed similar increases in their business. Likewise, the Milwaukee Better Laundries urged women workers to take advantage of its services. The company's advertising suggested that 20 percent of Canada's war plant absenteeism was caused by women who stayed home to do the daily wash; thus, every laundry worker released the equivalent of eight women for full-time war work. Whether the figures were accurate, the advertisement provided a graphic portrayal of the problems posed for women who did double duty as worker and homemaker.[54]

Although the rise in "double duty" workers resulted in increased business for certain service and retail industries, it also resulted in increased absenteeism and turnover just as the ad suggested. Based on information supplied by 16,000 factories, the WMC concluded that for every two women hired in October 1943, a third woman quit her job in a war plant. Observers on the national and local level agreed that the highest turnover occurred among workers unaccustomed to the regimen of the factory. Obviously, this included a large number of women, and manpower agencies suggested better training and exit interviews as possible ways to curb job turnover. Repeatedly during the last six months of 1943 the Milwaukee USES office studied the problem and concluded on each occasion that women left the workforce because they could not "withstand shop conditions" or because of family responsibilities.

In many cases, the USES believed absenteeism was simply a less serious manifestation of the same problems causing turnover. This was particularly true with women. As studies had found in Milwaukee and across the country, illness was the major cause of absenteeism. After illness, home problems were the most significant cause for women taking time off from work. During the fall of 1943 Milwaukee women showed a higher absence rate than men, and the USES attributed this poorer record to the problems inherent in maintaining a job and a home simultaneously.[55]

Unfortunately, the solutions proposed to ease the burden faced by many women workers fell far short of what was needed. Exit interviews conducted by company personnel departments succeeded in keeping some women on the job, but this was a persuasive tool and never really solved the problems posed by doing double duty. The CIO women's auxiliary studied the problem and submitted a program of sweeping solutions to the Women's Advisory Committee of the WMC. The CIO group concluded that many women left work or were absent because they needed time for basic duties such as shopping. The auxiliary suggested extended evening hours for stores, banks, doctors, beauty parlors, dentists, ration boards, and other similar establishments to enable workers to conduct daily business without skipping work. To assure that stores would have the supplies needed for a nutritious diet, the women's organization proposed reserving certain stores specifically for workers. In addition, the auxiliary noted the low quality of eating places near factories. For workers seeking nutritious meals, such establishments hindered the war effort. The Women's Auxiliary suggested that restaurants be established near factories where workers could get good, low-cost meals, and where working women could even pick up pre-cooked meals to take home to their families. Finally, the CIO women told the WMC that women were leaving their war jobs because of poor provisions for day-care and little knowledge of existing day-care facilities. Better facilities were needed.

Essentially, the CIO auxiliary suggested that the support system necessary to help women stay on the job did not exist. The solutions they proposed, however, often were institutionally oriented, and community institutions in Milwaukee were ill-prepared to meet the challenge. A few stores extended their hours, some factories established eating facilities, and Rhea Manufacturing Company even provided a beauty salon for its workers, but such examples were rare. In many ways, when women received support so they could continue working, it came from family, friends, and neighbors and not from any official, institutional, or organized source.[56]

Opposition to mothers working often meant that local institutions responded slowly to the needs of this group of workers despite stories of "latchkey children," poor child rearing practices, and juvenile delinquency, which raised questions about the future of America's youth. When the Works Progress Administration (WPA) sought to expand its nursery program in Milwaukee County, the board of supervisors reacted coldly. They neither wanted to encourage mothers to work nor wanted to shoulder the financial burden of running the program. Despite WPA assurances that the new child care facilities would operate on federal funds and user fees, County Supervisor Eugene Warnimont feared that the federal government eventually would withdraw its support and leave the nurseries "in the county's lap." As far as Warnimont was concerned, child care was a family matter. If the family could not handle the problem, then local communities should work to solve it. The county, however, should not get involved. Besides, Warnimont argued, married women with children were taking jobs from single women who needed them. The majority of his fellow board members seemed to agree. Several months later the supervisors accepted the concept of day-care in principle, but they remained adamant in the belief that local communities, not the county, should sponsor such facilities.[57]

The county board's reluctance to get involved in a day-care program only served to underscore the ineptness with which local institutions approached the program. After urging by federal officials, the Milwaukee County Defense Council and the Milwaukee Council of Social Agencies formed the joint Committee on the Care of Children of Working Mothers. As it sought to determine the needs of the community, the child-care committee acted on the philosophy that:

> Women with small children can make no finer contribution to the Nation than to remain in their homes, offering their children that love and care and security which only they can offer. The Nation should not recruit for industrial production the services of women with young children, except as a last resort.[58]

As late as February 1943, the committee continued to discourage companies from employing mothers, and had made little progress in assessing or meeting the needs of the community. During the first fifteen months of the war, the committee made two attempts to gauge the need for child care, but produced little usable information. Between April 1942 and April 1943 the committee solicited weekly reports from twenty-five health and welfare agencies regarding requests they received for assistance and the child-care needs they had observed. Only fifteen responded, many sporadically. To further skew the results, almost 60 percent of the reports came from the Family Welfare Association, which served as a screening agency for the Volunteers of America Day Nursery.[59]

Starting in the fall of 1942 the committee also sent questionnaires to 150 factories in Milwaukee. Approximately one-third responded to all questions. These fifty-four plants reported employing 12,396 women, of whom 2,103 (17 percent) had children. Fifty-nine companies answered the question regarding the satisfactory provision of care for the children of the women employed by the company. Only four thought parental arrangements were inadequate, compared with thirty plants that viewed the arrangements as satisfactory and twenty-five that had no information regarding the home situation of their employees. Unfortunately, the estimation of satisfactory arrangements was based only on the company's perception of the issue, and no attempt was made to determine the number of children of preschool age nor the manner of their care.[60]

As the Committee on the Care of Children of Working Mothers fumbled with its needs assessment, the city's four WPA day-care centers went out of business with their parent agency, leaving only six centers to serve Milwaukee. One of these centers was run by the West Allis school system, two by private secular organizations and three by religious organizations. When it became evident late in 1942 that the WPA would be eliminated and its day-care centers would be left without funding, no local sponsor came forward to save them. Under the Lanham Act, federal funding could be secured for the child-care facilities upon application by a "responsible" local sponsor such as a board of education or a mayor. The WPA centers had been housed in school buildings and attention immediately turned to the school board as the logical sponsor, but the board refused. The demands of angry citizens, civic organizations, civil defense units, and social service agencies could not convince the board members to commit the school system's financial resources to care for the children of women in war plants. Milton Potter, school superintendent, also questioned whether the taxpayers wanted their system to operate four centers for such a narrow constituency. Ultimately, the WPA nurseries closed for lack of a sponsor. Organizations such as the Milwaukee League of Women Voters, the Milwaukee Industrial Union Council (CIO), and the Milwaukee Council of Social Agencies pressured the Board of Education to absorb the centers, but no one volunteered as a sponsor when the board members refused.[61]

Shortly after the demise of the WPA nurseries, the Council of Social Agencies and the Defense Council concluded that further study was necessary "to learn more specifically to what extent the care of children of working mothers actually is a problem in this community." As a result, they hired Mary Kiely as Child Care Coordinator.[62] She immediately studied the needs of factory women directly, and the city acquired useful information regarding local child care needs. In June 1943 she instituted a new industrial survey, and interviewed twenty-six executives, employment directors, or personnel people in twenty-four companies. Thirteen of the companies perceived or anticipated a problem regarding child care for their women employees, but eleven companies observed no such problem. The employers generally were willing to make adjustments in working hours to accommodate a mother's home duties, but few believed it was their responsibility to provide child care facilities. As far as the industrial representatives were concerned, this was the community's responsibility.

Unlike earlier industrial surveyors, Kiely also reported direct information from 974 women in ten companies. Working mothers completed 808 of these reports, while one company filed 166 questionnaires based on its own files. For the first time, Milwaukee officials possessed statistical information upon which to base decisions. The 952 mothers who reported the number of children in their family averaged slightly under two children per mother. Out of 1,610 children whose ages were reported, 25 percent were preschoolers, 56 percent were between the ages of six and fifteen, and the remaining 19 percent were above the age of fifteen. Perhaps the most significant result of the survey was the finding that only 11 percent of the mothers were dissatisfied with the child-care arrangements they had made, and these women tended to work on the evening or night shift. In other words, the overwhelming majority of working mothers were satisfied with their child-care arrangements. The women who were displeased tended to work shifts during times when organized day-care, which might have helped to alleviate their concern, was unavailable. Out of 824 reports that indicated the type of care being provided, only 1 percent of the mothers reported that they used a day nursery. By contrast, 46 percent of the women relied on relatives; 11 percent employed a housekeeper, left the children with the landlady, or relied on a friend or neighbor; and in 3 percent of the cases the father and mother worked complementary schedules.

From her study of the problem, Kiely concluded that school-aged children posed the most serious child-care problem because they comprised the largest group of children of working mothers, and because these mothers had shown much less concern for the care of school-aged children than for their preschoolers. In addition, Kiely concluded that child-care problems would become more serious as companies hired more mothers, and that the community was ill-equipped to meet the needs of these women and their families. She recommended that the School Board be informed of her findings, that greater publicity be given to the needs of school-age children, that industry be brought into the planning process, and that the Child Care Committee begin thinking "in terms of general overall social planning for children."

With one exception, Mary Kiely's conclusions and recommendations simply reinforced what seemed to be the common wisdom among social agencies and the Child Care Committee. Unfortunately, her most significant conclusion was buried among ten others and did not form the basis for any final recommendation. Based on her direct survey of almost 1,000 working mothers, she concluded, "most mothers make arrangements which are satisfactory to themselves for the care of their children, and . . . in the final analysis the mother is the deciding factor in the arrangements that they are able to make for the care of their children."[63]

During the last four months of 1943, Kiely devoted much of her attention to following up on the recommendations made in her August report. She remained concerned over the lack of planning and facilities for adequate child care, but her work also reinforced the conviction that there was little public demand for such services. As she prepared to follow her husband, who had been transferred from his military post in Milwaukee, Mary Kiely submitted her final report to the child-care committee and found it difficult to reconcile her belief in the need for institutional child-care services with the fact that there was so little public demand for those services, Although she noted that professional social workers continued to express concern about the situation, their concern was not reflected by the general public. The social workers, she concluded, reflected "real need in terms of adequate standards." The lack of public concern "more accurately measures demand and acceptance." Existing day-care facilities remained underused, and a modified foster home program, inaugurated with great publicity, was discontinued when no women sought this solution to their child-care problems. Despite encouragement, not one of the women who expressed dissatisfaction with child-care arrangements ever contacted Mary Kiely for assistance. A survey of Milwaukee's schools indicated that 20 percent of the city's mothers were working full time by the middle of 1943, similar to the national average. With this level of employment, the public demand for day-care programs and facilities fell far short of what she perceived the actual need to be. As far as she could tell, social workers erroneously assumed that mothers wanted and needed help with child care problems, that parents misunderstood what constituted "adequate care," and that the community remained hostile to working mothers and to the concept of community responsibility for the children of such women. In short, although welfare officials perceived a pressing need for formal child-care facilities, parents did not perceive such a need, and the "culture of this community" inspired apathy or hostility to such programs.[64]

Further attempts were made to analyze the needs of working mothers and their children during 1944, but little was ever accomplished. Although existing programs continued to be underused, the Council of Social Agencies remained concerned that local needs were going unmet. The problem seemed beyond an institutional solution, and the organization's annual report explained, "The widely divergent ages of children, the work shifts, the place of residence, the place of work, all showed the difficulties of making plans in specific areas."[65]

By the summer of 1944 the Committee on Care of Children of Working Mothers was moribund, and was never revived. A local WMC survey of several major companies found an ongoing lack of corporate concern for day-care facilities, and the Council of Social Agencies decided against pressuring the Board of Education for use of a school building.[66]

Only the Milwaukee State Teachers College made an active attempt to alleviate the problem that the Defense Council and the social agencies spent so much time studying. With Lanham Act funding, the college opened its first nursery for thirty children of women war workers in July 1944. The program was so successful that the college opened a second center in January and a third in February 1945, both of which thrived.[67] Why the college's centers met with such a favorable response while other day-care facilities were underused remains a mystery. It may have been related to the positive publicity the centers received in the daily press; it may have been their location; it may have been the timing of their opening late in the war when husbands were being drafted and greater numbers of mothers entered the workforce.

Certainly some people availed themselves of the services offered by Milwaukee's child-care facilities, but most did not. Dorothy Keating worked as a coil winder at Allis-Chalmers and remembers, "They didn't have that many small nurseries in those days. If there were small babies and the women wanted to go to work, there'd be women in the neighborhood that would take them in and maybe some women would have six, seven babies or small ones."[68] Nellie Wilson had the same personal experience. A single parent with two small children, she went to work for A. O. Smith in 1943, and an older neighbor volunteered to watch her children. "She stayed with those kids until they [were] eleven and thirteen. . . . she was like a grandmother to them."[69]

Rose Kaminski also turned to an older woman for help. She remembers:

One of the women in the neighborhood was taking care of children for mothers that were in the service and she was up in her years. I would say she was about 65—an old grandmother—a little German woman who was just wonderful. . . .

This is where my daughter stayed. I don't think I would have gone into any work had I not been able to leave her with somebody as fine as this woman was. She devoted her time just to the children and in her old German brogue she always used to say, "I know that I am needed."[70]

Although the city's social agencies and its CIO unions repeatedly emphasized the need for more such assistance to working women, mothers in Milwaukee seemed to prefer their own arrangements to those made for them. Neighborhoods and kinship networks were little influenced by the war for this was not a boom town comparable to Willow Run or Seattle.[71] Milwaukee's economy thrived during the war, but its social fabric remained intact. Mothers who wished to work turned to their friends and relatives to solve the problem of child care. Social service workers may have disagreed with some of these arrangements, but they were satisfactory to the women involved. For Milwaukee, a large, well-developed system of day-care centers was unnecessary.

For the woman worker, the war provided greater opportunities than ever before. Her labor was essential to winning the war, but her participation in the workforce did not mark a fundamental change in the roles society expected her to play. Newspaper editors, government officials, employers, and union leaders reminded women that their first duty remained to serve their families. This basic message applied not only to mothers, but in many cases to married women in general.

The debate over women working permeated most discussions of postwar America and of reconversion to peacetime production. Few of the answers were simple, for any equitable solution required compromise and acceptance of fundamental changes in the social order. In August 1942 the *Milwaukee Journal* noted that many employers wanted their new women workers, who had proved to be efficient and competent employees, to continue working after the war. The *Journal* editorialized that such a development would "mean a major change in our social-industrial setup." The paper did not anticipate such a change occurring. Instead, it expected a repeat of the World War I experience, when servicemen returned to their old jobs and women returned home.[72] Over a year later, the *Journal* cited a *McCall's* magazine survey of women in several Detroit war plants to emphasize its view of the future role of women in America. Eighty-nine percent of the female workers surveyed believed a woman's proper place was in the home. "If this means anything," the *Journal* concluded, "it means that women by and large are unchanged by the war. Their present employment is emergency employment—nothing more. When the emergency is over, women will continue to work before marriage and will give up their jobs when they marry."[73]

Several months later the Milwaukee daily noted new evidence that contrasted sharply with the Detroit survey. Recent studies had indicated that as many as 71 percent of women workers intended to seek postwar employment. Although its editors accepted the right of women to work, the *Journal* predicated the exercise of this right on the ability of industry to provide such employment. Certainly, it suggested, the problem was difficult. To provide full employment for men alone would be a hard task. In addition, the paper worried about the survival of the American home and family "if great numbers of women no longer propose to sustain them."[74]

The *Journal*'s comments were indicative of the problems facing women as the war wound down. Most political, business, and labor leaders assumed at the beginning of the war that women would return home when peace finally came. Some surveys as late as October 1944, tended to support such a view. After taking an unofficial survey, the *Journal* reported: "Out of a cross-section of girls doing men's work in Milwaukee, about 99 percent of those interviewed said that they'd gladly give up their 'careers' for the role of housewife and mother."[75]

As the war progressed through its third year, surveys increasingly indicated that the majority of women wished to continue working after the war. Muriel Klein, a Milwaukee department store window designer, typified the attitudes of single women workers. "Certainly I hope to get married someday," she told an interviewer, "but I'd like to keep on with this work, too. I'm prepared to give the job up when the man whose place I took comes back for it, but I hope I can make a place for myself."[76]

To those critics who assumed that an inherent conflict existed between women workers and returning service personnel, Freda Miller, director of the Women's Bureau, explained that women respected the rights of returning soldiers, but they would continue to work even if it meant changing jobs. A variety of reports issued by women labor leaders, the Women's Bureau, and the WMC emphasized that women could not and should not be considered simply an emergency labor reserve to be discarded when the war ended. The women labor leaders did not expect women to be given preference over veterans, but to be treated the same as their male counterparts who were hired to meet emergency manpower needs.[77]

The Women in Industry Committee, chaired by Agnes Nestor of the International Glove Workers Union, warned of the consequences if labor ignored women's concerns and rights in the postwar era:

> There is a danger and a threat to the wage scale and working conditions in failure to establish the wage for the job rather than for the sex of the worker. . . . If unorganized through lack of union protection of their rights and interests, through ignorance, and through necessity, they will involuntarily become a brake on progress and a potential threat to all wage scales.[78]

Unfortunately, these labor leaders controlled neither corporations nor local unions. Women bore the brunt of the layoffs as Milwaukee companies

canceled contracts in preparation for the end of the war. They held low seniority, were recorded on separate seniority lists, or were employed heavily in industries created to meet specific wartime needs. The WMC's attempts to wring
male workers out of nonessential jobs paid off early in 1945, and employers
showed an immediate preference for hiring these men instead of women. The
USES reported that women continued to be in demand to replace workers
drawn into the armed forces, if men were unavailable. In July the Allis-
Chalmers' Supercharger plant and the Signal Battery Company each laid off almost 1,900 women as the plants ended production work. Although new employers immediately hired these experienced workers, they held the lowest
seniority on their new jobs and could expect little security when the war ended.
One Milwaukee company even began advertising for only male workers. The
level of experience was immaterial, but the company clearly did not want female applicants. The Nordberg Company went one step further. As soon as the
war ended, it fired all of its female production employees and reverted to a prewar pattern of hiring only men for such positions.[79]

Although Nordberg was extreme, the first months of peace offered little
encouragement to many women who wished to continue their industrial jobs.
The right of a single woman to participate in industrial work seemed to be generally accepted by the end of the war, but the influx of millions of married
women and mothers did not secure any general consensus on their right to
work. When Japan surrendered in September 1945, Milwaukee factories laid off
approximately 20,000 workers. By the end of September departure from the
paid labor force or reemployment had reduced the number of workers in the
labor market to approximately 10,000, and the USES reported that reconversion was almost completed in Milwaukee. Nonetheless, women comprised
more than 55 percent of the 10,000 workers who remained unemployed. Milwaukee companies told the USES that they would need a net of 8,947 workers
by the middle of November, but these companies expected to reemploy a net of
only 1,039 women during this time. The federal employment agency concluded
that "marginal" workers (housewives, young people, older and retired workers) comprised the majority of the unemployed. Male and female workers alike
in this group faced a labor market unfavorable to their reemployment. Once
sought after to fill the manpower shortage, these "marginal" workers found
employers tightening their hiring requirements as a surplus of workers developed. In addition, the non-manufacturing jobs that were available were unat-
tractive in comparison to the pay rate once earned in war plants.[80]

For the woman worker, especially the erstwhile housewife, the war had
brought unprecedented economic opportunities. She had performed well in
many jobs once considered the sole prerogative of men. Without question, her
participation in the workforce loosened the bonds restraining female economic
activity. Still, the bonds never really broke. Society continued to define
women's roles in terms of family duties, employers still preferred male workers,
and unions remained more concerned with the needs of male members than
with those of female members. In the final analysis, employers and unions alike

failed to implement any system that might have protected the economic rights of women. They were more concerned with protecting the wage rates of male workers and the seniority of servicemen.

The problem was unlikely to yield to any easy solution. Servicemen had a legal right to their old jobs. Plant-wide seniority systems would have eliminated some discriminatory practices, but in many cases women remained at the bottom of seniority lists and would have been transferred to their old jobs or laid off anyway. In addition, there was no consensus among women workers themselves regarding their basic rights. Few would have argued that they had any preemptive rights over returning veterans. Likewise, Milwaukee women workers did not hold one common view of their postwar role in the economy. Many women wished to continue working, but there were signs that they would give up their jobs in favor of raising a family.

The right to work was given lip service, but the socially acceptable role for a wife and mother remained the home. As the Women's Bureau survey of Midwestern factories had shown, union leaders and members generally adhered to this view. Men remained the accepted breadwinners, and unions acted to protect their interests. Even if women had held a common view of their own rights, they never held the power necessary to implement such a view. In the end, they were at the mercy of contract cutbacks, employer predilections for male workers, union concern for the economic security of male members, and social stereotypes that continued to define women as the preservers and protectors of social values. The future of the economy remained uncertain as the war drew to a close, and few people were willing to defend the rights of the "reserve labor force" against the rights of millions of veterans and of male breadwinners.

The debate over the role of women in the postwar economy not only reflected deeply held social values regarding the proper place of women in American society, but moreover it reflected lingering concerns for the role and economic welfare of male workers in that society. The debate over women's roles illustrated one of the subtler wartime social tensions through which we see industrial conflict more clearly.

CHAPTER SIX

WAR'S END

As Allied armies marched toward victory in Europe and Asia, there seemed every reason to believe that a new era of full employment and prosperity was about to dawn. Business surveys conducted by the Association of Commerce provided reassurance that Milwaukee's economic future would not return to the depression that had preceded the war. Well before the invasion of Normandy in June of 1944, the association issued a report, based on 1,052 questionnaires returned by industrial and commercial establishments in Milwaukee County, which estimated that local firms would employ approximately 248,500 people when full peacetime production resumed. To be sure, this estimate represented a reduction in the workforce of over 40,000 from the employment level of April 1944; but it also represented an increase of 27 percent over the employment level in 1940. Not only did there seem to be no hint of a depression in the making; on the contrary, the figures seemed to herald an unprecedented era of prosperity. As the end of the war drew nearer and as companies supplied more accurate information on their postwar employment plans, the Association of Commerce periodically revised its estimates. In July of 1945, with the defeat of Japan a little over a month away, the association surveyed county businesses again and issued an even more optimistic forecast. The postwar workforce was likely to reach 255,000, over 30 percent higher than in 1940. Given the nationally recognized goal of an economy capable of employing 60 million people, such an increase represented a fair step toward full employment in Milwaukee.[1]

Unfortunately, these same reports of the Association of Commerce also contained seeds of anxiety about the future. For example, the estimated future employment levels fell far short of the peak reached in November of 1943, and the association predicted that the sharpest decline would occur in Milwaukee's largest war industries. From a sample of 192 manufacturing firms, analysts predicted in April 1944 that retooling for civilian production would require an average of five months, during which unemployment would rise sharply. Particularly alarming was the fact that sixty-five companies—each of which employed more than 500 workers and accounted for over 105,000 wartime employees—reported that retooling would cut their workforce by 37.6 percent. After returning to full peacetime production, these firms expected to employ only 66,500 workers.[2]

For organized labor, such statistics raised troubling questions. What were industrial workers to do during the retooling process, and where were surplus workers to go when their skills were no longer needed by industry?

The surplus worker problem, analysts and businessmen agreed, might solve itself. Students would return to school; older workers would go back to retirement and women to their homes. In contrast to numerous surveys indicating that women wanted to continue in the workforce, business projections assumed that they would leave for the kitchen as soon as the war ended. In part, this was a self-fulfilling assumption, because industrial employers did not intend to continue employing women to the extent required during wartime. During the retooling process, planners also expected some unemployed workers to return to their old jobs in the commercial sector. Others would find work on municipal construction projects designed to cushion the blow of reconversion. Such estimates never became very well defined, and many workers could expect to endure temporary unemployment that might last a few days or a few months. Overall, this widespread certainty about some level of reconversion unemployment seemed uncomfortably like the prelude to a new depression.[3]

Shortly after V-E Day, CIO leaders asked Julius Krug of the War Production Board what would happen to the millions of workers who were being laid off. Krug responded, "Why they'll go back to what they were doing before." The *CIO News* replied indignantly,

> And from the absence of any national policy on reconversion unemployment, there appears to be more truth than poetry in what he has to say. Have we forgotten so soon that there were around ten million people pounding the pavements for jobs before the nation embarked upon war production?[4]

On August 14, 1945, the *Milwaukee Journal*'s headline announced in huge type "War Ended! Truman Tells Nation." The war was over. The time to convert the economy to peaceful pursuits had arrived. The nation's labor federations greeted the news with joy, but looked with a sense of bitterness at the problems facing America. Workers faced unemployment, industrial cutbacks, and decreased pay. Congress had failed to act in a manner labor felt satisfactory, and the country seemed on the verge of replaying the post–World War I experience. The *Milwaukee Labor Press* warned its readers that organized labor must not be complacent in the face of growing threats to labor's rights. The *CIO News* was equally strident in its demands for immediate action as it contemplated the future of American workers. After hailing victory over Japan, the paper told its readers,

> AND THEN COMES TOMORROW. Tomorrow is already here as the immediate cancellation of war contracts throws thousands of workers out of jobs in the state and leaves millions jobless in the nation.
>
> Tomorrow is here, and workers are clamoring for protection for the jobless days they will spend while machines that built weapons of war are swapped for those to build implements for peace.
>
> But there is no protection for them, nor any promise that the jobless period will be brief. Private industry has no program and Congress is on vacation.
>
> In short we have come upon tomorrow unprepared.
>
> The end of the war has brought great joy. But it also has brought great concern. For as millions of soldiers pack up to come home, their chances for jobs and security fade.
>
> Something must be done now—while the memory of the war is still fresh in our minds—to safeguard the security of our people.[5]

One week after V-J Day, almost 8,000 people stood outside the Milwaukee unemployment compensation office, waiting to fill out the forms that would help get them through a bad patch. As the government canceled contracts and companies closed plants, the fears that had fueled much of the industrial conflict during the war seemed to be coming to life. Each issue of Milwaukee's daily papers carried stories of unemployment. A. O. Smith alone laid off almost 6,000 workers late in August as it closed its plants to prepare for the production of water heaters, oil pipes, and automobile frames. Some industrial concerns, most notably the Signal Battery Company and the Froemming Brothers Shipyard, closed forever; they had been created for wartime production, and the government no longer needed their products. Thousands of workers registered with the United States Employment Service (USES) each day during the two weeks following the surrender of Japan.[6]

Despite routine accounts of unemployment, however, Milwaukee's daily papers also published stories that more accurately foretold the future course of the economy. As was the national pattern, many Milwaukee-area factories barely stopped production as they shifted from war matériel to consumer commodities. Clearly, these companies had been planning for reconversion. The depletion of consumer goods such as shoes, clothes, furniture, candy, and beer guaranteed immediate production for those plants that required little alteration as they shifted from war to civilian contracts. Even industrial concerns such as Harnischfeger awaited only the cancellation of their government contracts and the easing of controls on raw materials before producing for the civilian market. A. O. Smith also rapidly converted part of its production facility to peacetime pursuits. The same technology that had produced bomb casings could be used to produce pipes with only minor alterations. Likewise, the Square D Company's electrical control equipment remained in demand even as the federal government canceled military orders. With virtually no production changes required, the company began filling civilian orders that had accumulated during the last months of the war.[7]

Because many of Milwaukee's factories quickly converted their production facilities to domestic use, male workers immediately found new employment or returned to their old jobs. Although the Signal Battery plant and the Froemming Brothers Shipyard were spawned by the war and died with the end of the war, Milwaukee was not a boom town that had been turned upside-down by the conflict; its factories had existed before the war and drew workers primarily from local sources. Milwaukee industry and male workers therefore suffered relatively little dislocation. By October 1, 1945, the USES could report that reconversion in Milwaukee was almost completed.

For women workers, however, reconversion was not over, and the debate over the proper role of women in American society took on a new urgency. Many women who had entered the workforce during the war willingly returned to their household pursuits. Among them were the workers at the Signal Battery plant who had been hired after vigorous recruiting. The USES noted that they seemed to have left the workforce without even filing for unemployment. Working on behalf of the Fair Employment Practices Committee, Joy Schultz hypothesized that many of the women at Signal Battery were attracted to the plant because of its proximity to their middle-class neighborhood, and they went home without any fuss when the plant closed.

On the other hand, for those women who chose or needed to remain in the workforce, the immediate employment picture was bleak. At the end of September, approximately 10,000 people were in the labor market. Of these, more than 5,500 were women, and there seemed to be little demand for their labor in the industrial workforce. The demand for male workers remained strong, but the USES estimated that between September 15 and November 15 a net of only 1,040 women would be needed to meet industrial requirements. The agency assumed that most of the women in the labor market would find employment in non-manufacturing fields. In other words, women would return to a more traditional niche in the economy; they would either go home or seek clerical and retail jobs.[8]

In addition to the problems associated with reconversion of the economy to civilian production, V-J Day brought an end to the physical and psychological controls that had helped to keep labor conflict confined in non-disruptive channels. As both kinds of controls lifted, the nature of wartime industrial conflict became all too apparent. Arguing that sustained postwar recovery depended on the maintenance of workers' buying power, both labor federations—hoping to improve basic wage rates by 20 to 30 percent—demanded a return to free collective bargaining. With the end of the war and cancellation of the no-strike pledge, work stoppages skyrocketed. During the last four months of 1945, the number of work days lost through strikes exceeded 28.4 million—more than double the time lost during all of 1943, the war's worst year for strikes. Organized labor was stirring and flexing its muscles, as if to say that it was time to regain what it had given up in the name of national unity.[9]

Frank Ranney, general secretary of the Milwaukee Federated Trades Council, once warned that organized labor must carefully guard its rights, and the interests of its members, during the war, or risked losing gains won by decades of hard work. He had told readers of the *A.F. of L. Labor Press*

> Eternal vigilance is the watchword, if labor is to maintain its advances in the peace era to follow. It took long years of hard fighting, with organization—unions—to win as much as is possessed today. Tomorrow, when the war is over, the battle will be renewed by labor's foes, and the workers must be ready to fight to meet the onslaught, and drive back the attackers.[10]

Three disputes typified postwar conflict in Milwaukee. On the first of September 1,600 workers staged a spontaneous sit-down strike at the Heil Company to protest arbitrary changes in wage rates and a variety of other unnamed grievances that had been festering for some time.[11]

The Heil dispute was short-lived, but a strike by the Fabricated Metal Workers Union at Geuder, Paeschke and Frey was not. When the union began negotiating the 1945–1946 contract, a War Labor Board decision was still pending on wage rates for the 1944–1945 contract. The union hoped to secure a company commitment to honor the 1944–1945 contract wage rates recommended by the WLB panel. Instead, Geuder, Paeschke and Frey refused to make any commitments and proposed a ninety-day delay while it sought price increases from the Office of Price Administration. With no hope of a solution in sight and negotiations stalled, the workers voted overwhelmingly to strike. When they walked out on September 12, they began what proved to be one of Milwaukee's most protracted postwar strikes. After five months of stalemate and two weeks of intense negotiations in February 1946, the company capitulated. Geuder, Paeschke and Frey accepted the seven cents per hour WLB recommendation for the 1944–1945 contract and added five cents per hour for the new contract. The long struggle established a seventy-nine cent hourly minimum and equal pay for equal work for women.[12]

A third dispute, also in September, seemed to bear out many of organized labor's fears. Early in the war, dairy drivers had reluctantly accepted alternate-day delivery schedules imposed by dairies to comply with transportation restrictions. Now, with the war ended, the dairies wanted to maintain this money-saving practice. Officials of Truck Drivers Local 225 feared that the reemployment of veterans would force the layoff of drivers who had worked throughout the war unless the companies returned to a daily delivery schedule. It now appeared that the union would have to fight for the return to a schedule it had given up in support of the war effort.[13]

After the defeat of Japan, the basic conflict that had always existed between companies trying to maximize their profits and workers trying to maintain secure jobs at a livable wage came to life with a vengeance. Workers and unions sought to rebuild wage rates and to regain rights given up for the war effort. When the Japanese bombed Pearl Harbor four years earlier, Americans had united in a common enterprise. Unions relinquished the strike weapon, agreed to forgo double-time pay for Sundays and holidays, and sacrificed work standards. Workers toiled overtime to meet wartime production schedules, donated blood, bought war bonds, and assisted volunteer organizations. All these commitments were made voluntarily by workers and unions nationwide. They were the most visible signs that the country was united and that Americans shared a common patriotic interest in vanquishing the Axis powers.

Nonetheless, more subtle forces placed limits on national unity. Americans did not follow their government blindly. Generally, they accepted wartime controls on food, transportation, and housing because they understood the need to preserve raw materials for the war effort. People may have grumbled about such sacrifice, but they accepted it. They also gave their blood to the Red Cross and loaned their money to the government with the knowledge that both might save lives and end the war more quickly. Such sacrifices were made willingly because they represented a real contribution to the war effort.

On the other hand, Americans would not participate in activities that seemed to be a waste of time no matter how much government officials tried to persuade them to do so. Nowhere was this clearer than in Milwaukee's civil defense program. Situated in the nation's heartland, Milwaukeeans could no more conceive of being struck by an enemy air attack than of being shelled by a submarine in Lake Michigan. Civic leaders, civil defense officials, and military officers repeated a litany of threats, but Milwaukeeans ignored them. The threats made little sense and, after the impact of Pearl Harbor wore off, few people took them seriously. As a consequence, the civil defense system faltered for lack of full community support. In only two areas did civil defense preparation achieve much success: local citizens participated heavily in the air-raid warden program and, more significantly, in the fire protection program. Although the community auxiliary firefighter program failed to attract much support, the parallel project to train factory fire brigades achieved marked success. Few if any believed that Milwaukee would be bombed, but the development of an efficient factory fire brigade made practical sense in peace as well as war. An industrial fire could destroy lives, military supplies, and production capacity. This threat was real, and workers participated in far greater numbers than in the auxiliary firefighting program, which presupposed an enemy attack.

The sacrifices people made in the name of national unity, patriotism, and the war effort also created a sense of tension that pervaded wartime society.

America could not be at ease with itself and be at war at the same time. Too many problems came on the heels of the war, problems for which no solution existed as long as the war continued. Americans wrestled with a complex, often contradictory, mixture of feelings, beliefs, and actions. They understood the need for rationing, but as their paychecks grew ever fatter, they resented it as well. They could understand the need for controls on house construction, but that still left cities like Milwaukee to struggle with inadequate and substandard housing for many workers and minorities. When they at last were able to afford a better place to live, workers discovered they could not find such a place—and minorities found they could not move at all. Able to afford a new car, a refrigerator, new clothes, and better food, workers discovered that wartime controls made it difficult to find many items and impossible to find others.

The government not only restricted the purchase of material goods through rationing but also created a virtual job freeze. As the labor supply tightened, the government increased its controls on a worker's ability to move from one job to another until it achieved by administrative action what the Congress would not legislate. By war's end, a worker in Milwaukee could not change jobs without government approval. Americans made sacrifices every day to promote victory, and they felt good about their contributions to the war effort. At the same time, however, the war brought uncertainty to their lives, an uncertainty that effectively placed limits on national unity.

For the worker, the limits were all too clear. The war, despite providing fat paychecks and steady employment, did little to erase basic disagreements between employers and unions over proper compensation for daily production work and the proper application of contract provisions. The war-induced sense of national unity combined with wartime controls to promote new forms of labor-management cooperation and to alter the form of industrial conflict; but such conflict did not disappear.

Industrial conflict continued to exist despite the war because there was little change in the basic relationship between employers and workers. Employers still sought to maximize profits; workers still sought a secure future. Organized labor's fear of a future depression and its belief that prosperity rested on workers' buying power fueled much of the industrial conflict during World War II.

Workers and unions alike demonstrated the importance of economic security through their reactions to women workers, the cost of living, and industrial relations. By 1943 most people accepted the need for women industrial workers to replace the men drafted into military service. Nonetheless, neither workers nor unions—nor society as a whole, for that matter—expected women to be more than a reserve industrial labor force that would return to its former pursuits in the home, office, and department store at war's end. Women's employment in heavy industry was perceived as a wartime expediency; it was "for the duration," as the saying went. Although some unions fought for equal pay for women, such moves were designed to protect the security of male workers as much as to protect the jobs of newly hired women. Provisions for equal pay protected established wage rates and prevented companies from viewing women workers as a cheaper labor force that could be used to supplant higher-paid male workers or force unions into making wage concessions.

The rising cost of living also presented a real threat to the economic security of wartime workers. Basic wage rates did not keep pace with inflation, and the labor press repeatedly warned union members that unless wages were brought back in line with the cost of goods and services purchased by workers, postwar prosperity would dissolve and another depression would ensue. As far as organized labor was concerned, postwar prosperity depended on the preservation of worker buying power, and much of the wartime industrial conflict in Milwaukee revolved around this issue. Whether measured in terms of wage rates, piece rates, contract enforcement, seniority, grievance processing, or work rules, the workers' preeminent concern during the war was the preservation of economic security. Workers willingly sacrificed many things on behalf of the war effort, but they would not sacrifice their future. The pattern was the same for strikes and mediated disputes. Wages or wage-related issues caused the majority of conflicts in Milwaukee. To be sure, disputes also arose over work rules, non-pay grievances, union jurisdictions, and so on; but these issues trailed far behind wages as the cause of strife between labor and management. Even non-pay issues often could be related to economic security because they involved preservation of established work patterns or of a union's ability to defend its members.

World War II was a time of unity in America, and that unity brought out much of what was best about human nature and American society. But despite the sense of unity, a sense of tension also ran through American society during the war years. It was fueled by the very sacrifices it called forth, by the facts that social problems could not be addressed, and by the fact that the war could not erase inherent divisions between people. This tension helps to explain the labor-management conflict that developed as the cooperative feelings sparked by Pearl Harbor began to fade. The war neither changed the way people thought nor the way they perceived their basic interests. Corporate officials continued to plan for future markets and to advocate restrictive labor legislation. Organized labor continued to fear postwar legislative repression and to advocate controls on corporate profiteering. Given such divisions, it was remarkable that the level of conflict remained as low as it did. By any reasonable standard, organized labor abided by its no-strike pledge. When strikes occurred they tended to be short and spontaneous and reflected the frustration of workers who had found all other avenues closed.

Americans took the war very seriously. To many people whose sons were fighting in European foxholes or on coral islands in the Pacific, strikes by well-paid production workers seemed both incomprehensible and indefensible. And while they worried about husbands and relatives overseas, the press bombarded them daily with news of strikes, work stoppages, slowdowns, jurisdictional disputes, corrupt union bosses, and governmental permissiveness. The leaders of both the AFL and the CIO continually cited statistics that showed how well their unions had kept the no-strike pledge and supported the war effort, but the harsh judgment of the press and the opinion polls remained, a bitter residue of misperception and misunderstanding.

In truth, America's workers felt the same patriotism and the same sense of national unity as did the rest of their countrymen. Such feelings kept workers on the job day after day despite the tensions induced by the war and exacerbated by industrial conflict. By and large, organized labor had fulfilled its commitments to the nation during the war. Union members, male and female, had served in the armed forces, had worked long hours to create the production miracle, and had stayed on the job from the day after Pearl Harbor to the day Japan finally surrendered. Labor had earned the right to be treated as a full partner in American society.

As Milwaukee's first postwar strikes amply illustrated, traditional issues of conflict between labor and management quickly replaced the social and legal controls of wartime and catapulted America toward record work stoppages. In the end, in war and peace, labor's struggle for a secure economic future would be fought on the shop floor and the strike line.

Chapter One: Industrial Giant—Ready for War

1. John Gurda, *The Making of Milwaukee* (Milwaukee: Milwaukee County Historical Society, 1999), 308.
2. As quoted in Frederick Merk, *Economic History of Wisconsin During the Civil War Decade* (Madison: Wisconsin State Historical Society, reprint edition, 1971), 127. See also Bayrd Still, *Milwaukee: The History of a City* (Madison: State Historical Society of Wisconsin, 1948), 180–81. John Gurda, *The Making of Milwaukee*, 75–77, 84, 100, 107–8.
3. Still, *Milwaukee*, 191, 322, 328. Gurda, *Making of Milwaukee*, 113, 128. Roger D. Simon, "The City-Building Process: Housing and Services in New Milwaukee Neighborhoods, 1880–1910," in *Transactions of the American Philosophical Society*, Volume 68, Part 5 (Philadelphia: American Philosphical Society, 1978), 11.
4. Still, *Milwaukee*, 188–9, 332–33. Gurda, *Making of Milwaukee*, 120–22, 161–63.
5. Gurda, *Making of Milwaukee*, 119–20.
6. U.S. Bureau of the Census, *Report of the Manufactures of the United States at the Tenth Census: (June 1, 1880) General Statistics*, xxvi–xxvii and 374–75. See also Gurda, *Making of Milwaukee*, 112–16, 123–24. Still, *Milwaukee*, 335–36.
7. The company remained the Reliance Works of Edward P. Allis Company until Allis's death in 1889, when it was reorganized as a stock company: Edward P. Allis Company.
8. Walter F. Peterson, *An Industrial Heritage: Allis-Chalmers Corporation* (Milwaukee: Milwaukee County Historical Society, 1976), 7–10, 19–65, 101–13,

149–70, and 237–79. Also see Gurda, *Making of Milwaukee,* 123–24, 164–65, and Still, *Milwaukee,* 337–39.

9. A. O. Smith, "A Better Way," ca. 1949 (a promotional brochure on the history of the company).

10. Still, *Milwaukee,* 340.

11. U.S. Bureau of the Census, *Thirteenth Census of the United States Taken in the Year 1910, Manufactures 1909: General Report and Analysis,* vol. 8, 84.

12. Simon, *City-Building,* 11; Still, *Milwaukee,* 476.

13. By 1910 the total German community (first and second generations) numbered 199,922 and constituted 53.5 percent of Milwaukee's population. U.S. Bureau of the Census, *Thirteenth Census of the United States Taken in the Year 1910, Abstract of the Census: Supplement for Wisconsin,* 598.

14. Gurda, *Making of Milwaukee,* 197–202, 206–11.

15. *Wisconsin Vorwarts,* Dec. 24, 1899, as quoted in Thomas W. Gavett, *Development of the Labor Movement in Milwaukee* (Madison: University of Wisconsin Press, 1965), 96; see also 90–97. Gurda, *Making of Milwaukee,* 202–6.

16. Gavett, *Labor Movement in Milwaukee,* 111–13. Edward S. Kerstein, *Milwaukee's All-American Mayor: Portrait of Daniel Webster Hoan* (Englewood Cliffs, N.J.: Prentice-Hall, 1966), 23–26. Gurda, *Making of Milwaukee,* 213–21.

17. Hoan's attitude toward workers and industrial conflict marked a sharp departure from the attitude of Milwaukee's government officials during the nineteenth century. The most notable strike occurred when workers demanding an eight-hour workday marched on the Bay View Rolling Mills on May 5, 1886, one day after a bomb exploded in Haymarket Square in Chicago. Fearing mass social unrest, Governor Jeremiah Rusk responded to local demands and sent the Wisconsin National Guard. In the melee that ensued, the militia killed three protesters, an elderly man feeding his chickens a half-mile away, and a schoolboy watching from an adjoining railroad embankment. For accounts of the Bay View Strike, see Gurda, *Making of Milwaukee,* 146–56 and Robert C. Nesbit, *The History of Wisconsin. Volume III: Urbanization and Industrialization, 1873–1893* (Madison: State Historical Society of Wisconsin, 1985), 393–411.

18. Daniel W. Hoan, *City Government: The Record of the Milwaukee Experiment* (New York: Harcourt Brace, 1936), 212–23.

19. Still, *Milwaukee,* 477.

20. *Ibid.,* 477–84. Gurda, *Making of Milwaukee,* 276–90.

21. Gavett, *Labor Movement in Milwaukee,* 155–57; Hoan, *City Government,* 214–20; Still, *Milwaukee,* 498–99; Gurda, *Making of Milwaukee,* 290–92.

22. Hoan, *City Government,* 220.

23. *Ibid.,* 220–21; Gavett, *Labor Movement in Milwaukee,* 157; Still, *Milwaukee,* 499–500.

24. Gavett, *Labor Movement in Milwaukee,* 159–66.

25. As quoted in Gavett, *Labor Movement in Milwaukee,* 167. Of the companies mentioned, Marathon Electric, maker of motors and generators, was in Wausau; Highway Trailer, maker of truck bodies and trailers, was in Edgerton; Gisholt Machine Company, maker of lathes and other machine tools, was in Madison; Fairbanks-Morse, maker of diesel engines, motors, and pumps, was in Beloit. The remaining companies were in Milwaukee: Harley-Davidson made motorcycles, Evinrude made outboard motors, Milprint made paper and vinyl packaging materials, and Louis-Allis made electric motors and generators.

26. U.S. Department of Commerce, Bureau of the Census, *Sixteenth Census of the United States: 1940, Manufactures: 1939, Volume III, Reports for States and Outlying Areas,* 1082–1105; Still, *Milwaukee,* 476, 486–87.

27. *Milwaukee Journal,* Dec. 8, 1941, 18.

28. *Ibid.,* Dec. 28, 1941, II-5; Jan. 25, 1942, II-6.

29. Resurvey of the Milwaukee Labor Market Area, Aug. 21, 1942, and Bi-Monthly Demand-Supply Supplement (Wisconsin) for Milwaukee Labor Market Area, United States Employment Service, Labor Market Survey Reports, Milwaukee, Box 429, Record Group 183, in the National Archives (hereafter cited as USES Labor Market Reports). The survey covered 202 companies in Milwaukee and two in Waukesha.

30. Peterson, *An Industrial Heritage,* 331–35.

31. *Milwaukee Journal,* Dec. 3, 1941, L-1; Dec. 5, 1941, L-9; Dec. 10, 1941, L-11. Labor Market Development Report for the Milwaukee Area, Dec. 15, 1942 and Resurvey of the Milwaukee Labor Market Area, Aug. 21, 1942, USES Labor Market Reports.

32. Throughout World War II the *Milwaukee Journal* published its general business pulse articles about once a month in the Sunday paper. The index accounted for employment, payrolls, department store sales, credit reports, construction activity, and bank debits. *Milwaukee Journal,* Dec. 12, 1941, L-10; Dec. 14, 1941, G-11; Jan. 7, 1942, L-5; Feb. 8, 1942, II-5; Feb. 11, 1942, L-8; March 22, 1942, II-4; Dec. 28, 1941, II-5; March 29, 1942, II-6; April 12, 1942, II-6; April 26, 1942, II-6; May 24, 1942, II-5; June 28, 1942, II-6; July 26, 1942, II-6.

33. *Ibid.,* May 24, 1942, II-5.

34. *Ibid.,* March 19, 1942, L-8; March 23, 1942, L-7; April 3, 1942, L-11; May 21, 1942, L-1.

35. *Ibid.,* Dec. 7, 1941, II-6; Dec. 10, 1941, L-12; Dec. 11, 1941, L-12; Dec. 16, 1941, M-22; Dec. 19, 1941, L-7; Jan. 2, 1942, M-2; Jan. 5, 1942, L-5.

36. *Ibid.,* for quotation see: Feb. 11, 1942, L-8; see also: Jan. 13, 1942, Final 1; Feb. 26, 1942, L-1; Feb. 28, 1942, M-3; August 6, 1942, M-18; Sept. 30, 1942, L-1; Nov. 22, 1942, II-3; Nov. 24, 1942, M-12; Nov. 26, 1942, M-24 and L-1; Dec. 3, 1942, M-18; Dec. 23, 1942, M-1; Jan. 11, 1943, M-1; Feb. 8, 1943, M-7; July 15, 1943, M-1; March 19, 1944, II-4. *Milwaukee Sentinel,* Jan. 14, 1942, A-1 and A-3; Feb. 11, 1942, A-1; Jan. 12, 1943, A-5. *Wisconsin CIO News,* Jan. 19, 1942, 1; Jan. 4, 1943, 1. Telegram from George F. Adds (secretary-treasurer, UAW-CIO) to Fowler Harper (deputy administrator, War Manpower Commission [WMC]), Dec. 16, 1942, letter from Fowler Harper to George Adds, Dec. 18, 1942, War Manpower Commission, Administrative Service, Communication and Records Division, WMC Central Files, Region 6, Box 1289, Series 171, Record Group 211, Federal Archives and Records Center, Chicago.

37. *Milwaukee Journal,* May 13, 1942, L-9.

38. *Ibid.,* July 13, 1942, L-5; Jan. 3, 1943, II-6; Jan. 2, 1944, II-3.

39. *Ibid.,* Jan. 10, 1942, M-6; July 21, 1942, Final 1; Sept. 26, 1943, II-3, Dec. 19, 1943, II-3; Dec. 26, 1943, II-5; May 14, 1944, II-3; June 25, 1944, II-3; Dec. 17, 1944, II-3.

40. *Ibid.,* May 3, 1942, I-1; Aug. 27, 1942, M-6; Nov. 22, 1942, II-6; Dec. 20, 1942, A-14; Dec. 27, 1942, supplement "America at War—First Year," 16 and 27; Jan. 17, 1943, II-3; March 14, 1943, II-3; April 4, 1943, I-1; June 19, 1943, M-8; June 10, 1942, L-4; Sept. 12, 1943, II-3; Sept. 10, 1944, II-3.

41. Only construction activity took a serious beating after the United States entered the war. Figures for wage earners, payrolls, and weekly and hourly earnings are based on Wisconsin Industrial Commission, Statistical Releases, Manufacturing Industries in Selected Cities of Wisconsin. Specifically see: Statistical Release # 197 for December 1941 and Release # 288 for December 1942. See also: *Milwaukee Journal,* Jan. 24, 1943, II-3.

42. Gurda, *Making of Milwaukee,* 308.

Chapter Two: Unity and Tension on the Home Front

1. *Milwaukee Journal,* December 8, 1941, "Extra," M-2.

2. *Milwaukee Journal,* Dec. 8, 1941, "Extra," M-2; Dec. 8, 1941, regular edition, M-3, M-5, M-18, and L-1. *Milwaukee Sentinel,* December 8, 1941, 6-A.

3. Interview of Dorothy Tuchman Weingrod by Steve Kolman, August 3, 1992, transcript page 3, Wisconsin Women During World War II Oral History Project, Wisconsin Historical Society. For a published version of the interviews from this collection, see *Women Remember the War, 1941–1945,* Michael E. Stevens, ed. (Madison: State Historical Society of Wisconsin, 1993).

4. William F. Thompson, *The History of Wisconsin. Volume VI: Continuity and Change, 1940–1965* (Madison: State Historical Society of Wisconsin, 1988), 67.

5. *Milwaukee Journal,* December 9, 1941, L-12.

6. *Milwaukee Journal,* Dec. 7, 1941, M-1; and *Milwaukee Sentinel,* December 7, 1941, A-1. *The Gallup Poll: Public Opinion, 1935–1971.* Vol. I, 1935–1948 (New York: Random House, 1972), in particular see polls for Sept. 18, Oct. 6, Oct. 20, Oct. 23, and Dec. 8, 1939, and Sept. 26, Oct. 3, Oct. 5, Nov. 15, and Dec. 17, 1941.

7. *Milwaukee Journal,* Dec. 9, 1941, M-1, M-13, and L-1; Dec. 12, 1941, L-10.

8. *Ibid.,* Dec. 10, 1941, L-1; Dec. 11, 1941, L-1; Dec. 14, 1941, IIII-14; Dec. 16, 1941, L-1; Dec. 22, 1941, Final-1; Dec. 19, 1941, M-19.

9. *Ibid.,* Dec. 21, 1941, II-1 and II-2; Feb. 20, 1942, L-1.

10. *Ibid.,* Feb. 22, 1942, II-1 and II-2.

11. *Ibid.,* July 31, 1942, M-1, M-4, M-12, and M-13; Aug. 13, 1942, M-1 and L-1; Oct. 28, 1942, L-1; Oct. 29, 1942, M-1; Dec. 11, 1942, M-1; Dec. 27, 1942, of the supplement entitled "America at War—First Years", 8; May 27, 1943, M-1; May 28, 1943, M-1 and L-1.

12. *Ibid.,* April 2, 1942, M-17; April 24, 1942, L-15; April 27, 1942, M-13; July 6, 1942, Final-1; Sept. 3, 1942, L-1.

13. *Ibid.,* March 2, 1943, M-2. *Civilian Defense News,* March 26, 1943, Milwaukee County Council for Civilian Defense records, Milwaukee County Historical Society.

14. *Milwaukee Journal,* March 7, 1943, I-16.

15. *A.F. of L. Milwaukee Labor Press,* Sept. 3, 1942, 33; March 25, 1943, 1; April 8, 1943, 1. *Milwaukee Journal,* April 6, 1943, Final-1. *Wisconsin CIO News,* Feb. 9, 1942, 8; March 9, 1942, 8. Minutes of Meetings of Civilian Morale Committee, March 16, April 27, and May 18, 1942, Milwaukee Industrial Union Council records, Box 3, housed at the University of Wisconsin-Milwaukee Area Research Center, property of the Wisconsin Historical Society (hereafter cited as ARC-WHS).

16. *Wisconsin CIO News,* Feb. 23, 1942, 2. *Milwaukee Labor Press,* Oct. 29, 1942, 4; Aug. 6, 1942, 1; Nov. 26, 1942, 3.

17. *Milwaukee Labor Press,* Nov. 5, 1942, 12. *Milwaukee Journal,* March 7, 1943, I-16.

18. *Milwaukee Journal,* Jan. 18, 1942, II-2; June 7, 1942, II-2; Dec. 27, 1942, II-l.

19. *Ibid.,* Feb. 19, 1942, L-1; July 12, 1942, I-11; July 14, 1942, L-4; July 15, 1942, M-1.

20. Richard Polenberg, *War and Society* (Philadelphia: J. B. Lippincott, 1972), 29–30, Geoffrey Perrett, *Days of Sadness, Years of Triumph* (Baltimore: Penguin Books, 1974), 261 and 299.

21. *Wisconsin CIO News—Local 248 Edition*, April 2, 1945, 11; April 23, 1945, 2; Aug. 3, 1945, 7. *Milwaukee Labor Press*, Aug. 5, 1943, 4; July 26, 1945, 2.

22. *Milwaukee Labor Press*, Aug. 5, 1943, 4. Polenberg, *War and Society*, 30.

23. *Milwaukee Labor Press*, June 22, 1944, 2; Aug. 24, 1944, 7. *Wisconsin CIO News—Local 248 Edition*, June 28, 1943, 4.

24. *Milwaukee Labor Press*, Oct. 15, 1942, 1; Dec. 3, 1942, 4. *Wisconsin CIO News*, Nov. 2, 1942, 11; Nov. 9, 1942, 1 and 2.

25. Secretary (Fred Goldstein, Secretary of The Community-War Chest of Milwaukee County, hereafter when carbons are signed "Secretary" the writer will be cited as Goldstein) to William B. Uihlein (Campaign Chairman), August 8, 1942, Goldstein to Anthony Carpenter (Director of the Wisconsin Division of the National CIO Committee for American and Allied War Relief), August 12, 1942, "What is the CIO Program for War Relief," typed information sheet, August 17, 1942, "Cooperation of Labor Unions and War Chests," agreement reached between AFL, CIO, and Community Chests and Councils, Inc., August 17, 1942, "Memorandum of Understanding Reached between Committee for the CIO and the UWC," contained in Carpenter to Goldstone, August 22, 1942, and Goldstone to Will Ross (Will Ross, Inc.), September 1, 1942, in United Community Services of Greater Milwaukee records, Box 56, ARC-WHS.

26. Ed (presumably Edmund Fitzgerald, the only "Ed" involved in the discussions) to Fred Goldstone, Sept. 2, 1942, *ibid.*

27. Ralph Blanchard (administrative director, Community Chests and Councils, Inc.) to Fred Goldstone, Sept. 8, 1942, enclosed in Goldstone to Edmund Fitzgerald, Sept. 10, 1942, Goldstone to Fitzgerald, Sept. 23, 1942, M. J. Cleary (Chairman of the Executive Committee) to Anthony Carpenter, Sept. 23, 1942, Goldstone to Wm. W. Coleman (Bucyrus-Erie Co.), Sept. 26, 1942, *ibid.* An informational mailing had already been sent to the 79 plants with CIO unions. Goldstone's reference to using a "public addressograph system" probably refers to use of a public address system, and not a system for addressing envelopes.

28. List of AFL representatives on War Chest, April 6, 1943, F. H. Ranney to Charles Anger, Jan. 25, 1944, *ibid.*

29. Meyer Adelman to Charles Anger, April 16, 1943, Edmund Fitzgerald to Anger, July 7, 1943, Adelman to Anger, Dec. 7, 1943, *ibid.*

30. Untitled explanation of the United Community and War Fund, Inc. policy regarding nominations to the Board of Directors sent to the Industrial Union Council, ca. Jan. 1944, Charles Anger to Meyer Adelman, Jan. 10, 1944, Adelman to Anger, Jan. 21, 1944, internal memo regarding negotiations with the Milwaukee Industrial Union Council, March 1, 1944, membership list for the Milwaukee County War Chest Labor Relations Committee 1944, Aug. 23, 1944, all in *ibid.*

31. *Milwaukee Journal*, Oct. 18, 1942, II-1. "Report of Delegate King to the Milwaukee Housing Conference held Oct. 16, 1937," Anthony J. King papers, ARC-WHS; Interim Report of the Housing Committee to the Social Planning Committee, Sept. 1940, United Community Services of Greater Milwaukee records, Box 20, ARC-WHS.

32. Report and Recommendation of the Sub-Committee on Public Housing, Jan. 29, 1942, Report and Recommendation of the Sub-Committee on Private

Housing, Feb. 6, 1942, United Community Services of Greater Milwaukee, box 20, ARC-WHS.

33. Report and Recommendation of the Sub-Committee on Private Housing, Feb. 6, 1942, *ibid.*

34. *Milwaukee Journal,* Feb. 5, 1942, M-1.

35. Frank Kirkpatrick, Fred A. Mikkelson, and George L. Faber (Citizens' Committee for the Building Industry) to Mayor Bohn, May 25, 1942, John L. Bohn papers, Housing, Rents, Real Estate file, Milwaukee Public Library. *Milwaukee Journal,* June 15, 1942, M-1 and M-4.

36. Between May 29, 1942 and June 8, 1942 officials from Kearney and Trecker, Allis-Chalmers, Maynard Electric Steel Casting, and Nordberg responded to a letter sent by Mayor Bohn on May 27, 1942 asking for information regarding their need for in-migrant workers during the next six months, John L. Bohn papers, Housing, Rents, Real Estate file, Milwaukee Public Library. *Milwaukee Journal,* June 5, 1942, L-1; June 30, 1942, L-1; July 5, 1942, IIII-9.

37. A Milwaukee Citizen to Carl Zeidler, Feb. 8, 1942, Mrs. Carl J. Mucklinsky to Mayor Zeidler, Feb. 8, 1942, Mrs. Vogel to Carl Zeidler, March 18, 1942, Zeidler papers, Housing and Rents file, Milwaukee Public Library; Mrs. Harvey Conrad to John Bohn, ca. May 20, 1942, Nettie Strandt Otto to Bohn, Oct. 18, 1942, Bohn papers, Housing, Rents, and Real Estate file, *ibid. Milwaukee Journal,* June 6, 1942, M-14; Nov. 3, 1942, M-10; May 11, 1944, M-20; July 16, 1944, I-1 and I-3; July 17, 1944, M-1; July 21, 1944, M-16.

38. *Milwaukee Journal,* March 29, 1942, II-1.

39. Mrs. Carl J. Mucklinsky to Mayor Zeidler, Feb. 8, 1942, Zeidler papers, Housing and Rents File, Milwaukee Public Library.

40. *Ibid.,* June 5, 1942, M-22; June 18, 1942, M-1 and M-4; April 6, 1944, M-25. *Milwaukee AFL Labor Press,* June 1, 1944, 1.

41. *Wisconsin CIO News,* July 27, 1942, 2. *AFL Labor Press,* June 22, 1944, 1; June 29, 1944, 3. *Milwaukee Journal,* March 1, 1942, II-2; Sept. 3, 1942, L-1; Sept. 10, 1943, Green Sheet, 1; June 26, 1944, L-1.

42. Mayor Zeidler to J. A. Lippert (Ogden & Co., Inc.), March 24, 1942, memo from Wallace E. Maciejewski to Mr. Mayor, April 1, 1942, Zeidler papers, Housing and Rents file, Milwaukee Public Library; Mrs. Marion Lonn to Mayor Bohn, May 8, 1942, Bohn papers, Housing, Rents, and Real Estate file, Milwaukee Public Library. *Milwaukee Journal,* Dec. 15, 1941, 16; March 19, 1942, L-1; July 8, 1942, L-1; July 12, 1942, II-1 and II-2; July 14, 1942, Final-1.

43. *Milwaukee Journal,* July 22, 1942, M-1 and M-9; Aug. 1, 1942, M-3.

44. *Ibid.,* Dec. 20, 1942, V-4; Nov. 5, 1943, L-7; April 20, 1944, L-1. *Wisconsin CIO News—Local 248 Edition,* March 19, 1945, 2.

45. *Milwaukee Journal,* May 17, 1942, IIII-15 and IIII-16; Sept. 27, 1942, VI-3; Oct. 19, 1942, M-1; May 21, 1944, I-1 and I-13; July 26, 1944, L-1.

46. Frank Kirkpatrick to Carl Zeidler, Jan. 21, 1942, Zeidler papers, Housing and Rents file, Milwaukee Public Library. *Milwaukee Journal,* Dec. 20, 1942, I-20.

47. *Milwaukee Journal,* Oct. 18, 1942, II-1 and II-2; Jan. 5, 1944, L-1; Jan. 18, 1944, M-9; Jan. 24, 1944, Final-1; Jan. 25, 1944, L-1; Jan. 27, 1944, M-20; Feb. 13, 1944, V-4; March 12, 1944, II-1; April 4, 1944, M-17; April 12, 1944, M-1; April 13, 1944, L-1; April 14, 1944, M-1 and M-5; April 16, 1944, I-1 and I-10; April 21, 1944, M-1 and M-3; April 30, 1944, II-2; May 1, 1944, L-1; May 2, 1944, L-1; May 8, 1944, M-1. For a more detailed account of conditions in the Sixth Ward and race relations in Milwaukee during World War II, see: Joe William Trotter,

Jr., *Black Milwaukee: The Making of an Industrial Proletariat, 1915–1945* (Urbana: University of Illinois Press, 1985), 165–188.

48. Meyer Adelman to John J. Roache (secretary, Milwaukee Real Estate Board), April 21, 1944, Hy Cohen to Mrs. Ross Baum, April 11, 1944, Milwaukee Industrial Union Council papers, box 5, ARC-WHS. *Milwaukee Journal,* June 24, 1944, M-3; July 18, 1944, M-15; Oct. 27, 1944, M-1; Oct. 29, 1944, II-1; Oct. 30, 1944, M-6; Nov. 5, 1944, II-2; Nov. 14, 1944, L-1; Nov. 16, 1944, M-21; Nov. 15, 1944, L-1.
49. *Milwaukee Journal,* October 18, 1942, II-1 and II-2.
50. Observations on Housing Conditions in Milwaukee's Sixth Ward, A Report to Mayor Bohn and Common Council by E. R. Krumbiegel, Commissioner of Health, December 1944, Bohn papers, Housing Authority file, Milwaukee Public Library. *Milwaukee Journal,* Jan. 18, 1945, M-1 and M-8; Jan. 19, 1945, M-18; Jan. 29, 1945, L-1.
51. *Milwaukee Journal,* Feb. 4, 1945, I-17; March 6, 1945, L-1; April 1, 1945, I-19; May 1, 1945, M-1; June 13, 1945, M-1; June 15, 1945, Final-1; June 16, 1945, M-8.
52. *Ibid.,* Jan. 2, 1942, M-1, M-2, and L-1.
53. *Ibid.,* Jan. 22, 1942, L-1.
54. *Ibid.,* Feb. 8, 1942, I-1 and I-12; Feb. 6, 1942, M-1.
55. *Ibid.,* Aug. 2, 1942, II-1; Oct. 2, 1942, L-1; Oct. 25, 1942, II-1; Jan. 7, 1943, M-1 and M-3.
56. *Ibid.,* March 18, 1942, L-1; June 10, 1942, L-1; July 14, 1942, L-1; July 24, 1942, L-1; July 31, 1942, L-1; Sept. 6, 1942, II-1; Sept. 8, 1942, L-1.
57. *Ibid.,* July 23, 1942, Final-1; Nov. 22, 1942, I-1.
58. *Ibid.,* Dec. 1, 1942, M-1 and M-20; Dec. 2, 1942, M-1 and M-10; Dec. 3, 1942, L-1; Dec. 4, 1942, L-1; Dec. 8, 1942, L-1; Dec. 27, 1942, supplement "America at War—First Year," 12; Jan. 19, 1943, M-1 and M-3; Jan. 20, 1943, M-1 and M-2.
59. Progress Report, Study Committee on Staggered Hours, submitted to the Committee on Public Utilities—Health of the City of Milwaukee, May 15, 1943, filed under Defense-Milwaukee County Council in the Bohn papers, Milwaukee Public Library. *Milwaukee Journal,* Oct. 10, 1943, I-1 and I-20; Oct. 23, 1943, M-8; April 4, 1944, M-17; Oct. 15, 1944, II-1; Dec. 12, 1944, M-1 and M-3. *Civilian Defense News* (official bulletin of the Milwaukee County Council of Defense), November 1943, Council of Defense records, Milwaukee County Historical Society. Report on Public Transportation, Milwaukee Metropolitan Area, Nov. 16, 1943, issued by the Study Committee on Staggered Hours and Transportation, under the cover letter: Howard F. Ilgner (committee chairman) to Leo Tiefenthaler (civic secretary of the City Club), Nov. 24, 1943, Progress Report on Public Transportation to Study Committee on Staggered Hours and Transportation, Dec. 15, 1944, contained under the cover letter: Ilgner to Tiefenthaler, Jan. 30, 1945, City Club of Milwaukee records, box 29, ARC-WHS.
60. *Milwaukee Labor Press,* Dec. 17, 1942, 1; Jan. 7, 1943, 1. *Milwaukee Journal,* Oct. 11, 1942, I-21; Nov. 25, 1942, M-7; Dec. 2, 1942, M-16 and M-20; Jan. 5, 1943, M-1; Jan. 7, 1943, M-1, M-3, and Final-1; Jan. 8, 1943, L-1; January 9, 1943, M-9.
61. *Milwaukee Journal,* Jan. 10, 1943, II-1 and II-4; March 3, 1943, L-1; March 11, 1943, M-1; July 20, 1943, L-1; Oct. 26, 1943, L-1; Dec. 1, 1943, L-1. *Wisconsin CIO News—Local 248 Edition,* March 1, 1943, 2. *Labor Press,* March 18, 1943, 7.
62. *Milwaukee Journal,* Dec. 28, 1942, M-1 and M-6; Feb. 14, 1943, II-1; Feb. 22, 1943, M-1 and M-3; Feb. 23, 1943, L-1; Feb. 24, 1943, L-1.

63. *Ibid.*, March 12, 1943, M-1 and M-10; March 24, 1943, M-1, M-5, and M-6. Also see: Amy Bentley, *Eating for Victory: Food Rationing and the Politics of Domesticity* (Urbana: University of Illinois Press, 1998), 9–29.

64. *Ibid.*, Jan. 23, 1942, M-1; Feb. 15, 1942, II-5; Nov. 21, 1942, M-1 and M-2; Nov. 22, 1942, I-1; Nov. 30, 1942, L-1; Dec. 28, 1942, M-1; Dec. 29, 1942, L-1; Feb. 9, 1943, L-1; March 12, 1943, M-1 and M-10; March 22, 1943, M-1; March 24, 1943, 1 and 6; March 25, 1943, L-1; Aug. 15, 1943, I-1; May 3, 1944, M-1; May 4, 1944, M-4; May 5, 1944, M-5; May 9, 1944, M-1; June 30, 1944, L-1; July 2, 1944, I-1; Dec. 31, 1944, II-1; March 1, 1945, M-1 and M-4.

65. *Milwaukee Journal,* Sept. 12, 1943, I-1 and I-5; Oct. 12, 1943, L-1; Oct. 29, 1943, L-4; July 23, 1944, I-1; Dec. 26, 1944, M-1; Oct. 15, 1943, M-1; Feb. 23, 1944, M-11. *Wisconsin CIO News,* June 15, 1942, 1. *Milwaukee Labor Press,* Dec. 3, 1942, 7; Aug. 5, 1943, 5; Oct. 14, 1943, 7; Oct. 28, 1943, 2. Also see: William F. Thompson, *The History of Wisconsin, Volume VI: Continuity and Change, 1940–1965* (Madison: State Historical Society of Wisconsin, 1988), 74–80.

66. *Milwaukee Journal,* March 7, 1943, II-1; March 11, 1943, L-1; March 31, 1943, L-1; April 8, 1943, L-1; April 29, 1943, L-1; July 4, 1943, II-3; July 21, 1943, M-13; March 18, 1945, I-1; March 25, 1945, I-16; April 20, 1945, M-1 and M-13; April 26, 1945, M-1 and M-24. Claude Keim (recording secretary of local 75, UAW-CIO) to Hy Cohen (CIO labor coordinator for the OPA), May 25, 1945, Milwaukee County Industrial Union Council papers, box 7, ARC-WHS.

67. *Milwaukee Journal,* June 19, 1945, L-1. *Milwaukee Labor Press,* June 21, 1945, 1; June 28, 1945, 1 and 6. Bentley provides an excellent discussion of the importance Americans placed on food rituals and particular foods; in particular, see pp. 85–113.

68. *Labor Press,* July 5, 1945, 1; July 12, 1945, 1; July 19, 1945, 1.

69. *Milwaukee Journal,* March 16, 1945, M-1 and M-8; March 17, 1945, M-1; March 18, 1945, I-18; March 21, 1945, M-1; March 22, 1945, M-18; March 23, 1945, M-1; March 25, 1945, I-16; March 27, 1945, M-1.

70. *Labor Press,* July 5, 1945, 1; July 12, 1945, 1; July 19, 1945, 1.

71. *Milwaukee Journal,* Feb. 14, 1943, II-1; *Labor Press,* July 26, 1945, 1. Chris L. Christensen, "Butter in National Health," *Wisconsin Labor,* 1942, 139–143, reprinted from a special supplement of the *Wisconsin Medical Journal,* June 1942.

72. Nagorsne to Affiliated Central Bodies, April 19, 1943, Wisconsin State Federation of Labor papers, Wisconsin Historical Society. *Wisconsin CIO News—Local 248 Edition,* June 28, 1943, 7.

73. Interview with Agnes Zeidler by Kathy Borkowski, March 12, 1992, transcript page 9, Wisconsin Women During World War II Oral History Project, Wisconsin Historical Society. For a published version of the interviews from this collection, see *Women Remember the War, 1941–1945,* Michael E. Stevens, ed. (Madison: State Historical Society of Wisconsin, 1993).

74. Interview with Rose Kaminski by Kathy Borkowski, March 9, 1992, transcript pages 18–23, *Ibid.*

75. Interview with Dorothy Keating by Kristina Ackley, July 18, 1992, transcript pages 33–34, *Ibid.*

Chapter Three: The Struggle for Economic Security

1. For daily reports on the Milwaukee municipal employee's strike, see the *Milwaukee Journal,* Nov. 1 through Dec. 6, 1943.

2. *Milwaukee Labor Press,* April 15, 1943, editorial, 6.

3. The phrase "basic pay rate" means the hourly rate for a job, excluding any additional compensation for overtime or shift differential. If a worker took home $40 for a 40-hour week in 1941, the base pay rate would be $1 per hour. If the worker received a 10 percent raise in 1942, and worked an average of 45 hours a week, the worker's take-home pay would rise by almost 29 percent. Although this is a useful figure when gauging wartime living standards, it is a poor gauge of long-term economic security because one could assume neither continued overtime nor high-paid war work. Recognizing that the wartime economy was an anomaly and remembering their experience during the Great Depression, workers prudently evaluated current compensation based on the basic rate paid for a job.

4. Wisconsin Industrial Commission, *Statistical Releases.* In particular, see releases 115 and 302. Bureau of Labor Statistics, *Consumer's Prices in the United States, 1942–1948,* Bulletin no. 966, 54. Throughout this chapter, hourly rates have been adjusted to remove the effect of overtime pay. Estimates of hourly pay rate increases made by this method actually overestimate the real wage rate increases by an unknown amount. During the war, it was generally recognized that average weekly and hourly earnings for the entire industrial labor force were skewed upward by the dramatic increase in the number of high-paying jobs in heavy industry. It also was generally recognized that many such jobs would be eliminated by postwar reconversion. As a consequence, an accurate measure of wage rate increases should adjust for the average increase due to the creation of high-paying war jobs. Unfortunately, this cannot be quantified from available statistics.

5. *Milwaukee Labor Press,* editorials, Jan. 7, 1943, 6.

6. Harvey C. Mansfield and Associates, *A Short History of OPA. Historical Reports on War Administration* (Office of Price Administration, General Publication no. 15, Washington, D.C., 1947), 13–23.

7. *Labor Press,* April 8, 1943, 1 and 4. Although the AFL contended that food and clothing were up 84.4 percent, the BLS estimated the increase at approximately 34 percent for food and 24 percent for clothing. Wage rates trailed far behind, but weekly earnings increased 48.6 percent, which helped to cushion most workers' standard of living. See Wisconsin Industrial Commission, *Releases,* nos. 115 and 302.

8. *Milwaukee Journal,* May 8, 1943, M-1 and M-2; May 9, 1943, I-1 and I-20; May 10, 1943, M-1; May 12, 1943, M-1 and M-22; May 16, 1943, I-1 and I-24; May 19, 1943, L-3. *Labor Press,* April 8, 1943, 4; May 13, 1943, 1. In many cases, the OPA established different ceiling prices for different brands of the same product. The AFL survey listed only one price for each product and did not list brand names, making direct comparison difficult.

9. *Milwaukee Journal,* May 20, 1943, M-1; May 21, 1943, L-1. *Labor Press,* May 27, 1943, editorial, 6.

10. *Labor Press,* June 3, 1943, 1. *Journal,* editorial cartoon, June 8, 1943, M-1.

11. Joel Seidman, *American Labor from Defense to Reconversion* (Chicago: University of Chicago Press, 1953), 55–73.

12. *Ibid.,* 81–85.

13. Directive Orders and Opinions delivered in connection with Little Steel Companies Case Nos. 2148-D (30), 2152-D (31), 2157-D (34), 2159-D (35) as contained in Appendix G-2, *WLB Termination Report,* Vol. 2, 288–322. See also the *Wisconsin CIO News,* July 6, 1942, 4, and July 20, 1942, 3 and 5. For a general ac-

count of the Little Steel case and its implications, see Seidman, *American Labor,* 110–111.

14. The term "Little Steel" was used to distinguish Bethlehem, Republic, Youngstown, and Inland from their bigger rival, the United States Steel Company and its subsidiaries. For a concise discussion of the Little Steel case, see Seidman, *American Labor,* 109–130.

15. *Milwaukee Journal,* April 9, 1943, M-1, M-3, and M-4; April 14, 1943, M-1 and M-10. For examples of labor reaction, see *Journal,* April 10, 1943, M-3; *Labor Press,* April 22, 1943, 1; April 29, 1943, 1; May 13, 1943, 3; and *Wisconsin CIO News—Local 248 Edition,* April 26, 1943, 2 and 5.

16. *Wisconsin CIO News—Local 248 Edition,* Feb. 8, 1943, 4; March 8, 1943, 6. *Milwaukee A. F. of L. Labor Press,* March 18, 1943, 2; March 25, 1943, editorial, 6. Seidman, *American Labor,* 109–120.

17. "Report and Selected Documents of the President's Cost of Living Committee," Appendix K-6, *WLB Termination Report,* Vol. 2, 1052–1053.

18. George Meany and R. J. Thomas, "Cost of Living." This is a pamphlet edition of their "Recommended Report for the Presidential Committee on the Cost of Living," January 25, 1944, contained in the pamphlet collection of the State Historical Society of Wisconsin. See especially pages 1–12.

19. *Wisconsin CIO News—Local 248 Edition,* editorial, Jan. 31, 1944, 4; Feb. 7, 1944, 5–8; *Labor Press,* Feb. 3, 1944, 1.

20. *Labor Press,* Jan. 27, 1944, 2; April 6, 1944, 1; April 13, 1944, 1. Wisconsin Industrial Commission statistical release number 451. *Wisconsin CIO News—Local 248 Edition,* Feb. 7, 1944, 5–8; Feb. 14, 1944, 5; March 27, 1944, 4–9; April 3, 1944, 3–8; April 10, 1944, 3–4; April 17, 1944, 3.

21. "Report and Selected Documents of the President's Cost of Living Committee," Appendix K-6, *WLB Termination Report,* Vol. 2, 1052–1068; Seidman, *American Labor,* 123–125. See also: "Comments by the American Federation of Labor Members on the Public Members' Report to the President on the Modification of the Little Steel Formula," contained in a press release of March 4, 1945, formulated by George Meany, Matthew Woll, Robert Watt, and James Brownlow, in Series 8, Files of the Director of Research, box 31, AFL records, State Historical Society of Wisconsin; *American Federationist,* July 1944, 7.

22. "Report to the President on the Wartime Relationship of Wages to the Cost of Living," Feb. 22, 1945, as contained in *The Termination Report of the National War Labor Board,* Vol. 2, 843–849 and 898–912.

23. Comments by the American Federation of Labor Members on the Modification of the Little Steel Formula contained in a news release for March 4, 1945, and prepared by George Meany, Matthew Woll, Robert Watt, and James A. Brownlow, in the American Federation of Labor Papers, Series 8, File A, box 31, State Historical Society of Wisconsin.

24. "Report and Selected Documents of the President's Cost of Living Committee," Appendix K-6, *WLB Termination Report,* Vol. 2, 1052–1068; Seidman, *American Labor,* 123–125. See also: "Comments by the American Federation of Labor Members on the Public Members' Report to the President on the Modification of the Little Steel Formula," contained in a press release of March 4, 1945, formulated by George Meany, Matthew Woll, Robert Watt, and James Brownlow, in Series 8, Files of the Director of Research, box 31, AFL records, State Historical Society of Wisconsin; *American Federationist,* July 1944, 7.

25. Progress and Final Reports by Despins, March 28 and April 23, 1945, case no. 455–962, International Harvester, in CS Case Files.

26. *Labor Press,* Aug. 3, 1944, 1; Aug. 10, 1944, 1; Sept. 28, 1944, 1; Oct. 5, 1944, editorial, 6; Nov. 16, 1944, 4; Nov. 23, 1944, 1; Dec. 28, 1944, 15; Jan. 4, 1945, 4; March 8, 1945, 1; March 22, 1945, 1; May 10, 1945, 1; May 17, 1945, 2; June 21, 1945, 1 and editorial, 6. *Wisconsin CIO News—Local 248 Edition,* Feb. 12, 1945, 5; Feb. 26, 1945, 7; May 28, 1945, 3 and 4; June 18, 1945, 5.

27. *Consumers' Prices in the United States 1942–48* (BLS Bulletin no. 966), 3–8. Hereinafter, Bureau bulletins are cited as BLS Bulletin.

28. Measures rejected by labor such as gross weekly earnings, gross hourly earnings, and adjusted hourly earnings advanced 53.3 percent, 45.4 percent, and 37.1 percent, respectively. *Trends in Urban Wage Rates April 1946* (U.S. Department of Labor, Bureau of Labor Statistics, Bulletin no. 891). BLS Bulletin no. 966, 44. *Milwaukee Sentinel,* Dec. 25, 1944, II-6.

29. Federal Mediation and Conciliation Service Dispute Case Files in the Federal Archives and Records Center, Suitland, Maryland. (Hereinafter cited as CS Case Files.)

30. Progress Report by J. J. O'Brien, Dec. 30, 1943, case no. 302–45, Harnischfeger; Final Report by Paul L. White, Aug. 24, 1945, case no. 455–3384, Cutler Hammer; Final Progress Report by MacDonald, May 26, 1943 and Final Report by Badenoch, March 27, 1944, case no. 300–4755, Chain Belt; all in CS Case Files.

31. Final Progress Report by Pierson, March 30, 1944 and Final Report by Pierson, May 30, 1944, case no. 445–1466, Allis-Chalmers; Progress Report by James A. Despins, July 14, 1944 and letter from J. R. Steelman to Harold Christoffel, Aug. 3, 1944, case no. 445–3890, Allis-Chalmers; Final Progress Report by O'Brien, Sept. 5, 1944, case no. 445–4775, Briggs and Stratton; Final Progress Report by Despins, June 15, 1945, case no. 455–2018, Briggs and Stratton; Final Progress Report by Holmes, July 31, 1944, Memo: E. R. McDonald to M. J. O'Connell, Aug. 16, 1944 and Final Report by Holmes, Sept. 29, 1944, case no. 445–3579, Chain Belt; all in CS Case Files.

32. Progress Report by Holmes, Oct. 17, 1944 and Final Report by Holmes, Oct. 17, 1944, case no. 445–5654, Automatic Products; Final Report by MacDonald, June 23, 1943, case no. 300–6652, Cudahy; Special Report by MacDonald, Sept. 2, 1943, case no. 301–4419, Cutler Hammer; Final Report by James P. Holmes, Sept. 2, 1943, case no. 301–3367, Geuder, Paeschke and Frey; Preliminary Report by J. J. O'Brien, Dec. 3, 1943 and Final Report by J. J. O'Brien, Dec. 4, 1943, case no. 301–9145, Geuder, Paeschke and Frey; Final Report by Holmes, April 18, 1944, case no. 445–2017, Geuder, Paeschke and Frey; Progress Report by Holmes, March 31, 1943 and Final Report by Holmes, April 1, 1943, case no. 300–4174, Globe Union; Special Report by Holmes, Sept. 30, 1942, case no. 209–7159, Milwaukee Ordnance; letter from Claude Keim (Recording Secretary for UAW-CIO local 75) to Honorable Madam Perkins, Dec. 22, 1942, case no. 300–820, Seaman Body; all in CS Case Files.

33. See Harley-Davidson case file nos. 209–198, 209–1439, 209–7633, 301–6679, 445–2033, 455–532, 455–1726, and 455–3664, all in CS Case Files.

34. See the following articles listed by company: Crucible Steel Casting Co./USA; *Milwaukee Journal* (hereinafter abbreviated *MJ*), Sept. 7, 1944, L-1. Globe Steel Tube Co./Steelworkers' Cooperative Union 18499-AFL; *MJ* Dec. 19, 1944, Final 1; Dec. 20, 1944, M-10 and L-1; Dec. 21, 1944, M-1 and M-2 and editorial M-14; Dec. 22, 1944, L-1. Milwaukee Foundry Equipment Co./UAW-CIO local 361; *MJ* July 19, 1944, M-10; July 20, 1944, M-1; July 25, 1944, L-1; July 26, 1944, L-1. Petroleum Transport Co., Inc./Teamsters local 695; *MJ,* July 27, 1944,

7. Harley-Davidson Motor Co./UAW-AFL local 209; *MJ,* June 7, 1944, M-1 and M-17; June 8, 1944, M-22; *Milwaukee Sentinel,* June 8, 1944, I-1; June 9, 1944, I-7; Progress Report by Ries, June 12, 1944 and Final Report by Ries, June 13, 1944 in case file no. 445–3377; Harley-Davidson, in CS Case Files.

35. The commentator is unknown, but from the language of the document it must have been a union official and probably was Alois Mueller. Untitled commentary on WLB case #III–1047-D between local 360 and the Cleaners & Dyers Association of Milwaukee, ca. Nov. 1943; records of the Laundry and Dry Cleaning Drivers local 360; Box 4; housed at the University of Wisconsin—Milwaukee Area Research Center, property of the Wisconsin Historical Society (hereafter cited as ARC-WHS).

36. Report of the National WLB Trucking Commission (Douglas Soutar, examiner) in the matter of Cleaners and Dyers Association and Local No. 360 IBTCWHA, WLB case # III–1074-D, Aug. 27, 1943; Untitled commentary on WLB case # III–1047-D, ca. Nov. 1943; Alois Mueller to OPA (re: WLB case # III–1047-D), Jan. 5, 1944; Mueller to NWLB, 6th Region, Chicago, Feb. 3, 1944; telegram, Bernice Harvey (NWLB Trucking Commission) to Mueller, Feb. 23, 1944; *Ibid.*

37. *Labor Press,* Nov. 12, 1942, 11; Nov. 4, 1943, 3; March 23, 1944, 1. Progress Report by Arthur H. Pierson, Dec. 3, 1943, case no. 301–8929, Vilter Mfg. Co., in CS Case Files. *Milwaukee Journal,* Nov. 1, 1943, L-1; July 24, 1945, L-2; Aug. 7, 1945, L-2. *Milwaukee Sentinel,* Nov. 1, 1943, I-1.

38. Progress Report by Cleland on behalf of McDonald, Oct. 28, 1943; Final Report by Cleland on behalf of McDonald, Nov. 6, 1943, case no. 301–6315, Nordberg, in CS Case Files. *Milwaukee Journal,* July 24, 1945, L-2; Aug. 7, 1945, L-2.

39. For information on the dispute at A. O. Smith, see: *Labor Press,* June 7, 1945, 1; and Werner J. Schaefer to Marsh (no last name but may be associated with IUOE president Maloney), March 20, 1945; records of the International Union of Operating Engineers, Local 311, box 9, in ARC-WHS. For other strikes, see: Luick Dairy Co. and Dairy Distributors, Inc./Milk and Ice Cream Drivers and Dairy Employees Local 225; *Milwaukee Journal* (hereinafter abbreviated *MJ*), May 17, 1944, M-1; May 18, 1944, M-1; May 19, 1944, M-1; May 20, 1944, M-8; *Milwaukee Sentinel,* May 17, 1944, I-1, May 18, 1944, I-3. Evinrude Motors Division of Outboard Marine and Mfg. Co./USA Local 1302; *MJ,* May 19, 1944, M-10; June 8, 1944, M-1 and M-26; June 9, 1944, M-22; June 26, 1944; M-1; *Wisconsin CIO News—Local 248 Edition,* April 2, 1945, 2. Gridley Dairy Co./Teamsters Union; *MJ,* April 7, 1944, M-1. Worden-Allen Co./Bridge, Structural and Ornamental Iron Workers' Local 471-AFL; *MJ,* July 25, 1944, L-1; *Milwaukee Sentinel,* July 24, 1944, L-1. Coal and Ice Drivers and Helpers Local 257 (Teamsters), *MJ,* June 12, 1944, M-1; June 13, 1944, L-1; Nov. 7, 1944, M-1; Nov. 8, 1944, L-1. Koehring/Bridge, Structural and Ornamental Iron Workers Local 471; *MJ,* June 30, 1944, L-2; *Labor Press,* July 6, 1944, 2.

40. *Milwaukee Journal,* July 26, 1942, II-1; July 31, 1942, L-1; Aug. 16, 1942, I-16; Aug. 30, 1942, II-1. For a detailed account of disputes between Milwaukee's municipal workers and the city government during wartime, see Edwin Layne Cling, "Industrial Labor Relations Policies and Practices in Municipal Government, Milwaukee, Wisconsin" (doctoral dissertation, Northwestern University, 1957), 629–666.

41. *Milwaukee Journal,* quote from May 29, 1943, M-4.

42. *Ibid.*, May 14, 1943, L-1; May 20, 1943, L-1; May 27, 1943, M-1; May 28, 1943, M-1; May 29, 1943, M-4; June 1, 1943, M-1; June 2, 1943; L-1; June 22, 1943, L-1.

43. *Ibid.*, July 6, 1943, Final 1; July 8, 1943, M-1; July 7, 1943, L-1; July 13, 1943, M-9.

44. *Ibid.*, July 7, 1943, M-11; July 9, 1943, M-15; July 13, 1943, L-1; July 20, 1943, L-1; July 24, 1943, M-14; July 26, 1943, L-1; July 28, 1943, L-1.

45. *Ibid.*, July 26, 1943, L-1; July 27, 1943, M-1; July 28, 1943, L-1; July 31, 1943, M-9; Aug. 3, 1943, L-1.

46. *Ibid.*, Oct. 19, 1943, M-1; Oct. 20, 1943, M-1 and M-8; Oct. 22, 1943, Final 1; Oct. 23, 1943, M-2.

47. The "Council Capitulates!" editorial appeared in the *Milwaukee Journal*, Nov. 19, 1943, M-1. For other *Journal* editorials, as well as daily reports on the dispute, see: the *Journal* for Nov. 1 through Dec. 6, 1943. For earlier *Journal* editorials on municipal strikes, see: June 1, 1943, M-1; July 8, 1943, M-1; Aug. 15, 1943, V-2; Oct. 20, 1943, M-8; Nov. 2, 1943, M-1.

48. *Ibid.*, Nov. 19, 1943, M-1 and M-3; Nov. 23, 1943, L-1; Nov. 24, M-1 and M-3; Nov. 25, 1943, L-1; Nov. 26, 1943, L-1; Dec. 1, 1943, M-1 and M-3; Dec. 2, 1943, M-1 and 6 and Final 1; Dec. 3, 1943, M-1 and M-3.

49. *Ibid.*, Dec. 4, 1943, M-1 and M-3; Dec. 4, 1943, Final 1; Dec. 5, 1943, I-1 and I-14; Dec. 6, 1943, L-1; Dec. 23, 1943, L-1; Jan. 10, 1944, M-1; Jan. 11, 1944, M-1.

50. *Ibid.*, Dec. 8, 1943, M-1; Dec. 9, 1943, M-1; Dec. 10, 1943, M-1; Dec. 15, 1943, M-1; Dec. 18, 1943, M-1; Dec. 20, 1943, M-12; Dec. 23, 1943, L-1; Jan. 10, 1944, M-1; Jan. 11, 1944, M-1; Jan. 12, 1944, M-1 and M-5; Feb. 21, 1944, M-10; Feb. 29, 1944, L-1.

51. *Ibid.*, March 12, 1945, M-4; March 29, 1945, L-1; April 17, 1945, L-1; April 23, 1945, L-1; April 25, 1945, L-1; April 26, 1945, L-1; May 10, 1945, Final 1; May 11, 1945, M-18; June 29, 1945, M-1; June 30, 1945, M-1; July 1, 1945, II-1; July 2, 1945, M-1; July 2, 1945, Final 1; July 3, 1945, M-1 and M-5; July 5, 1945, M-1; July 11, 1945, L-1; July 24, 1945, L-1; July 27, 1945, L-1; July 31, 1945, M-1; July 31, 1945, Final 1; Aug. 1, 1945, L-1; Aug. 2, 1945, L-1.

52. *Milwaukee Journal*, Nov. 16, 1943, M-14. *Wisconsin CIO News—Local 248 Edition*, Dec. 6, 1943, 2. *Labor Press*, April 15, 1943, 6; Jan. 25, 1945, editorial, 6. See also: *Wisconsin CIO News*, Sept. 14, 1942, 14. *Wisconsin CIO News—Local 248 Edition*, Feb. 22, 1943, editorial, 4; March 27, 1944, 4; July 31, 1944, 3. *Labor Press*, March 18, 1943, editorial, 6; July 1, 1943, 3 and 5; Jan. 27, 1944, editorial, 6; Nov. 30, 1944, editorial, 6. See also John Morton Blum, *V Was for Victory: Politics and American Culture During World War II* (New York: Harcourt-Brace Jovanovich, 1976), 122.

53. *Milwaukee Journal*, March 11, 1945, II-3. See also: March 15, 1942, II-6; June 15, 1942, L-5; July 30, 1942, L-7; Nov. 28, 1942, M-8; April 2, 1943, L-13; June 21, 1943, L-5; Aug. 5, 1943, L-7; Jan. 16, 1944, II-2; March 10, 1944, L-10; April 23, 1944, II-2; Nov. 20, 1944, L-9; Jan. 22, 1945, L-4; March 15, 1945, L-10; May 11, 1945, L-11. See also Lester V. Chandler, *Inflation in the United States: 1940–1948* (New York: Harper & Brothers, 1951), 83–113.

54. *Milwaukee Journal*, Aug. 24, 1943, M-10.

55. *Ibid.*, Nov. 19, 1943, M-20.

56. Randolph E. Paul, *Taxation for Prosperity* (New York: Bobbs-Merrill, 1947), 107–109, 177–78, 185–87, 215, 387–89.

57. Securities and Exchange Commission, *Survey of American Listed Corporations, Data on Profits and Operations, 1936–1945.* Beginning in January 1944, the Securities and Exchange Commission published reports on data supplied by corporations required to report under the Securities Act of 1933 and the Securities Exchange Act of 1934. The first report covered 1936–1942. Three successive reports published information covering 1942–1943, 1943–1944, and 1944–1945. The series includes data on fourteen Milwaukee companies, and it is upon

these reports that the conclusions are based. In particular, see reports for International Harvester, Chain Belt, Harnischfeger, Bucyrus-Erie, and Briggs and Stratton. Also see: *Milwaukee Journal,* Dec. 27, 1944, L-8; March 22, 1944, L-9; March 9, 1945, L-10; July 31, 1945, L-5; Aug. 9, 1945, L-9; Feb. 25, 1945, II-2.

58. See reports for A. O. Smith and for Cutler-Hammer in Securities and Exchange Commission, *Survey of American Listed Corporations, Data on Profits and Operations, 1936–1945; Milwaukee Journal,* March 11, 1945, II-3.

59. *Milwaukee Journal,* June 21, 1943, L-5; Oct. 20, 1943, L-10; June 9, 1944, L-10; May 22, 1945, L-4; July 17, 1945, L-3; July 20, 1945, L-5.

60. *American Federationist,* June, 1943, 26; December, 1943, 3–5.

61. *Milwaukee Journal,* Nov. 16, 1943, M-14. *Wisconsin CIO News—Local 248 Edition,* Dec. 6, 1943, 2. *Milwaukee Labor Press,* April 15, 1943, editorial, 6; Jan. 25, 1945, editorial, 6.

62. "Report to the President on the Wartime Relationship of Wages to the Cost of Living," *WLB Termination Report,* Vol. 2, 832–33; Seidman, *American Labor,* 122–130; and the following from the *American Federationist:* Boris Shishkin, "Inflation Crisis," April 1943, 3–6; "Change the Wage Formula," May 1944, 20–21; George Meany, "Labor Must Have a Real Cost-of-Living Index," July 1944, 4–7; William Green, "Postwar Wages," Oct. 1944, 25; "The Wage Freeze Must Go," Oct. 1944, 9–10; William Green, "America's Wage Policy," March 1945, 3–4 and 29–30.

Chapter Four: Worker Militancy and Wartime Industrial Conflict

1. *Wisconsin CIO News,* June 15, 1942, 2. Also see excellent discussion in Stephen Meyer, *"Stalin Over Wisconsin:" The Making and Unmaking of Militant Unionism, 1900–1950* (New Brunswick, N.J.: Rutgers University Press, 1992), 134–41.

2. U.S. Department of Labor, Bureau of Labor Statistics, Bulletin no. 741, *Strikes in 1942,* 4.

3. *Wisconsin CIO News,* Dec. 15, 1941, 1, 3 and 5; Dec. 22, 1941, 3 and 5. *Milwaukee Journal,* Dec. 8, 1941, M-3; and Dec. 16, 1941, M-22. Letters and telegrams supporting the war are contained in William Green's correspondence files, 1941–1942, World War II Policy, Pledges of Support, in the American Federation of Labor records (hereinafter cited as AFL records), Series 11, File B, box 9, Wisconsin State Historical Society. "Proceedings of the Conference of International Officers of the American Federation of Labor," Dec. 16, 1941, Series 11, File B, box 10, AFL records. See also: "War Labor Policy," contained in William Green to Officers of State Federations of Labor, City Central Bodies, Directly Affiliated Local Unions, Dec. 18, 1941, World War II Policy, Special Executive Council Meeting, Series 11, File B, box 9, AFL records. For a good discussion of this general period, see Joel Seidman, *American Labor from Defense to Reconversion* (Chicago: University of Chicago Press, 1953), 77–90.

4. *Milwaukee Journal,* Dec. 24, 1941, M-7. *Wisconsin CIO News,* Dec. 22, 1941, 3; Dec. 29, 1941, 1 and 3. *Milwaukee Sentinel,* Dec. 28, 1941, B-8; Dec. 30, 1941, A-10.

5. U.S. Senate, *Wartime Record of Strikes and Lock-outs, 1940–1945,* by Rosa Lee Swafford, 79th Cong., 2d Sess., 1946, Document no. 136, 3–9.

6. Nelson Lichtenstein, *Labor's War at Home: The CIO in World War II* (New York: Cambridge University Press, 1982), 178–202.

7. Preliminary Report, July 28, 1944 and Final Report, September 5, 1944 by J. J. O'Brien; case number 445–4352, Heil; Federal Mediation and Conciliation

Service Dispute Case Files; Federal Archives and Records Center, Suitland, Maryland. Hereafter cited as CS Case Files.

8. Final Report by Thomas J. Cleland, Jan. 5, 1943; case number 300–644, Nordberg; CS Case Files.

9. Final Report by Paul L. White, June 12, 1944; case number 445–2828, Globe Union; *Ibid.*

10. *Labor Press,* Oct. 15, 1942, 4; April 8, 1943, 1. *Wisconsin CIO News—Local 248 Edition,* March 1, 1943, 2. *Milwaukee Journal,* Jan. 7, 1943, L-1; March 5, 1943, L-2; March 11, 1943, L-5; March 16, 1943, M-6; April 3, 1943, M-16.

11. Untitled notes from two contract negotiation meetings with United States Rubber Company—Mil. Ordnance Plant by Werner J. Schaefer (bus. rep. for IUOE # 311), April 21, 1943; telegram H. T. Colvin (acting director of U.S. Conciliation Service) to W. J. Schaefer, Sept. 6, 1943; Mrs. Tommy L. Runyon (Administrative Officer Disputes Division of Region 6, WLB) to W. J. Schaefer, Sept. 15, 1943; Untitled union brief "Re: U.S. Rubber Co. (Operating Milwaukee Ordnance Plant) and International Union of Operating Engineers, Local No. 311, A. F. of L.", War Labor Board Case #111–3670, Sept. 27, 1943; Report and Recommendations of the Panel (Region 6, WLB) Dec. 2, 1943 in the matter of US Rubber Co.—Milwaukee Ordnance Plant and IUOE # 311, WLB case # 311–3670-D; Directive Order of the Region 6 War Labor Board in the matter of U.S. Rubber and IUOE 311, WLB Case #311–3670-D, May 6, 1944; Records of the International Union of Operating Engineers, Local 311; Box 5; housed at the Area Research Center at the University of Wisconsin-Milwaukee, property of the State Historical Society of Wisconsin.

12. *Strikes in 1942* (U.S. Department of Labor, Bureau of Labor Statistics, Bulletin No. 741 [Washington, D.C., 1943]). *Strikes in 1943* (U.S. Department of Labor, Bureau of Labor Statistics, Bulletin No. 782 [Washington, D.C., 1944]). *Strikes and Lockouts in 1944* (U.S. Department of Labor, Bureau of Labor Statistics, Bulletin No. 833 [Washington, D.C., 1945]). *Work Stoppages Caused by Labor-Management Disputes in 1945* (U.S. Department of Labor, Bureau of Labor Statistics, Bulletin No. 878 [Washington, D.C., 1946]).

13. For this comparison I chose the cities for which the BLS reported at least fifty strikes during each year of the war, and I chose the six cities (listed in the BLS strike reports) that had the closest number of wage earners to Milwaukee (three above and three below) as reported in the 1939 Census of Manufacturers. In addition, figures for 1945 have been adjusted to exclude the impact of postwar strikes. BLS Bulletin No. 878 lists only strikes and man days idle for all of 1945, but reports that 25 percent of the idleness and 62.5 percent of the strikes for 1945 occurred before V-J Day. These figures were used as multipliers to derive the information for these graphs.

14. I located newspaper accounts for sixty-five strikes between the beginning of 1942 and the end of September 1945, approximately 75 percent of the number registered by the BLS. Based on these accounts, I was able to determine the causes of 80 percent of Milwaukee's strikes during 1942, 1943, and 1944. Because I stopped searching the newspapers in September 1945, I can account for only 60 percent of the strikes noted by the Bureau of Labor Statistics during the last year of the war. In graph 2 strikes caused by WLB delays were usually wage related in some way. The category of strikes caused by grievances includes strikes over working conditions, seniority, work rules, and other traditional grievance issues.

15. See the following articles arranged by company: AFL Structural Steel Workers'
    union; *Milwaukee Journal* (abbreviated *MJ*), Dec. 14, 1941, M-24; Dec. 18, 1941,
    L-1. Blackhawk Mfg. Co./IAM lodge 66; *MJ*, Oct. 26, 1944, Final 1; Oct. 27,
    1944, L-5; Oct. 30, 1944, L-1. Federal Malleable Co./UAW-CIO local 264; *MJ*,
    May 12, 1944, L-1; May 13, 1944, M-3; May 17, 1944, M-1. Filer and Stowell
    Co./USA local 1563; *MJ*, Sept. 1, 1944, L-1. Froemming Brothers shipyard/Erec-
    tor Machinists local 1667-AFL; *MJ*, Aug. 2, 1945, Final 1. General Foundries/In-
    ternational Molders and Foundry Workers union local 125; *MJ*, Aug. 2, 1943,
    L-1. Heil Co./USA; *MJ*, July 5, 1944, final 1; July 6, 1944, M-1 and L-1; July 10,
    1944, L-4; July 12, 1944, M-12; *Milwaukee Sentinel* (abbreviated *MS*), July 6,
    1944, I-1; July 7, 1944, I-3. Louis Allis Co.; *MJ*, April 13, 1944, L-1. Metal Spe-
    cialties Co./UAW-CIO; *MJ*, June 15, 1945, L-1; *MS*, July 28, 1945, I-4. George J.
    Meyer Mfg. Co./USA local 1258; *MJ*, Jan. 4, 1945, M-1; Special Report by Mac-
    Donald, May 24, 1943; case number 300–8806; CS Case Files. Nash-Kelvinator;
    Labor Press; Nov. 19, 1942, 2. Nordberg International Molders' and Foundry
    Workers union local 125; *MJ*, Sept. 16, 1944, M-1; Sept. 18, 1944, L-1. R & M
    Mfg. Co./UAW-AFL; *MJ*, Jan. 7, 1943, M-2; Jan. 9, 1943, M-3. Schlitz/Brewery
    Workers' union local 9; *MJ*, Sept. 26, 1944, L-1; Sept. 27, 1944, L-1; S, Sept. 27,
    1944, I-1. Wisconsin Bridge and Iron Co./Bridge/Structural and Ornamental
    Iron Workers local 471—AFL; *MJ*, June 19, 1945, M-1; June 21, 1945, M-20.
16. *Milwaukee Journal,* July 20, 1944, M-1; July 25, 1944, L-1; July 26, 1944, L-1.
17. This is an excellent example of a common phenomenon. For a particularly ap-
    propriate commentary see: Ruth Milkman's discussion of the UAW (CIO) atti-
    tude toward equal pay in *Gender at Work,* 74–77. The Harley-Davidson exam-
    ple suggests that Milkman's observations apply to more than just the CIO.
    Harley was organized by the AFL auto workers union.
18. *Milwaukee Journal,* June 7, 1944. M-1 and M-17; June 8, 1944, M-22. *Milwaukee
    Sentinel,* June 8, 1944, I-1; June 9, 1944, I-7. Progress Report and Final Report
    by Holmes, November 18, 1943, case file 301–6679; Progress Report, June 12,
    1944 and Final Report, June 13, 1944 by Ries; case file 445–3377; Harley-
    Davidson; CS Case Files.
19. Local 19340 was a federal labor union affiliated directly with the AFL rather
    than with a craft union. The AFL used this structure when organizing non-craft
    production workers.
20. August K. Paeschke (manager of Defense Division of Geuder, Paeschke and
    Frey) to Walter Norbeck, Feb. 4, 1942; John Schmidt (secretary, local 19340) to
    George Meany, Feb. 15, 1942; records pertaining to the Fabricated Metal Work-
    ers Federal Labor Union 19340 in Series 10, File C, Box 1, AFL records.
21. Telegram, Walter Norbeck (business representative of local 19340) to William
    Green, April 21, 1942; David Sigman to Green, June 1, 1942; Series 7, Box 23, *Ibid.*
22. Telegram, Paeschke 19340 to John R. Steelman, June 14, 1942; Progress Report
    by R. G. MacDonald, June 30, 1942; Final Report, July 27, 1942; case number
    3275, Geuder, Paeschke and Frey Co.; CS Case Files. *Labor Press,* Sept. 10, 1942, 3.
23. Walter Norbeck (bus. rep. local 19340) to Steelman, Nov. 18, 1942; Final Re-
    port by MacDonald, March 26, 1943; case number 300–467; and memo on a
    telephone call from Mr. Marshall (WLB) to Mr. Sheehan, Feb. 5, 1943;
    telegram Cleland to Steelman, Feb. 6, 1943; Special Report by Cleland, Feb. 9,
    1943; case number 300–2273, Geuder, Paeschke and Frey; CS Case Files. *Labor
    Press,* Dec. 3, 1942, 1.
24. Final Reports by Holmes, Aug. 4, 1943; case numbers 301–865 and 301–1391,
    Geuder, Paeschke and Frey; CS Case Files. *Labor Press,* Aug. 5, 1943, 1.

25. Preliminary Report by Holmes, May 13, 1944; Final Report by James P. Holmes, May 13, 1944; case number 445–2701, Geuder, Paeschke and Frey; CS Case Files. *Milwaukee Journal,* May 12, 1944, L-1; May 13, 1944, M-3. *Labor Press,* May 18, 1944, 2.

26. *Milwaukee Journal,* April 6, 1945, M-8. Final Report by Holmes, Sept. 2, 1943; case number 301–3367; and Preliminary Report by J. J. O'Brien, Dec. 3, 1943; Final Report by O'Brien, Dec. 4, 1943; case number 301–9145; and Final Report by Holmes, April 18, 1944; case number 445–2017; Geuder, Paeschke and Frey; CS Case Files.

27. For quote see: Opinion in Arbitration and Report to N.W.L.B. by H. Herman Rauch, July 22, 1944. Also see: the Report and Recommendations of the [WLB] Panel, November 24, 1943; both documents relate to WLB case III–3328-D; in the file for Geuder, Paeschke and Frey Company vs. Fabricated Metal Workers' Union 19340, Fair Employment Practices and Stabilization (H. H. Rauch File), Wisconsin Industrial Commission records, Wisconsin State Historical Society. Additional information is also available in: Progress Report by Holmes, July 5, 1943; JRS (John R. Steelman) to Milton Barlament (president of local 19340), Aug. 20, 1943; case number 300–9228; Geuder, Paeschke and Frey; CS Case Files.

28. Final Opinion in Arbitration and Report to the N.W.L.B., October 10, 1944, by Rauch, WLB Case III–3328-D; and H. Herman Rauch to Geuder, Paeschke and Frey and Fabricated Metal Workers Union, October 7, 1944; in file for Geuder, Paeschke and Frey Company vs. Fabricated Metal Workers' Union 19340, Fair Employment Practices and Stabilization (H. H. Rauch File), Wisconsin Industrial Commission records.

29. Final Progress Report by J. J. O'Brien, Nov. 24, 1944; case number 445–5556; Geuder, Paeschke and Frey; CS Case Files.

30. Final Report by Holmes, March 14, 1946, case number 445–3632 in the CS Case Files; *Labor Press,* Aug. 9, 1945,1; and the file for Federal Labor Union 19340 in Series 7, Box 23; AFL records.

31. Case I, No. 694, A-29, Ampco Metal, Inc. and Employees' Mutual Benefit Association of Ampco Metal, Inc., recorded March 1, 1943 and closed March 26, 1943; Case II, No. 748 Ce-121, Edward Hanleck v. Ampco Metal, Inc. and Employees' Mutual Benefit Association of Ampco, sworn complaint dated Oct. 29, 1943; Case III, No. 752, R-264, Decision No. 528, Certification of Referendum, Nov. 24, 1943; Closed Labor Disputes Case Files, 1939–1951, Wisconsin Employment Relations Board; Wisconsin State Historical Society.

32. Summary of Company Position in Arbitration; Case IV, No. 931, A-35; *Ibid.*

33. Memo to Edward Mesarich from Charles E. Funk (supervisor of departments 200 and 210), Nov. 10, 1944; Arbitration Award, Ampco Metal, Inc. and Employees' Mutual Benefit Association, Dec. 1944; Victor M. Harding (attorney for the EMBA of Ampco) to L. E. Gooding (chairman, Wisconsin Employment Relations Board), Dec. 5, 1944; Summary of Company Position in Arbitration; Case IV, No. 931, A-35; *Ibid.* Final Report by Holmes, Jan. 29, 1945, Case Number 455–170, Ampco Metal, CS Case Files.

34. Company's Memorandum Brief, March 2, 1945, In the Matter of Arbitration of the Dispute Between Ampco Metal, Inc. and Employees' Mutual Benefit Association; Case V, No. 947, A-36; Closed Labor Disputes Case Files, 1939–1951, Wisconsin Employment Relations Board; Wisconsin Historical Society.

35. Hearing before the Arbitration Board, testimony taken on Feb. 14, 1945; Union's Brief, March 26, 1945; *Ibid.*

36. Arbitration Award, ca. April 1945; "Opinion" of the chairman of the arbitration board elaborating on the arbitration award, April 25, 1945; *Ibid. Milwaukee Journal,* May 6, 1945, I-II.

37. Fred Witney, *Wartime Experiences of the National Labor Relations Board, 1941–1945* (Urbana: University of Illinois Press, 1949), 240–248.

38. John Grochowski (president of Pulp and Sulphite local 193) to John Burke, May 9, 1944; Valeria Brodzinski (international union organizer) to Burke, June 20, 1944; Brodzinski to Burke, July 2, 1944; Records of the International Brotherhood of Pulp, Sulphite and Paper Mill Workers Union, microfilm edition, Wisconsin State Historical Society. International Brotherhood of Firemen and Oilers local 125 petition to determine bargaining agent for Hummel and Downing Company, May 23, 1944; Results of Secret Ballot for Representation of Maintenance Workers at Hummel-Downing Held by the Wisconsin Employment Relations Board on July 10, 1944; Hummel-Downing Case I No. 835 E-293; Closed Labor Disputes Case Files, 1939–1951, Wisconsin Employment Relations Board records, Wisconsin State Historical Society. *Milwaukee Journal,* June 18, 1944, II-4. *Milwaukee Labor Press,* June 22, 1944, 4.

39. *Milwaukee Journal,* Jan 23, 1943, M-1 and M-3; Jan. 24, 1943, I-9; Jan. 25, 1943, M-4; Jan. 26, 1943, Final 1; Jan. 29, 1943, L-1. *Milwaukee Labor Press,* Jan 28, 1943, 1; March 25, 1943, 1.

40. *Milwaukee Journal,* May 27, 1942, M-1.

41. *Milwaukee Journal,* May 27, 1942, M-1; April 27, 1943, M-1; May 6, 1943, M-1; May 7, 1943, M-12; May 8, 1943, M-8; May 10, 1943, M-1 and M-9; Aug. 4, 1943, L-1.

42. Executive Board Minutes, March 22, 1942; Special Meeting Minutes, March 30, 1942; Richards to Simon P. Obrien (Buffalo, N.Y.), March 31, 1942; Daniel D. Sobel (attorney) to local 815 International Longshoremen's Association, April 6, 1942; Milwaukee Circuit Court order in the case of Johnson, Toliver, Altman, Watson, Potter, Biddle, and Wdowicki vs. International Longshoremen's Association local 815, April 18, 1942; Trial Meeting Minutes, April 30, 1942; International Longshoremen's Association records; ARC-WHS.

43. For quote see Werner J. Schaefer to John Berry, Jan. 20, 1943; Werner to Sherman Baird, Jan. 21, 1943; Schaefer to Hyson Cornelius, Jan. 21, 1943; Schaefer to Henry W. Byerly, Jan. 21, 1943 (Box 10); Untitled memo from Werner J. Schaefer, Oct. 16, 1942; Supplemental decision of the NLRB in the matter of Nash Motors Parts Plant, Div. of Nash-Kelvinator Corporation and the International Union of Operating Engineers local 311, Case No. R-4682, March 2, 1943 (Box 5); four letters from Werner J. Schaefer to Arthur Sellnow dated Jan. 20, 1943, and to Thomas J. Sheppard, Oscar Sanburg, and Walter Szymkowski dated Jan. 21 1943 (Box 29); records of the International Union of Operating Engineers, Local 311; ARC-WHS. *Milwaukee Journal,* Feb. 4, 1943, M-1. *Wisconsin CIO News,* Dec. 8, 1941, 2.

44. For examples see: *Milwaukee Journal,* Dec. 6, 1941, M-1; March 21, 1942, M-1; March 22, 1942, I-1 and I-6; March 24, 1942, editorial cartoon, M-1 and editorial, M-10; March 19, 1943, M-1 and M-3; Oct. 20, 1942, Final 1; Oct. 22, 1942, M-2; Oct. 24, 1942, M-4. *Wisconsin CIO News,* Oct. 26, 1942, 5.

45. *Milwaukee Sentinel,* Dec. 1, 1941, A-12; Dec. 4, 1941, A-18; Dec. 6, 1941, A-12; Dec. 10, 1941, A-14. Minutes of the Board of Directors, Dec. 22, 1941; Metropolitan Milwaukee Association of Commerce; ARC-WHS. *Weekly Bulletin,* July 26, 1944; Wisconsin Manufacturer's Association papers; Wisconsin State

Historical Society. *Milwaukee Labor Press,* May 6, 1943, 1; July 1, 1943, 4; July 27, 1944, 5; April 12, 1945, 1.

46. *Wisconsin CIO News,* Feb. 16, 1942, 1; March 16, 1942, 1; May 4, 1942, 8; Aug. 17, 1942, 1; Dec. 21, 1942, 1. Preliminary Report, Oct. 2, 1942; letter from George Bradow (international union representative) to John R. Steelman, Oct. 7, 1942; letter from James P. Holmes to John R. Steelman, Oct. 8, 1942; Telegram from Steelman to Bradow, Oct. 30, 1942; letter from Nathan Witt (attorney for the union) to Steelman, Nov. 21, 1942; NWLB Directive Order, Aug. 28, 1943; case number 209–6407; Final Report by Edward A. Egan, Nov. 13, 1943; case number 301–7368; Progress Reports by Pierson, Dec. 21 and 29, 1943; case number 301–9335; Greenebaum Company Plant # 2; CS Case Files. Edmund V. Bobrowicz (president of local 260, International Fur and Leather Workers Union) to Meyer Adelman, May 5, 1943; Milwaukee County Industrial Union Council, Box 4; ARC-WHS. *Wisconsin CIO News—Local 248 Edition,* Sept. 6, 1943, 8; July 3, 1944, 10; July 17, 1944, 8; Dec. 11, 1944, 6. *Milwaukee Journal,* Feb. 23, 1944, L-4.

47. For quote see the Final Report by Holmes, March 22, 1945; case number 455–518; also see: Progress Report by James P. Holmes, Jan. 26, 1943 and Final Report by Holmes, Feb. 3, 1943; case number 300–150; Smith Steel Foundry; CS Case Files. *Milwaukee Journal,* July 3, 1942, Final 1; July 6, 1942, L-1; Dec. 16, 1942, L-1; April 21, 1944, M-8; July 25, 1944, L-1; July 26, 1944, L-1; Aug. 1, 1944, Final 1; Aug. 2, 1944, M-1; Aug. 4, 1944, L-5; Aug. 6, 1944, II-1; Aug. 7, 1944, L-1; Sept. 21, 1944, Final 1. *Milwaukee Sentinel,* Dec. 1, 1942, B-6. *Wisconsin CIO News—Local 248 Edition,* May 1, 1944, 2; April 16, 1945, 6.

48. Meyer, *Stalin Over Wisconsin,* 27–34.

49. As quoted in Meyer, 34–35, also see 3–4.

50. As quoted in Meyer, 41–44.

51. As quoted in Meyer, 50–52.

52. Meyer, 45–62, 67. Robert Ozanne, "The Effect of Communist Leadership on American Trade Unions" (unpublished doctoral dissertation, University of Wisconsin, 1954), 189–221.

53. Meyer, 67–104.

54. Ozanne, 221–29.

55. Meyer, 105–146. Ozanne, 225–69.

56. As quoted in Meyer, 109.

57. *Ibid.,* 134–46.

58. Harold Story to Schmitty, February 17, 1943; and Story to Leroy B. Lorenz, February 19, 1943; Harold W. Story Collection, Box 2, File 9, Milwaukee County Historical Society.

59. *The CIO News—Local 248 Edition,* November 6, 1944, 1.

60. Company Statement to Panel, vol. 1, Allis-Chalmers Manufacturing Co. (West Allis Works) and Allis-Chalmers Workers Union, Local 248, UAA&AIWA (CIO), War Labor Board Case No. 111–9878-D, January 15, 1945, Exhibit 1, 17.

61. *Milwaukee Journal,* March 19, 1942, M-10; July 8, 1945, II-2. *Wisconsin CIO News—Local 248 Edition,* June 28, 1943, 10; Feb. 7, 1944, 11; April 3, 1944, 10; June 12, 1944, 10; June 26, 1944, 6; March 12, 1945, 1.

Chapter Five: The Response to Women Workers

1. *Milwaukee Sentinel,* quote cited from Nov. 7, 1942, A-4. Other articles dealing with "Miss Victory" were published on the following dates during 1942: Nov. 7, A-4; Nov. 8, B-5; Nov. 10, A-10 and A-12; Nov. 11, A-4; Nov. 13, A-6; Nov. 15,

A-10; Nov. 26, A-11; Dec. 4, A-5; Dec. 5, A-16; Dec. 6, A-1 and A-6; Dec. 7, A-1 and A-6; Dec. 9, A-4; Dec. 13, A-18.

2. *Ibid.*, Nov. 8, 1942, A-8.

3. Interview with Dorothy Keating by Kristina Ackley, July 18, 1992, transcript page 17, Wisconsin Women During World War II Oral History Project, Wisconsin Historical Society. For a published version of the interviews from this collection see *Women Remember the War, 1941–1945,* Michael E. Stevens, ed. (Madison: State Historical Society of Wisconsin, 1993).

4. Interview with Rose Kaminski by Kathy Borkowski, March 9, 1992, transcript pages 5–13, *Ibid.* Mrs. Kaminski returned to work at Harnischefer as a crane operator in 1950 and retired in 1981.

5. D'Ann Campbell, *Women at War with America: Private Lives in a Patriotic Era* (Cambridge: Harvard University Press, 1984), 72–73. Maureen Honey, *Creating Rosie the Riveter: Class, Gender, and Propaganda during World War II,* second edition (Amherst: University of Massachusetts Press, 1984), 19–24.

6. Labor Market Development Report, June 17, 1943; United States Employment Service (USES), Labor Market Survey Reports; National Archives. "Women and the War," Special Intelligence Report # 62, August 6, 1942; Special Reports and Special Memoranda, 1942–1943, Media Division Reports; records of the Office of Government Reports, United States Information Service, Bureau of Intelligence, Office of War Information; Box 1845, Record Group 44; Federal Archives and Records Center, Suitland, Maryland. *Milwaukee Labor Press,* Sept. 17, 1942, 3. *Milwaukee Journal,* March 15, 1942, II-6; May 12, 1942, M-16. *Wisconsin CIO News—Local 248 Edition,* Sept. 4, 1944, 17.

7. Katherine Archibald, *Wartime Shipyard: A Study in Social Disunity* (Berkeley: University of California Press, 1947), 15–39. Susan M. Hartmann, *The Home Front and Beyond: American Women in the 1940s* (Boston: Twayne Publishers, 1982), 63–64.

8. For excellent accounts of women workers and attitudes toward their proper role see: Karen Anderson, *Wartime Women: Sex Roles, Family Relations, and the Status of Women During World War II* (Westport, Conn.: Greenwood Press, 1981). Ruth Milkman, *Gender at Work: The Dynamics of Job Segregation by Sex during World War II* (Urbana: University of Illinois Press, 1987). D'Ann Campbell, *Women at War with America.*

9. William Chafe, *The American Woman, Her Changing Social, Economic, and Political Roles, 1920–1970* (New York: Oxford University Press, 1972), 148. Also see: Milkman, *Gender at Work,* 92–94.

10. "Women in Unions in a Mid-West War Industry Area," unpublished survey report, July 10, 1945; contained in "Women in Unions in a Mid-West War Industry Area Trade Union Survey," Records of the Women's Bureau; Record Group 86, Acc. 56-A-50; National Archives. Much of this chapter is based on survey information accumulated during 1944 for this report. The Women's Bureau surveyed eighty-one unions representing ninety-two factories in Illinois, Indiana, and Michigan to learn what these unions were doing to meet the needs of women members. Each union studied by the Bureau was given a "schedule number," and the findings of surveyors generally were arranged by schedule number. Hereafter this report and its documentation will be cited as WB Midwest Unions Survey; Record Group 86; National Archives.

11. Campbell, *Women at War,* quote from 146; also see 141–61. Milkman, *Gender at Work,* 84–88. Hartmann, *Home Front and Beyond,* 65. Anderson, *Wartime Women,* 55–60.

12. "Women in Unions in a Mid-West War Industry Area," unpublished survey report, July 10, 1945; WB Midwest Unions Survey; Record Group 86; National Archives.

13. Although her work focused on the auto and electrical workers unions in the CIO, one of the best discussions of this point is in Milkman, *Gender at Work,* 65–83. Also see: Hartmann, *Home Front and Beyond,* 65–66. Campbell, *Women at War,* 141–61.

14. Women's Bureau interviewer's comments regarding IUUAWA local 322 at Globe Union Inc., schedule # 69, WB Midwest Unions Survey; Record Group 86; National Archives. In contrast to Anderson, *Wartime Women,* 57, numerical superiority on the local level guaranteed very little power to women workers.

15. WB interviewer's comments regarding UAWA local 232 at Briggs and Stratton Co., schedule # 71, *Ibid.*

16. WB interviewer's comments regarding IUAAAIWA local 335 at Fulton Company, schedule # 101, *Ibid.*

17. Women's Bureau surveyor's summary of union comments regarding equal pay; IUAAAIWA (UAW-CIO) local 469 at Master Lock Co.; *Ibid.*

18. WB interviewer's comments regarding the Smith Steel Workers Union, Federal Labor Union local 19806 at A. O. Smith Corporation, schedule # 72; and WB interviewer's comments regarding IUUAWA local 209 at Harley-Davidson Co., schedule # 70; *Ibid.* For additional information regarding Smith Steel Workers see *Milwaukee Labor Press,* Sept. 17, 1942, 3.

19. WB interviewer's comments regarding IUAAAIWA local 409 at Mueller Furnace and Boiler Manufacturers, schedule # 104; and WB interviewer's comments regarding UAWA local 75 at the Seaman Body plant of Nash-Kelvinator, schedule # 105; WB Midwest Unions Survey, Record Group 86, National Archives.

20. WB interviewer's comments regarding IUAAAIWA local 248 at Allis-Chalmers Manufacturing Company, schedule # 102, *Ibid.* Also see: Section 5 and Exhibit 8, Allis-Chalmers Manufacturing Company's statement to the War Labor Board Panel, Jan. 15, 1945, filed in the National War Labor Board, Region 6, Case No. 111–9878-D; in the possession of the author.

21. WB interviewer's comments regarding the Smith Steel Workers Union, Federal Labor Union local 19806 at A. O. Smith Corporation, schedule # 72; and WB interviewer's comments regarding IUAAAIWA local 248 at Allis-Chalmers Manufacturing Co., schedule # 102; WB Midwest Unions Survey, Record Group 86, National Archives.

22. Interview with Rose Kaminski by Kathy Borkowski, March 9, 1992, transcript page 16, Wisconsin Women During World War II Oral History Project.

23. WB interviewer's comments regarding employment of women and seniority in the following unions: IAM lodge 66 at Jambor Tool and Stamping, schedule # 64, at Clum Manufacturing Co., schedule # 65, and at Perfex Corporation, schedule # 66; IAM lodge lo61 at Cutler Hammer Inc., schedule # 63; IBEW local B-1169 at Square D Co., schedule #67; UERMWA local 1111 at Allen Bradley Co., schedule # 100; also see comments contained elsewhere in schedule # 100 and in schedule # 107 (USA local 1258 at George Meyer Manufacturing Co.); comments regarding equal pay in schedule # 103 for IUAAAIWA (UAW-CIO) local 469 at Master Lock Co.; *Ibid.*

24. For the best treatment of this subject see Campbell, *Women at War.* Also see: Hartmann, *Home Front and Beyond,* 53–99 and 163–86.

25. WB interviewer's comments regarding IAM lodge 66 at Jambor Tool and Stamping, schedule # 64 and at Perfex Corporation, schedule #66; WB Mid-

west Unions Survey, Record Group 86, National Archives. Anderson, *Wartime Women,* 43–65.

26. Milkman, *Gender at Work,* 77–83. The United Electrical Workers supported comparable worth nationally, but it too had difficulty implementing the program.

27. For the poster cited and for other examples of glamorized war jobs see: Employment Campaign Posters, War Manpower Commission records; Series 195, Record Group 211; National Archives. W. H. Spencer to Executive Director, Activity Report for the Week of July 11–17, contained in W. H. Spencer to Executive Director, July 20, 1943; Periodic Progress and Activity Reports from Regional Office Division Heads, War Manpower Commission Records, Region 6; Box 3211, Series 272, Record Group 211; Federal Archives and Records Center, Chicago. For excellent discussions of the themes used in recruiting campaigns see: Leila J. Rupp, *Mobilizing Women For War* (Princeton, N.J.: Princeton University Press, 1978), 137–66 and Honey, *Creating Rosie the Riveter,* 24–59.

28. Valeria Brodzinski (international union organizer) to John Burke (international union president), May 17, 1942; Brodzinski to Burke, Sept. 21, 1942; Walter Trautmann (international organizer) to Burke, Oct. 30, 1942; Burke to Trautmann, Nov. 1, 1942; Burke to Brodzinski, Nov. 2, 1942; Records of the International Brotherhood of Pulp, Sulphite and Paper Mill Workers Union, microfilm edition; Wisconsin Historical Society.

29. Raymond Richards (international vice president for Wisconsin) to Burke, June 2, 1942, *Ibid.*

30. Burke to Richards, June 4, 1942; Richards to Burke, June 8, 1942; Brodzinski to Burke, June 17, 1942; Burke to Richards, June 25, 1942; Burke to Richards, July 17, 1942; *Ibid.*

31. Brodzinski to Burke, Aug. 26, 1942; *Ibid.*

32. Quote from Brodzinski to Burke, June 4, 1945; also see: Brodzinski to Burke, March 23, 1942; Brodzinski to Burke, Nov. 13, 1944; Brodzinski to Burke, Dec. 18, 1944; Brodzinski to Burke, July 31, 1945; *Ibid.*

33. Conference Report of "Meeting between International Paper Company, Book and Bond and Groundwood Specialties Divisions, and the International Brotherhood of Paper Makers, the International Brotherhood of Pulp, Sulphite and Paper Mill Workers, and the International Brotherhood of Firemen and Oilers;" held in Glen Falls, New York on May 25–26, 1942; *Ibid.*

34. For information regarding the views of Pulp and Sulphite union leaders see: circular from Burke TO ALL LOCAL UNIONS, Aug. 27, 1942; Richards to Burke, Sept. 16, 1942; Trautmann to Burke, Oct. 14, 1942; Burke to Trautmann, Oct. 16, 1942; Richards to Burke, Oct. 27, 1942; Burke to OUR LOCAL UNIONS AND FIELD REPRESENTATIVES IN THE UNITED STATES, Nov. 13, 1942; Richards to Burke, Dec. 18, 1942; Burke to Richards, Dec. 22, 1942; Minutes of a meeting with Menasha Carton, April 9, 1943 contained in Richards to Burke, April 16, 1943; Richards to Burke, April 18, 1943; Brodzinski to Burke, July 31, 1943; Herbert Sullivan (international union vice president for New York) to Brodzinski, Sept. 15, 1944. For specific examples of contracts negotiated by Trautmann and Brodzinski see: Trautmann to Burke, May 18, 1942, Trautmann to Burke, June 18, 1942; Trautmann to Burke, July 17, 1942; Otto Mueller (recording and corresponding secretary for local 295) to Burke, July 24, 1942; Brodzinski to Burke, Nov. 13, 1943; *Ibid.*

35. *Milwaukee Journal,* Feb. 7, 1942, M-14. Milkman, *Gender at Work,* 49–64. Milkman has demonstrated clearly that even where old gender-segregation broke down, it often was replaced by new gender-segregation and discrimination

practices. She focuses on the UAW and the UE, two CIO unions. The pattern in Milwaukee suggests that union affiliation had little to do with the discriminatory practices faced by women.

36. *Milwaukee Sentinel,* May 2, 1942, A-3. Anderson, *Wartime Women,* 43–47.

37. *Weekly Bulletin,* vol. 22, no. 15 (July 29, 1942); publication of the Wisconsin Manufacturers' Association; Wisconsin Manufacturer's Association papers, Wisconsin Historical Society.

38. *Milwaukee Journal,* Dec. 29, 1943, M-12. For other examples see: *Milwaukee Journal,* April 9, 1944, VII-6; July 7, 1943, L-4; Jan. 19, 1943, L-2. *Milwaukee Labor Press,* June 15, 1944, 10.

39. WB Midwest Unions Survey; Record Group 86; National Archives.

40. Minutes of the International Association of Machinists Wisconsin State Council, Nov. 14, 1942; records of the Wisconsin State Council of Machinists, microfilm edition; Wisconsin Historical Society. Milkman, *Gender at Work,* 61–64. Campbell, *Women at War,* 72–83.

41. WB interviewer's comments regarding IAM lodges 66 and 1061, schedule #s 63, 65, and 66; WB Midwest Unions Survey; Record Group 86; National Archives.

42. Press release issued by the Office of War Information and the War Manpower Commission following a two-day conference of the Women's Advisory Committee devoted to postwar employment issues, May 17, 1943; files of the AFL economist; Series 5, File C, Box 26; American Federation of Labor Papers; Wisconsin Historical Society.

43. *Milwaukee Journal,* March 12, 1944, II-1 and II-4.

44. Lynn Y. Weiner, *From Working Girl to Working Mother: The Female Labor Force in the United States, 1820–1980* (Chapel Hill: University of North Carolina Press, 1985), 110–12. Anderson, *Wartime Women,* 5 and 36. Campbell, *Women at War,* 81–82.

45. *Milwaukee Journal,* Sept. 26, 1942, M-7; Oct. 19, 1942, M-2; Nov. 7, 1942, M-3; and Nov. 8, 1942, II-7. Manual of Operations, War Manpower Commission, Amendments to Policy on Employment in Industry of Women with Young Children, Jan. 13, 1943; Defense Council File from Box 15; papers of the United Community Services of Greater Milwaukee; housed at the University of Wisconsin-Milwaukee Area Research Center, property of the Wisconsin Historical Society (ARC-WHS).

46. *Milwaukee Journal,* Nov. 7, 1942, M-3; Nov. 29, 1942, VII-4; Jan. 29, 1943, L-2; April 17, 1943, M-3.

47. Report to the Executive Committee (of the Milwaukee County Community Fund and Council of Social Agencies) on the Proposal to Include in a War Fund, Experimental Child-Care Centers for Children of Working Mothers (written by Louise Root), July 28, 1942, Box 12; papers of the United Community Services of Greater Milwaukee; ARC-WHS.

48. *Milwaukee Journal,* quote from Jan. 28, 1943, M-16; also see editorials on Oct. 25, 1942, V-2; Nov. 20, 1942, M-22; Nov. 28, 1942, M-4; Dec. 13, 1942, V-2; Jan. 31, 1943, V-2.

49. *Milwaukee Journal,* Aug. 13, 1944, V-1; Aug. 29, 1944, L-1; Aug. 31, 1944, L-10.

50. Anderson has provided one of the most thorough studies of child care during the war. Her study focuses on three boom towns: Detroit, Seattle, and Baltimore. Conditions in Milwaukee, which was prosperous but not a boom town, paralleled those outlined by Anderson, *Wartime Women,* 91–92 and 122–53. Campbell, *Women at War,* 82.

51. "Employment Facts Concerning Women: What employment is doing to home life," November 7, 1942, Box 49; Also see: "Summary of Contacts with Social Agencies Relative to Types of New Cases Coming to Their Attention," September 16, 1943; and "Summarized Report of the Study by the Committee on the Alleged Increase in Juvenile Problems in Milwaukee County to the Social Planning Committee Milwaukee County Community Fund and Council of Social Agencies," March 14, 1944, Box 21; papers of the United Community Services of Greater Milwaukee; ARC-WHS.

52. Campbell, *Women at War,* 77–100. Hartmann, *Home Front and Beyond,* 53–99 and 163–86. Doris Weatherford, *American Women and World War II* (New York: Facts on File, 1990), 161–76.

53. Chafe, *The American Woman,* 145. *Wisconsin CIO News—Local 248 Edition,* July 5, 1943, 2. Also see: *Milwaukee Sentinel,* April 27, 1943, A-11; Nov. 15, 1943, I-7. *Milwaukee Journal,* Oct. 18, 1942, "Journal Magazine," 4–5; Jan. 3, 1944, L-2; Dec. 31, 1944, VII-4. *Milwaukee Labor Press,* March 4, 1943, 10.

54. *Milwaukee Journal,* March 1, 1943, M-15; April 5, 1943, M-3.

55. *Ibid.,* Oct. 6, 1943, M-15. Labor Market Developments Reports, Aug. 16, 1943; Oct. 16, 1943, and Dec. 17, 1943; Labor Market Survey Reports, Milwaukee, Wisconsin; United States Employment Service, Box 426, Record Group 183; National Archives. Also see: Hartmann, *Home Front and Beyond,* 84. Campbell, *Women at War,* 132–33.

56. *Wisconsin CIO News—Local 248 Edition,* Sept. 27, 1943, 5. *Milwaukee Labor Press,* March 18, 1943, 4.

57. *Milwaukee Labor Press,* Oct. 22, 1942, 2. *Milwaukee Journal,* Oct. 20, 1942, M-15. *Wisconsin CIO News,* Dec. 14, 1942, 12.

58. *Wisconsin Defender,* official publication of the Wisconsin Council of Defense, September 1942, included in the papers of the Milwaukee County Council for Civilian Defense; Milwaukee County Historical Society. Summarized Report of the Wartime Child Care Coordinator taken from the Report of August 25, 1943 approved by the Committee on the Care of Children of Working Mothers of the Welfare Committee of the Milwaukee County Defense Council and the Milwaukee Council of Social Agencies (hereafter cited as the Report of the Child Care Coordinator); Box 10, papers of the United Community Services of Greater Milwaukee; ARC-WHS.

59. Minutes of the Board of Directors, Milwaukee County Council of Defense, Feb. 3, 1943; John L. Bohn papers; Milwaukee Public Library. Report of the Child Care Coordinator, Aug. 25, 1943, found in Box 10; the following items are located in Box 15: Outline of suggested publicity program on care of children of working mothers, ca. 1943; Report of the Committee on Care of Children of Working Mothers under the Community Welfare Committee of the Milwaukee County Defense Council, June 12, 1942; Henry J. Whiting to Executive of Health and Welfare Agencies, Dec. 4, 1942; Circular letter to service agency executives from Cornelia Heise, chairman of the Committee on Care of Children of Working Mothers of the Community Welfare Committee of the Health and Welfare section of the County Defense Council, April 6, 1942; Rev. Henry J. Whiting (chairman of the Committee on Care of Children of Working Mothers) to Executives of Health and Welfare Agencies which failed to return day care survey forms, June 20, 1942; A Preliminary Report from the Family Welfare Association of Milwaukee to the Council of Social Agencies on the project of Counseling Service for Working Mothers, July 15–Sept. 1, 1942; the following items are located in Box 16: Progress Report of the Community Welfare Committee of the Health and

Welfare Section of the County Defense Council, April 14, 1942; Progress Report/Welfare Committee of the Citizens Service Corps/Milwaukee County Defense Council, Dec. 1942; papers of the United Community Services of Greater Milwaukee; ARC-WHS. *Civilian Defense News,* official bulletin of the Milwaukee County Council of Defense, May 26, 1943; filed with the records of the Council for Civilian Defense, Milwaukee County Historical Society.

60. Plant Survey (returns as of Nov. 24, 1942) revised as of Dec. 16, 1942; Box 15, papers of the United Community Services of Greater Milwaukee; ARC-WHS.

61. *Milwaukee Journal,* Dec. 9, 1942, L-3; Jan. 27, 1943, L-1; Jan. 28, 1943, L-9; Feb. 3, 1943, L-1; Feb. 6, 1943, M-4; Feb. 16, 1943, L-1; Feb. 17, 1943, M-12; Feb. 25, 1943, L-1; March 2, 1943, L-1; March 3, 1943, L-1; April 7, 1943, M-16. *Wisconsin CIO News—Local 248 Edition,* Feb. 8, 1943, 1; Feb. 22, 1943, 1; March 8, 1943, 12. "Report on the School Board Meeting in Regards to the Day Nursery," apparently a report by the representative from UAW local 75 to the County Industrial Union Council, ca. June 1943; Milwaukee County Industrial Union Council papers, Box 4; ARC-WHS. Report of the Child Care Coordinator, Aug. 25, 1943, Box 10; Ruth G. Strickland (Senior Specialist in Extended School Services for the Federal Security Agency, Office of Defense Health and Welfare Services) to Louise Root (associate executive secretary of the Council of Social Agencies), March 12, 1943, and Memorandum on Day Care of Children Beyond Nursery School Age, ca. 1943, both are located in Box 15; Report to the Executive Committee on the Proposal to Include in a War Fund, Experimental Child-Care Centers for Children of Working Mothers (written by Louise Root), July 28, 1942, Box 12; Report to the Board of Directors-Milwaukee County Council of Defense by the Special Committee Appointed by the Chairman of the Council to Study Present Status of Nursery Schools and Possible Suspension of Continuation of Them, Feb. 23, 1943, Box 15; papers of the United Community Services of Greater Milwaukee; ARC-WHS. Minutes of Board of Directors, Milwaukee County Council of Defense, Feb. 24, 1943; John L. Bohn papers; Milwaukee Public Library. Civilian Defense News, March 26, 1943; Minutes of the Milwaukee County Council of Defense, Aug. 20, 1942; Milwaukee County Council for Civilian Defense records; ARC-WHS. For a detailed account of the problems encountered in implementing day care in three boom towns see: Anderson, *Wartime Women,* 122–146.

62. *Civilian Defense News,* March 26, 1943; included in the papers of the Milwaukee County Council of Defense; Milwaukee County Historical Society. Progress Report/Welfare Committee Citizens Service Corps/Milwaukee County Defense Council, May 1943, Box 16; Fred D. Goldstone (executive vice president, Milwaukee County Community Fund and Council of Social Agencies) to Company Presidents, June 21, 1943, Box 15; United Community Services of Greater Milwaukee; ARC-WHS.

63. Report of the Child Care Coordinator, August 25, 1943; papers of the United Community Services of Greater Milwaukee, Box 10; ARC-WHS.

64. Progress Report/Welfare Committee/Citizens Service Corps, Oct. 1943 and Nov. 1943, Box 16; Louise Root to Agencies and Interested Individuals, Feb. 11, 1944, Box 15; *Ibid. Civilian Defense News,* Dec. 1943 and Feb. 1944; included among the papers of the Milwaukee County Council for Civilian Defense; Milwaukee County Historical Society.

65. The quotation is taken from the Annual Report of the Council of Social Agencies for the period May 1943 to May 1944, written by Louise Root, June 10, 1944; papers of the United Community Services of Greater Milwaukee, Box

49; ARC-WHS. Also see: Progress Report/Welfare Committee/Citizens' Service Corps/War Services Division, April 1944, Box 16; and Louise Root to Ione Quinby Griggs (columnist for the *Milwaukee Journal*), April 5, 1944, Box 15; papers of United Community Services. *Civilian Defense News,* April 1944 and May 1944; included in the papers of the Milwaukee County Council for Civilian Defense; Milwaukee County Historical Society.

66. *Civilian Defense News,* July 1944. Survey—RE: Need for Child Care Centers—Milwaukee, Aug. 1944, Box 15; Progress Reports/Welfare Committee/Citizens' Service Corps/War Services Division, for the period May to Sept. 1944 and for Jan. 1945, Box 16; papers of United Community Services.

67. *Civilian Defense News,* Jan. and March 1944. *Milwaukee Journal,* March 17, 1944, M-23; June 12, 1944, L-1; June 27, 1944, L-3; Dec. 8, 1944, L-13; Feb. 2, 1945, L-1; Feb. 6, 1945, L-1; March 25, 1945, I-6; Nov. 9, 1944, M-19. *Milwaukee Sentinel,* July 2, 1944, A-3; July 6, 1944, II-8; April 22, 1945, C-1 and C-3.

68. Interview with Dorothy Keating by Kristina Ackley, July 18, 1992, transcript page 16, Wisconsin Women During World War II Oral History Project.

69. Interview with Nellie Wilson by Kathy Borkowski, September 7, 1993, transcript pages 13–15, *Ibid.*

70. Interview with Rose Kaminski by Kathy Borkowski, March 9, 1992, transcript pages, *Ibid.*

71. For an excellent review of child care in Baltimore, Detroit, and Seattle, see: Anderson, *Wartime Women,* 122–53. Also see: Lowell Juilliard Carr and James Edson Stermer, *Willow Run: A Study of Industrialization and Cultural Inadequacy* (New York: Harper, 1952). Robert J. Havighurst and H. Gerthon Morgan, *The Social History of a War-Boom Community* (New York: Longmans, Green, 1951).

72. *Milwaukee Journal,* Aug. 30, 1942, V-2.

73. *Ibid.,* Nov. 2, 1943, M-14.

74. *Ibid.,* Feb. 26, 1944, M-8.

75. *Ibid.,* Oct. 1, 1943, L-2; Aug. 1, 1943, "Journal Magazine," 4 and 5; Jan. 25, 1944, L-2; Oct. 27, 1944, M-22.

76. *Ibid.,* January 25, 1944, L-2.

77. *Ibid.,* Jan. 24, 1944, M-10; Feb. 20, 1944, V-4; Dec. 3, 1944, VII-12; Jan. 21, 1945, V-4; July 25, 1945, M-15. *Wisconsin CIO News—Local 248 Edition,* Aug. 14, 1944, 11; Dec. 18, 1944, 8; Aug. 10, 1945, 2. *Milwaukee Labor Press,* Dec. 28, 1944, 14. Press Release by OWI and WMC, May 17, 1943, Files of the Economist AFL, Series 5, File C, Box 19; "Reconversion Blueprint For Women," adopted at a conference held on Dec. 5, 1944 by officials from the Women's Bureau and from thirty national women's organizations affiliated with the AFL and the CIO; Files of the Director of Research, General Files, Series 8, File A, Box 32; American Federation of Labor papers; Wisconsin Historical Society.

78. "Women in Industry After the War," ca. 1944, Report Submitted by Women in Industry Committee (Agnes Nestor—Director of Research and Education for the International Glove Workers Union of America, chair; Florence C. Thorne, Rose Schneiderman, and Sallie D. Clinebell), from the files of the A.F.L. Director of Research; Series 8, File A, Box 32; American Federation of Labor Papers, Wisconsin Historical Society.

79. Bi-Monthly Demand-Supply Supplement, March 1945 and Labor Market Developments Report, Sept. 1945; United States Employment Service; Labor Market Survey Reports, Milwaukee, Wisconsin; Record Group 183; National Archives. Joy Schultz, memo for the files, Dec. 13, 1945, Nordberg Manufactur-

ing Company, Closed Cases, Regional Files, Region 6, Records of the Committee on Fair Employment Practice, Record Group 228; National Archives. *Milwaukee Sentinel,* July 2, 1945, II-3; July 20, 1945, I-4.

80. Labor Market Developments Report, Sept. 1945; USES, Labor Market Survey Reports, Record Group 183; National Archives. Wisconsin Industrial Commission Statistical Releases numbers 466 and 470.

Chapter Six: The War's End

1. *Milwaukee Journal,* April 9, 1944, I-1 and I-10; April 23, 1944, II-3; July 8, 1945, II-4. Joel Seidman, *American Labor from Defense to Reconversion,* 214.
2. *Milwaukee Journal,* April 9, 1944, I-1 and I-10; April 23, 1944, II-3.
3. *Milwaukee Journal,* April 23, 1944, II-3; April 27, 1945, L-10. Report of the Steering Committee of the Mayor's Post-War Planning Conference; post-war planning file, John L. Bohn papers; Milwaukee Public Library.
4. *Milwaukee Labor Press,* July 13, 1944, 1. Seidman, *American Labor,* 215. *Wisconsin CIO News—Local 248 Edition,* July 27, 1945, 1.
5. *Milwaukee Journal, extra edition, Aug. 14, 1945, 1. Milwaukee Labor Press, editorial, Aug. 16, 1945,* 6. *Wisconsin CIO News—Local 248 Edition,* Aug. 17, 1945, 4.
6. *Milwaukee Journal,* Aug. 15, 1945, L-1; Aug. 16, 1945, L-1; Aug. 17, 1945, M-1 and L-1; Aug. 18, 1945, M-2; Aug. 22, 1945, L-1. *Milwaukee Sentinel,* Aug. 16, 1945, I-1 and I-6; Aug. 17, 1945, I-1 and I-14; Aug. 19, 1945, I-1 and I-3; Aug. 22, 1945, I-1.
7. *Milwaukee Journal,* Aug. 16, 1945, M-1, M-5, and L-8; Aug. 19, 1945, II-3; Aug. 21, 1945, M-1 and M-4; Aug. 24, 1945, L-1. *Milwaukee Sentinel,* Aug. 30, 1945, II-6.
8. Labor Market Developments Report, September 1945; United States Employment Service, Labor Market Survey Reports, Milwaukee, Wisconsin; Box 429, Record Group 183; National Archives. Memo: Joy Schultz to Elmer W. Henderson, regarding the Milwaukee Employment Picture, Oct. 10, 1945; Records of the Committee on Fair Employment Practice, Regional Files, Region 6, Administrative Correspondence, Organizational Contacts, War Manpower Commission 6, Wisconsin; Box 711; National Archives.
9. Seidman, *American Labor,* 213–232.
10. *A.F. of L. Milwaukee Labor Press,* Sept. 2, 1943, 3.
11. *Milwaukee Journal,* Sept. 1, 1945, M-1.
12. J. F. Friedrick (AFL regional organizer) to William Green, Sept. 13, 1945; J. F. Friedrick to William Green, February 25, 1946; Strikes and Agreements File, Series 7, Box 23; American Federation of Labor papers; Wisconsin Historical Society.
13. *Milwaukee Journal,* Sept. 2, 1945, I-9.

The writing of history is the analytical process of converting records into a story that illuminates the past. The historian does not recreate the past, but only a version of the past that is as good as the sources from which that history is drawn. This essay is a commentary on the primary sources used to create this history of Milwaukee's labor movement during World War II. It is a reflection on the value of different kinds of sources and the ways in which information flows together to inform the historian's analysis and to shape history itself.

I relied on the records of labor unions, business organizations, civic groups, community leaders, local governments, and federal agencies. These manuscript collections and records series provided many details essential to understanding the nature of industrial conflict and the relationship between that conflict and living on the home front during America's most important war. Government publications provided statistical data necessary for comparing Milwaukee to other cities and for understanding events within Milwaukee during the war years. As essential as all of these sources were, newspapers provided the basic fabric without which this study would have been isolated events without context.

NEWSPAPERS

Milwaukee's newspapers, flawed as they are with reporting errors and editorial bias, provide the foundation for understanding daily events. The strength of newspapers as a source of information lies less in their factual accuracy or their depth than in their breadth of coverage. As one turns the pages, life unfolds. The reader is immersed in stories of major events of the day—military strategy, battlefield victories and losses, political campaigns and conflicts, American industrial and military power, manpower shortages and migration to industrial production centers, industrial conflict and work stoppages. Newspapers also document the many small ways in which individuals and families participated in the war effort and sacrificed in the name of a national cause—grief of personal loss, rationing and hoarding, prices for groceries, new factory construction, civil defense, war bond and scrap drives, mothers caring for families, and mothers working. We see the surge of patriotic fervor that brought an angry nation to its feet after Pearl Harbor, and the more subtle, enduring patriotism that fueled the long fight for victory over true, malevolent, malignant evil.

Four newspapers were essential for this book: the *Milwaukee Journal,* Milwaukee's most respected daily; the *Milwaukee Sentinel,* a Hearst newspaper; the *A.F. of L. Milwaukee Labor Press,* principal organ of the Milwaukee Federated Trades Council; and the *CIO News—Wisconsin Edition* (later the *CIO News—Local 248 Edition*), mouthpiece for the Milwaukee Industrial Union Council and UAW Local 248, Milwaukee's most significant union. By their nature, newspapers not only report the news but shape public opinion through what is reported and how it is represented. Although we are seldom able to judge the true impact of this reporting and opinion shaping on the readers of newspapers, a thorough reading provides the historian not only with factual information but with a clear picture of what the residents of Milwaukee read on a daily basis.

Newspapers provide details on the causes and outcomes of many labor disputes and, for many events, may be the only record in existence. For example, the most comprehensive record of strikes and worker discontent among Milwaukee's government employees appears in the pages of the city's newspapers.

The *Milwaukee Journal* provides the most thorough coverage of city life. Reporters generally worked to a high professional standard; factually accurate when information can be checked against other sources. For example, the *Journal* regularly reported summary information drawn from United States Employment Service, Labor Market Development Reports. When compared with these reports, the news stories are not as complete as the official records, but the newspaper accounts are invariably accurate. Indicative of the free flow of information in American society, the National Archives' copies of the USES Market Development Reports were stamped "confidential," but clearly were not treated as such in the nation's hinterland. Although its reporting was generally accurate, the *Journal* clearly conveyed an editorial bias that was staunchly pro-business and anti-labor, while remaining politically liberal on most domestic issues. The *Journal* editorialized against most issues important to organized labor, especially related to economic conditions and maintenance of union rights.

The *Milwaukee Journal* also published a "Business Pulse" column in the Sunday paper approximately once a month. These articles provide an easy mechanism through which one can track local employment, payrolls, department store sales, credit reports, construction activity, and bank debits. These newspaper accounts often add details to information available in government statistical reports.

I relied on the *Milwaukee Sentinel* to supplement coverage provided by the *Journal*. The *Sentinel* belonged to William Randolph Hearst. *Sentinel* reporting was seldom as thorough as that provided by the *Journal,* and often carried a sensational undertone. As with all Hearst papers, it was rabidly opposed to the administration of Franklin Roosevelt and to "fuzzy headed" academics and new dealers in general. One could count on editorialists such as Westbrook Pegler to inveigh against all things Roosevelt, New Deal, or labor oriented. The attack on Pearl Harbor gave legitimacy to Hearst's warnings about the "yellow peril." The Hearst organization was openly self-promotional and prone to organizing campaigns that produced "news" reported in the paper. For example, the search for "Miss Victory" cited in chapter 5 was an event created by the Hearst organization and reported in its newspapers.

The *A.F. of L. Milwaukee Labor Press* and the *CIO News* are the most important sources of labor reporting and opinion available to a Milwaukee researcher. These weekly newspapers conveyed a regular stream of information about significant events into the city's labor households. The labor papers explained rationing and price controls, recruited civil defense workers, and reported on union participation in every aspect of the home front. In many cases, stories in the *Labor Press* and *CIO News* contain the only news about the way in which average people, through their unions, participated in the war effort, and about many small conflicts inevitable in labor-management relations. More importantly, these newspapers gave voice to organized labor's view of events. While the *Milwaukee Journal* stated a mainstream view of labor's record on wages, price controls, work stoppages and postwar reconversion, the labor press provided workers with a counterpoint. For example, numerous articles regularly analyzed the disparity between price and wage controls. As labor's representatives on the Presidential Committee on the Cost of Living, George Meany (AFL Secretary-Treasurer) and R. J. Thomas (President of the CIO Auto Workers) issued a report highly critical of the Bureau of Labor Statistics' Cost of Living Index and government attempts to control wages. Both labor papers ran extensive articles highlighting the findings and implications of the report. This level of information from a labor perspective was unavailable in the *Journal* or *Sentinel*. As the war ended, the *Milwaukee Journal* focused on corporate conversion to peacetime production while the *Labor Press* and *CIO News* took up the issue of protecting economic security for workers during the period of postwar reconversion. Just as the mainstream press reflected the community as a whole through the eyes of managing editors, the labor press reflected events important to the union community with a particular emphasis on labor's perspectives. In addition, the *CIO News* was a major source of information about the ongoing struggle between UAW Local 248 and management at Allis-Chalmers.

GOVERNMENT RECORDS AND PUBLICATIONS

Newspapers provide a rich record for the social historian because of their breadth. Government records and publications provide a rich record because of the depth, focus, and accuracy of information accumulated as agencies and offices went about fulfilling their duties. Not only do these sources provide a window into specific events, but also allow us to make generalizations about events and attitudes based on patterns derived from these sources. Any broad study of home front life must ultimately turn to government statistical reports for data on prices, cost of living, strikes and lockouts, manpower shortages, and corporate assets. Newspapers provide stories, causes, and explanations; statistics allow the researcher to place the anecdotal information drawn from newspapers into a more analytical context.

The Bureau of Labor Statistics' *Consumer's Prices in the United States, 1942–1948* provides excellent information on changes in consumer prices over time, a significant component of any cost of living analysis. Similarly, the Wisconsin Industrial Commission *Statistical Releases* document wage information for Wisconsin workers. The availability of this data also allowed for comparison of federal, state, and labor survey data and of organized labor's claims regarding the decline of buying power during the war.

The United States Securities and Exchange Commission's *Survey of American Listed Corporations: Data on Profits and Operations* provided invaluable information about the operations, profits, assets, and postwar reconversion reserves for many of Milwaukee's biggest corporations. Without this information, it would have been impossible to assess the financial impact of the war on corporations in Milwaukee and the ways in which those corporations prepared financially for the end of the war. By comparing corporate profits and operations with consumer price, cost of living, and wage data, I was able to place concerns regarding economic security expressed by organized labor and business alike into comparative context.

The unpublished United State Employment Service's "Labor Market Development Reports" provide detailed reporting and analysis of the manpower needs in the Milwaukee area throughout the war. As mentioned earlier, the trends noted by USES analysts are reflected directly in news stories, especially in the *Milwaukee Journal*. The combination of USES "Labor Market Reports" and newspaper stories (which often contain information drawn from interviews with corporate, union, federal, or city officials) provides the researcher with statistical and anecdotal data necessary to create a historical assessment of employment conditions and their impact on home front life.

Wartime Record of Strikes and Lock-Outs written by Rosa Lee Swafford for Congress provides excellent comparative information on the level of strikes and lock-outs in Milwaukee and other major industrial cities. Swafford's data are essential for placing strike activity and the losses resulting from this activity into the context of total industrial production. Likewise, these data are essential for placing Milwaukee into context with other major industrial centers.

If government publications provide context and allow for generalization, government records provide stories that bring statistics to life and give them meaning. Strikes, by their nature, are public events. In wartime, they take on added visibility as a breach in national unity. They are reported in the press, they are recorded in statistical summaries, and they are adjudicated by the National War Labor Board. War Labor Board case files and reports, particularly the board's *Termination Report,* provide excellent information on significant strikes and industrial conflicts requiring the board's action. In addition, the *Termination Report* documents the board's policies, procedures, orders, opinions, and its defense of wage controls.

Labor unions and workers reduced the number and shortened the duration of open conflicts through their commitment to the no-strike pledge, to the patriotic pursuit of wartime production, and to victory. Because I am concerned not only with the relatively small number of conflicts that became strikes, but also with the far greater number of disputes that never burst into open view, the dispute case files of the Federal Mediation and Conciliation Service were essential for this study. Indeed, my heavy use of these records distinguishes this work from other studies of wartime industrial conflict. The Conciliation Service closed case files contain detailed notes by conciliators assigned to work with companies and unions to facilitate the resolution of conflicts and thereby avoid strikes or the need for War Labor Board involvement. These files often track disputes from their beginning through numerous negotiations and clearly document the issues important to the parties involved. The conciliation case files are perhaps the richest source of information on individual industrial conflicts available anywhere. No other source provides the combination of breadth and detail.

The detailed notes of federal conciliators are invaluable when trying to assess the nature of wartime industrial conflict. In specific cases, other records augment the Conciliation Service Case Files or provide details of behind the scenes negotiating. Records of the Wisconsin Employment Relations Board, another agency working to adjudicate and mediate industrial disputes, were essential to understanding the slowdown at Ampco Metal, Inc. and the jurisdictional dispute at Hummel and Downing. The files of Federal Labor Unions, contained within the records of the AFL, contributed to assessment of the long-running dispute between Fabricated Metal Workers Local 19340 and Geuder, Paeschke and Frey, to which records of the Wisconsin Industrial Commission also contributed. Records of the International Brotherhood of Pulp, Sulphite and Paper Mill Workers and of International Longshoremen's Association Local 815 helped define the jurisdictional dispute issues these unions faced in Milwaukee during the war. Records of the Milwaukee County Industrial Union Council also augment Conciliation Service information on the struggle between the Greenebaum Tanning Company and the Fur and Leather Workers Union.

What the Conciliation Service case files contribute to the study of industrial conflict, the "Women in Unions in a Mid-West War Industry Area" study conducted by the Women's Bureau offers to our understanding of the relationship between working women, their unions, and male union leaders. The Women's Bureau survey project gathered data that make it possible to generalize about the relationships between women workers, male workers, and their unions. Because Women's Bureau staff talked with female and male union leaders representing large and small AFL and CIO unions, the resulting survey data are essential for understanding the ways in which men and women viewed their participation in the industrial workforce and in their labor unions. In addition, these data allow researchers to generalize about the perceptions of men and women alike, as well as women's satisfaction levels regarding their roles and representation by their unions.

MANUSCRIPTS

Newspapers provide broad context and information about specific events. Government records and publications support generalizations about wartime patterns. The records of organizations provide detailed perspectives on narrow events and on issues of interest to the organizations and their members. The papers of individuals play a relatively small part in this study. Although they reflect a well focused view of specific events, it is that very focus that limits the usefulness of individual's records in this project.

Understanding conditions on the home front in Milwaukee requires weaving together information from newspapers, government statistics, and manuscript collections. Records of the United Community Services of Greater Milwaukee are the best single source for information on social conditions on the home front. When combined with accounts in the *Milwaukee Journal* and with records from Anthony King, Mayor Carl F. Zeidler, and Mayor John L. Bohn, records of the United Community Services provide excellent analytical information on housing conditions in the city. The governmental and social work perspectives reflected in these records were augmented by the work of *Journal* reporters who did an excellent job of investigating housing conditions and developing the human side of the story. Similarly, articles in the *Milwaukee Journal* and records from the John L. Bohn, City Club of Milwaukee, and the Milwaukee County Council for Civilian Defense collections all provided information essential to understanding wartime transportation problems. The Council for Civilian Defense records document fears of German air attack and actions taken to help protect the city from such an eventuality. Defense council records also contributed substantial information to the discussion of women working in war jobs and problems associated with child care for working mothers.

Records from United Community Services provide the best source for assessing Milwaukee's child care needs, social worker attitudes about appropriate care, and the attitudes of working mothers themselves. Mary Kiely's reports offer a clear analysis of the problems working women faced in caring for children and attempts to ameliorate those problems. With unvarnished candor, she assessed the local situation and, despite her professional judgement favoring organized childcare, concluded that Milwaukee women workers were finding non-institutional ways of caring for their children.

The records of the United Community Services also offer a unique window into the minds of business leaders who played critical roles in the organization. Without the Community Services records researchers would have no access to the exchange over labor participation in war-relief/community-war chest activities and the tensions this created within the business community. The records also provide far greater detail than records of labor organizations themselves regarding union participation in War Chest campaigns. Two small collections of materials related to Harold Story (vice president for industrial relations at Allis-Chalmers), also contributed to this rare view of the businessman's perspective.

When combined with accounts in the *A.F. of L. Milwaukee Labor Press,* records of the American Federation of Labor are particularly useful in documenting the official position of the federation, as well as the views of some of its most prominent leaders on issues such as support of the war effort, protecting worker buying power, and planning for the postwar era. The records provide detailed information on the federation's development and implementation of the no-strike pledge. Similarly, the AFL records document labor's view of the Little Steel formula and the struggle over how to best protect worker buying power against the ravages of inflation. These files are augmented by the pamphlet "Cost of Living" (authored by George Meany and R. J. Thomas), the most succinct and widely available joint AFL/CIO statement on the weaknesses of the Bureau of Labor Standards Consumers' Price Index. As the employment of women in war industries became increasingly essential to production, the records also reflect the fact that women within the AFL leadership began voicing concern for protecting the rights of these workers after the war. Records from the offices of the AFL economist and research director document concerns about reconversion in general as well as the role of women workers in the postwar era.

Milwaukee boasted a strong Federated Trades Council (AFL) and Industrial Union Council (CIO). Although the records of the Federated Trades Council of Milwaukee were of only modest usefulness for this study, the records of the Milwaukee County Industrial Union Council (IUC) provide particularly valuable information about labor's commitment to the war effort, participation in civil defense activities, debates over housing and meat shortages, and policies of the Office of Price Administration. Milwaukee IUC records demonstrate the active participation of labor leaders in home front affairs, their views regarding solutions to such social problems as housing shortages, and their incredulity that such shortages could be solved by the real estate industry without government involvement or assistance. The *CIO News* reflects these points of view as well, colored by editorial perspective. As with most manuscript collections, records of the IUC reflect views of events uncolored by interpretations prepared for public consumption. Similarly, two small collections of Harold Story papers document the personal views of an influential business leader, as related to labor management relations in general, and the conflict between Allis-Chalmers and UAW Local 248 specifically.

The AFL combined industrial style unions for production workers with craft unions for skilled workers in the same factories. As a consequence, records of a union such as Local 311 of the International Union of Operating Engineers illuminate disputes at the Milwaukee Ordnance Plant and the Nash Motors Parts Plant. Similarly, the records of Local 311 shed light on conditions or issues seemingly unrelated to that union, as was the case when an official from the Operating Engineers commented on a work stoppage by A. O. Smith employees who were members of an AFL Federal Labor Union called the Smith Steelworkers. Local 311 represented the operating engineers at A. O. Smith. That insight is available nowhere else.

The records of Laundry and Dry Cleaning Drivers Local 360 (Teamsters) and of International Longshoremen's Association Local 815 document several different wartime disputes beyond conventional industrial settings. Records of Local 360 amply demonstrate that workers outside the conventional factory (such as teamsters) struggled under the same government wage constraints as did their brothers and sisters working at industrial concerns. The Longshoremen's records document an internal union dispute that never surfaced in public and for which the union's records may well be the only source.

The records of the Women's Bureau survey of Midwestern labor unions supplied information essential to generalizing about the relationships between women workers and their unions. The records of the International Brotherhood of Pulp, Sulphite and Paper Mill Workers, on the other hand, allowed me to delve in depth into the relationship between one woman, Valaria Brodzinski, and her union. The detailed correspondence between Brodzinski, the international union vice president to whom she reported, and the international's president allows us to witness the way in which a talented organizer viewed herself and the male dominated world in which she operated. These records also provide a unique window into the thoughts of men around her and their evaluation of her work in light of her gender. Although much more limited, the records of the Wisconsin State Council of Machinists also provided a male perspective on the likely role of women in postwar industry.

ORAL HISTORY INTERVIEWS

As a form of social history documentation, oral histories help place a human face on events. This is true of the Wisconsin Women in World War II project run by the Wisconsin Historical Society in 1992–1993. As the Historical Society contemplated publishing a volume on the role of women in World War II, researchers realized that conventional written sources were insufficient for the project. In comparison to men who served in the armed forces, relatively few women's letters have survived. Transcriptions of interviews conducted with women who worked in Milwaukee factories provided valuable personal insights into factory work, gender roles, rationing, child care, and general home front conditions. These insights added to the richness of this story.

This study has been an exercise in understanding the home front, labor's role, and industrial conflict during World War II by focusing on Milwaukee, Wisconsin. To write this social and labor history has required bringing together the diverse resources of newspapers, government publications, government records, and manuscript collections. To all of the archivists and librarians who have collected, processed, and cataloged the primary sources needed for my work, many of whom are employed by the Wisconsin Historical Society, I owe a great debt. In the end, those who preserve the records of the past make it possible for us to write history.